Consumer and Quality

Consumer and Quality

(Second Edition)

D.B.N. Murthy

PUBLISHING FOR ONE WORLD

NEW AGE INTERNATIONAL (P) LIMITED, PUBLISHERS

(formerly Wiley Eastern Limited)

New Delhi • Bangalore • Chennai • Cochin • Guwahati • Hyderabad
Jalandhar • Kolkata • Lucknow • Mumbai • Ranchi
Visit us at **www.newagepublishers.com**

Published by New Age International (P) Ltd., Publishers
First Edition: 2001
Second Edition: 2007

ISBN 13 : 978-81-224-2133-0

ISBN 10 : 81-224-2133-4

Rs. 160.00

C-07-06-1627

Printed in India at Nisha Enterprises, Delhi.
Typeset at In-house, Delhi.

PUBLISHING FOR ONE WORLD
NEW AGE INTERNATIONAL (P) LIMITED, PUBLISHERS
(formerly Wiley Eastern Limited)
4835/24, Ansari Road, Daryaganj, New Delhi - 110002
Visit us at **www.newagepublishers.com**

To

All those who value quality

in every human activity

PREFACE TO THE SECOND EDITION

When the book was published in the year 2001, winds of change were already blowing across the country, thanks to the regime of liberalization and globalization. Consumers who are used to a choice in the products/ services of superior quality will not accept anything less. Products made in India for international market are being exported from our shores earning valuable foreign exchange. There is now thriving market for the BPO industry in the country, thanks to the abundant availability of qualified personnel.

Consumers are learning a new language of e-commerce and up-to-date technology. The fear of technology is slowly but surely diminishing. More consumers are opting for ECS and use of ATM cards. There is a strange problem the consumers in India are facing now—the problem of plenty! The more knowledgeable and informed customer is better for investing wisely. When the book was published in the year 2001, the idea was to give the consumers inputs that could help them to improve their decision-making. The main purpose of the revision, which has been done totally is to include the latest information. We can provide only a few guidelines, as ground reality could be different. You must remember that each purchase decision is unique and so there cannot be a uniform set of rules to cover every possible situation.

Chapter 1, "Importance of Quality" highlights the attention paid to quality by our ancients and how somewhere down the time, we lost that quest and accepted shoddy goods and services. Quality is an eternal quest for excellence from time immemorial. They had laid a solid foundation for quality. From the initial definition of 'fit for use', quality now means 'total and continuous customer' satisfaction. The chapter contains a discussion on the much touted liberalization and globalization.

"Consumer Rights and Responsibilities" is the subject of Chapter 2.

The present consumer is confronted with a plethora of goods and services. The consumer rights should be understood which are detailed. Consumer education is woefully inadequate in our country and a discussion gives details how this could be improved to make consumerism meaningful.

Paradoxically, a consumer is having problem in making the right choice. This issue is getting more and more important, which is discussed in Chapter 3, "Making the Right Choice". Dealers and sellers are trying their best to woo customers by unleashing advertisements and by offering inducements to customers for buying their products. Here is where a customer has to make up his own mind armed with information so as to get the best value for the money invested. This is equally of concern when deciding health-care issues and financial matters.

Chapter 4 is about "Returns, Warranty and Product Liability". A customer should read the warranty/guarantee terms thoroughly and understand the implications. The discussion presented is an attempt to equip the customer on these issues that could make a difference to a purchase decision. Examples of warranty/guarantee terms are given as illustrations. Product liability is well established in the advanced countries.

When a product/service is not up to the expectation of a consumer he/she has no choice but to complain. How such a complaint should be redressed is the topic of discussion in Chapter 5, "Complaint Redress". Consumer Protection Act passed some years ago has benefited many consumers over the years. When every persuasion fails, then the Act through its various fora, help customers to get their complaints redressed. Examples of cases settled in various courts and other fora are given as illustrations.

Chapter 6, "The Role of Consumers" highlights what informed consumers can and should do to get the maximum out of any purchase. Those who buy 'green products' and energy-efficient products/services are doing a great service to the environment. Mere low price should not influence a purchase decision but quality in all its over-arching definition of 'total and continuous satisfaction'.

A fact that is becoming more and more clear is that consumers once used to better quality products/services won't be induced, by any means, to go in for poor quality despite price reductions and other enticements.

Chapter 7, "What the Future Holds for Consumers" is an attempt to look into the future and predict what awaits consumers of the coming generations. We can expect the pace of liberalization and globalization to pick up that would offer more choices for consumers.

Our economy is poised for more growth with the service sector already leading the manufacturing sector in the GDP. The future is bright for consumerism in India. However, we need responsible consumerism that does not deplete our natural resources fast. The ideas and suggestions presented in the book, hopefully, would enhance the decision-making capability of consumers. It is hoped that the revised book would come in handy, as a useful guide that would serve the interests of the consumers well.

D.B.N. MURTHY

Preface to the First Edition

The market situation for the consumer has changed dramatically in the past ten years, especially in the last five years with India's new approach to economic reforms which has revolutionised thinking and caught the imagination of one and all. With the ushering in of the regime of liberalisation, the consumer is in a position to pick and choose the product of his liking from a multiplicity of brands and varieties. Considering the volume of our middle class buyers with money power, which in terms of sheer numbers is more than the total population of several advanced countries put together, business firms have realised the huge potential of the market to be tapped. No wonder many global players are keen to set up shop in India, either by way of direct investment or tie-ups with Indian partners. A few years ago, it was common to see everyone coming from the Gulf walking in at the arrival lounge with TVs, two-in-one cassettee players or even refrigerators. But things have changed now. Now bringing 'white goods' or electronic goods into the country from abroad is no longer an attractive proposition. That's because many international brands are available locally at a competitive price. That is not all. Even some of the domestic brands have established a reputation for themselves in international markets.

With such a multi-choice marketplace the decision to buy should be easier. Strange as it may sound, that 'choice' which the Indian consumer had been waiting for, is now becoming more and more difficult! Reason—the consumer is confused with too many brands, all of which seem to be similar with hardly any price difference. Given the level of sophistication of products/services, an average consumer just seems lost in a welter of new terminology. Now the market speaks a new language of E-Commerce, ECS, DEMAT, ATM, E Mail, Internet, Networking, Quadra Focus, Dolby, Golden Eye which sounds Greek and Latin to a common man. But no dealer or retailer can take a customer for a ride as long as he is equipped with some knowledge of the terminology of the globalised era or at least makes a pretense of it.

The consumer of today and tomorrow needs the right kind of help and support when it comes to making a choice. But dealers/retailers who are more concerned about their own commissions with each brand they sell, may not be particularly open about the demerits of the brand they are selling. The dealer may even go to the extent of persuading the buyer to take the brand for which he gets a better commission, by listing the demerits, real or imaginary of the particular brand the customer is interested in and overrating the brand he is interested in selling. This is where the government and the NGOs should step in to help the consumer in decision-making, by periodically issuing reports of comparative ratings in the performance/quality/price of each and every household item or goods/services available in the market. This is where the consumers of the advanced countries have an advantage as they have access to the kind of information which helps them to make a wise choice. In the absence of such objective rating reports, the Indian consumer is guided more by his personal experiences and that of his friends and relatives.

This book is meant to provide general information on quality vis-a-vis consumers. It seeks to provide information on what a consumer should look for while shopping for goods, how he can avoid the hidden traps and pitfalls and how he can get better value for his money. With some useful tips on various issues of interest to consumers and information inputs, an attempt is made to equip the consumer for better decision-making. It is emphasised, however, the subject of consumer decision-making is too vast to be covered in one book. All that can be done is to equip him with information on how to be an alert consumer and how to avoid the hidden traps and be ever vigilant so as not to be swept away by glittering products, aggressive advertisements, misleading talk and juicy freebies. The book can only provide broad guidelines and the suggestions offered are indicative and not mandatory. Each buying situation is unique and for the consumer to make an informed choice he should be armed with the necessary information and knowledge.

Quality is all about the quest for excellence. In olden days, much emphasis was laid on quality in all human activites, whether it was the *gurukula* system of education, *gharana* style of music and dance, building monuments or crafting art objects. The creed of excellence was the accepted norm and any deviation from this was unthinkable. This is true not only of our civilisation but other ancient civilisations too. Chapter 1 discusses these issues under the title "Importance of Quality". It is a matter of concern for all of us that we have come down several notches from such great heights. It's only in recent times that quality is given its due importance.

"Consumer Rights and Responsibilities" discussed in Chapter 2 focusses on what consumers should expect as a matter of right. It's true they have been denied such rights for long. When a simple illiterate farmer wants to buy a thresher, the onus is on the dealer to sell only those brands which have buit-in safety devices. He should not expect the farmer to read a manual or follow instructions in writing.

Consumers are in a dilemma when confronted with several similar looking/performing products/services. Often TVs look alike with almost the same price. "Making the Right Choice" in Chapter 3 provides guidelines to help consumers in making wise decisions.

Ideally, a product/service should work well when used for the first time and every time till it becomes obsolete. But in reality things are not so simple. More often than not, when you test a product in the shop, it seems fine. But the moment you bring it home it may turn faulty. It can be quite frustrating, especially if you have paid a hefty sum for it. That may not be the end of it. Even after setting it right, it may break down off and on, depriving you of the enjoyment of uninterrupted service. Another problem faced by a consumer is the how-to-use manual provided by suppliers. "Start the computer and insert the CD-ROM", may seem to be sufficient for a proessional. But a consumer who is not so well versed in computers may confront a variety of problems just trying to instal some software as per instructions. Finally, in frustration, he has no choice but to seek professional help which, in general, is tardy in coming becuase they are all 'too busy' to attend to consumers problems.

Fortunately, there is a mechanism for getting such deficiencies attended to. Chapter 4 "Returns, Warranty and Product Liability" is all about services offered by a dealer/service shop when the product/service fails to work.

Earlier a dissatisfied consumer had little or no recourse to redress when faced with the negative attitude of sellers who sold faulty products/services. Fortunately, the Consumer Protection Act (1986) came as a godsend to consumers who can now get their complaints settled, albeit within two to three years, and generally in their favour.

This is the topic discussed in Chapter 5 "Complaint Redress". A number of case studies are presented showing how the consumer courts and other agencies have disposed of consumer complaints.

"The Role of Consumers" is the subject discussed in Chapter 6, the penultimate chapter of the book. With business firms focussing on the consumer as never before, consumers will be wooed with more and better incentives. But at the same time the consumer must be aware of his responsibilities towards the society as a whole and the importance of his role in improving the quality of products/services while safeguarding the scarce resources of the earth.

The final Chapter 7 is titled "Trends in Consumerism" which is an attempt to crystal-gaze into the future and what it holds in store for the Indian consumers in the millennium. From the experience of the consumerism of the advanced countries we can predict the shape of things to come. The consumer will be in a situation of a wide choice of complex goods and services.

If this book helps consumers appreciate the importance of quality, informs them about their rights, suggests methods to fight consumer disputes and finally proves beneficial in making the right choice, the purpose of this hook shall be suitably served. I shall appreciate any feedback from the readers (after all they are my consumers) which may help in improving the quality of the next edition of the book.

D.B.N. MURTHY

ACKNOWLEDGEMENT

Consumer related issues have fascinated me for a long time. We are all consumers and do want the best when we make a purchase decision. How to get the best value for money is what the book is about. Needless to state that quality professionals, who are all consumer-friendly and espouse the cause of consumers, have influenced me on consumer matters. Dr J.M. Juran, an internationally known quality and management expert, taught us the importance of quality in its all-encompassing features. I had interface with consumer and quality experts over decades, both domestically and internationally, that has given me the inputs needed to bring out the book "Consumer and Quality" that was first published in the year 2001. I am grateful to these men for their valuable inputs.

The present book is a total revision of the book "Consumer and Quality". The inputs have been gathered for a few years that enabled me to rewrite the book totally. I am grateful for discussions with consumer activists and quality and management experts over the years that have given me the urge to rewrite the book that is up-to-date. My recent visit to the U.S.A (2006) was an eye-opener as I was amazed at the choice before a consumer. The customer service centre in departmental stores was, as before, a place a customer simply walks in and gets replacement, refund or exchange of whatever the goods/service purchased. How I wish we too could have such a simple and easy way of getting complaint redressed.

My family, as always, has played a supporting role in seeing that the revision of the book was completed fast. I am grateful to them for their encouragement and cooperation. Uday and Shalini, who hosted our recent visit to the U.S.A., gave me interesting perspective to the latest consumer trends in that country where there is plenty of choice for consumers. I am thankful to them for the latest inputs.

The publisher was the trigger for the revision and I am thankful to them for taking up the project. But for the full cooperation and professional work, this revised book could not have come up fast and so well. I thank the publishers for the interest in getting the book revised for the benefit of the consumers. The publishing team deserves my thanks for the professional manner in which this project was completed.

I have made extensive use of the newspapers, magazines, journals, websites, too numerous to list, for the information that has enabled me to update the book in a proper manner. I would be thankful to the readers if they bring to my/publisher notice any error of omission/commission so that these could be corrected in the next issue of the book.

D.B.N. MURTHY

CONTENTS

CHAPTER 1

IMPORTANCE OF QUALITY

Quality is the business of doing business
—Anonymous

The importance of quality, be it in product or service, cannot be over-emphasized. Just study some of the tips given from time to time to make matters easier for everyone. For instance, Indian Government's Postal Department, one of the most extensive, popular and efficient in the world issues guidelines such as *"PIN Code helps speed up your mail. If the PIN Code in your address is missing or inaccurate, please send us the addressed portion of this wrapper indicating the correct PIN Code. This will enable faster delivery of your mail."* PIN Code in our country is equivalent to ZIP Code in USA.

Quality is the buzzword these days and everybody talks about it, the politicians from public platforms, the company executives from business fora, and of course, the common man on the street. Nevertheless, few understand the true meaning of the word quality and fewer still are able and willing to put quality in its true perspective in the changing context of the liberalization and globalization where the national boundaries for freer trade and commerce are slowly, but surely, breaking down. In the olden times, quality had a simple definition — a product or service should fit the purpose for which it was intended. For example, a part should fit another part without much effort. Thus a standard or specification was all that was necessary for the part to meet, nothing else. So many an industrial designer/manufacturer was concerned with making a product/service to meet its standard or specification. This resulted in making the customer a secondary objective to be satisfied. "Fitness for use" was the predominant concept, to the exclusion of everything else. This went on for quite some-time and consumers did a get a raw deal when confronted with statements like "Our product/service is fit for the purpose for which it was intended. If that does not satisfy you, tough luck. We can do very little about it," would be the bland statement. Strangely, often it was the producer/manufacturer who decided such a 'fitness for the purpose' to the exclusion of the customer.

Fortunately, we have come a long way by now in understanding the true meaning of quality and customer satisfaction. Consequently, the all-encompassing meaning of the word quality means: *"Total and continuous satisfaction"* while using a product/service. Such a holistic concept for quality is universally accepted that benefits the customer since he/she is the focus of attention by everyone in the design/manufacture/sale/distribution chain.

Quality means the product has, preferably, all or most of the under-mentioned **characteristics** as detailed below:

- It has the right quality.
- Is safe, reliable, and long lasting.
- It's economical to the customer to use it till it lasts.
- It's delivered on time.
- Its price is right.
- Its customer support is good, polite, quick and responsive.
- Its after-sales service is polite and competent with availability of genuine spare-parts and repair cost is affordable.
- Disposal of product/service presents no problem and is environmentally friendly.
- 'Buy-back' schemes of used items for new are user-friendly.
- The total life-cycle cost to the customer (the 'cradle-to-grave' cost) is optimum.
- Conforms to norms of ethics and does not infringe on any trademark or patent laws and is genuine. Its potential for pollution is within acceptable limits.
- No unethical practices like underhand dealings, employment of child labour, exploiting the employees/workers are used as business practices.

In brief, stages in the evolution of the concept of quality may be seen as depicted in the chart below:

Meets Specifications/Standards

↓

Fit for use

↓

Meets or exceeds total customer satisfaction

As stated earlier, quality is the business of doing business. The race is on to capture a bigger slice of the market pie with competition hotting up from domestic as well as foreign business. More and more industries are re-orienting their focus on customers' needs to make them satisfied and keep them as their loyal customers. Quality is the bandwagon as we are into the 21st century. Customers expect a better deal in the coming years. Quality is thus the enchanted *mantra* for salvation for both the customers and businesses. It should be clearly understood that quality is an attitude of mind and a way of life where "excellence is a journey, not a destination."

CUSTOMER AND QUALITY

Quality is what a customer expects in the product/service he/she is buying. If a customer expects 'excellence' in everything he/she purchases, then his/her expectations are high. However, this could prove to be elusive to a customer when he actually gets a product/service that he has paid for. For instance, a passenger travelling in an economy class on a flight cannot expect service like a passenger who is travelling in the first class. We should appreciate the fact that a first class passenger has paid two to three times more for the fancy first class and that person has every right to be pampered on the flight. That applies to hotels where a five star hotel guest expects and wants star treatment unlike a budget hotel occupant who is satisfied with basic amenities. A customer who receives something more than he has paid for would be delighted. This is how a brand loyalty is built up where the product/service provider puts in that little extra effort to make the life of a customer better and happier.

A question arises which quality a Mercedes Benz luxury car owner expects. He wants safety, smooth noiseless ride, many features like GPS, luxury fittings like leather upholstery, top class music system and the list is endless. On the other hand, a Maruti 800 car owner has fewer expectations. Yet he too expects some features that would make his drive smooth and with no problems. We have to remember that a Mercedes Benz vehicle costs many times more than a simple Maruti 800 car. So the quality as perceived by a customer depends upon the money he has invested. The higher the investment, the higher is the expectation on quality. If that is not meet, we have a dissatisfied customer on our hands. Though a customer has invested modest money, he still has every right to expect quality as perceived by him. If it falls below what he had expected, he becomes an aggrieved dissatisfied customer looking for a better quality of product/service than what he got from a particular organization.

The relation between quality and price might be seen from Fig. 1.1 below:

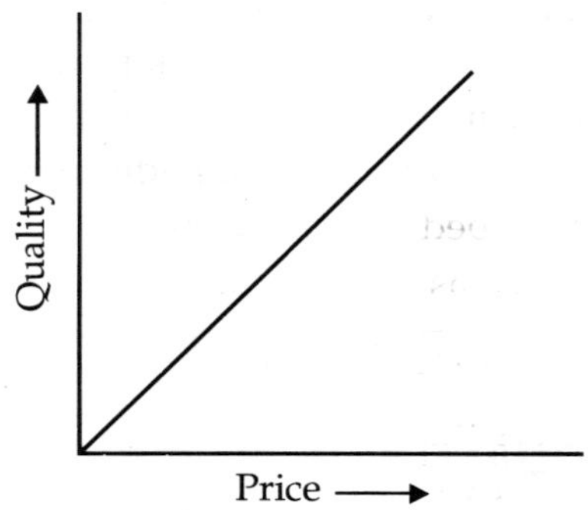

Fig. 1.1

In brief:

Higher price = Higher quality

When a customer pays a higher price for a service/product, he is paying for not only quality which he can see, feel, or judge, known as 'tangibles', but also the 'intangibles' such as the 'esteem' value. While a standard Maruti 800 car and a Mercedes Benz limousine perform more or less the same function, with some difference in 'tangibles', both perform the same function of transporting people, the difference between the two being that the latter has a higher 'esteem' value. Another example could be a meal in a modest *dhaba* costing Rs. 20 whereas a regular meal in a five star hotel, even without drinks, could run up to Rs. 1500 or more. It is not that the food in that starred hotel is superior, though to some extent that is true, but the customer is paying for the 'intangibles' such as the exotic food menu, ambience, the music, the air-conditioning, the décor, the fine plates and cutlery, as well as liveried attendants. It is quite possible that a modest *dhaba* food could be tastier and more like home food than a fine restaurant. However, the rich and the mighty would like to shell out more money to be seen in such splendid hotels and posh restaurants, the rendezvous of the Page 3 people.

Such intangibles affect even ordinary purchases such as cheap art objects, costume, jewellery, dresses, domestic appliances and the like. Here too the higher priced items is supposed to have higher 'esteem' value than cheap imitation stuff, though to the eyes of a lay person there may not be much to distinguish between real diamonds and American diamonds. However, for the connoisseur the esteem value and prestige associated with the highly priced real glittering diamonds are important.

Thus, there is a market for such high priced, high esteem valued items that could end up in elite homes where such items are regarded highly. That could also be a matter of 'keeping up with the Joneses'. Take for example, the VVIP, in whose perception his prestige in the society is enhanced when he travels in a chauffer-driven car, preferably with a flag and a red light on top. He would abhor the idea of driving a small Maruti 800 car, or worse, be dropped by a taxicab.

In brief, quality is seen as:

Quality = Tangible + Intangible (esteem) value

It is interesting to note that a customer attaches various values to the product/service he purchases. These are defined as given below:

- Cost value
- Use value
- Exchange/Resale value
- Esteem value

While some of the above values are easily understood, the intangible factor such as 'esteem' value could pose a problem to the uninitiated. However, this factor alone could decide whether some item is worth buying or not by those who value such esteem value, though some might call it 'snob' value by those who do not attach any value to such luxury items.

The role of quality

The importance of quality in every walk of life cannot be overemphasized in this global economy. Dr. J.M. Juran, an international expert in quality and management put it succinctly: "We live behind the dykes of quality". It may be recalled Dr. J.M. Juran and Dr. W.E. Deming were responsible for the quality revolution in Japan, which had the pre-war, dubious distinction of a producer of poor quality and shoddy goods. All that changed after Dr. Juran and others taught the Japanese the importance of quality in the goods and services they produced. Dr. Juran's prediction that one day Japan would surpass the advanced countries like Germany, UK, and USA, in quality has been proved right.

During our daily life we presume so many things: milk is not adulterated, the food we consume does not contain harmful substances, vegetables do not have pesticides and herbicides, the transportation is safe and reliable, we can occupy the seat as indicated in the railway reservation chart and a flight on a particular day and time would take off as scheduled, our money is safe in the banks we trust so much, investment in a sound mutual fund is not risky but will give attractive returns, the refrigerator which we bought by investing a hefty amount would produce ice and keep the stuff inside cold at all times without consuming too much power or making too much noise.

All these suppositions would go awry if something goes wrong. For example, an unscrupulous trader mixes a dangerous substance in cooking oil that turns deadly and results in serious sickness or death. Air travel is generally safe but a minor pilot error could prove disastrous with the tragic loss of hundreds of passengers. Thus, we have taken quality as being reliable and safe in whatever activity we are involved. Take for example, the gym equipment we exercise. If a minor problem exists unnoticed, then someone sometime is bound to face a serious injury. In these days of technological inventions, supposed to improve the quality of life, quality is given a high degree of importance as one mistake could put an end to that invention in which millions of rupees have been invested. For instance, the new passenger Airbus 380, supposed to carry five hundred and more passengers, has yet to prove its reliability and so its official launch has been delayed by a couple of year. A few product inventions have been hastily introduced, though without wide field trials, while the customers' feedback forced the manufacturer to recall the products prematurely with consequent financial losses and loss of reputation. There cannot be any short cut to quality despite offer of attractive schemes, low prices and freebies. A responsible and intelligent customer will always choose quality and reliable products as he/she knows the quality of a product/service will endure as long that customer has it, whereas the price paid is forgotten within a short time.

It is wise to be reminded what W.A. Foster stated some years ago:

> *"Quality is never an accident. It is always the result of high intention, sincere effort, intelligent direction and skilful execution. It represents the wise choice of many alternatives."*

No doubt there are still people who would like to go back to the 'good old days'—no vehicles but only bullock carts, no telephone, no electricity, and no processed food. They would like, if possible, to turn the clock back. But these diehard 'conservatives' have to realize the world is moving towards a technological society. For instance, e-mail has almost replaced the traditional 'snail mail'. Bank clerks and tellers are being made redundant by increasing use of automatic ATMs, which work 24 hours a day throughout the year. If some people are reluctant or unhappy with the rapid changes, tough luck on them as some of these changes are irreversible. Either you try to catch up with the changes or you would be isolated and left far behind. However, a point to remember is that any technological change has to be user-friendly, safe and reliable. This is where quality counts. For instance, if a person wants to draw cash from an ATM, all that he needs his credit/debit card, the password which only he/she knows, the amount to be drawn. If that person wishes to draw Rs. 1000, then he/she should get it without fail. That customer cannot be short-changed due to a glitch in the system. Of course, the customer cannot be given extra cash by machine error either.

CREED OF EXCELLENCE

It is the desire to excel that has been the hallmark of many ancient civilizations, including our own. This is nothing but quality at its best. For example, the *gurukul* system of ancient education was practiced by which the learned teachers, the gurus, took a number of pupils under their tutelage who would spend their childhood and youth in the ashram not only learning everything that has to be learnt but become a member of that guru or sage's family carrying out domestic chores. The students served their master and his wife well for a number of years. To be accepted as a *shisya* (student) in such a system, especially under renowned *acharya* was difficult. The *gurus* (teachers) taught their pupils all that they knew while the students in turn devoted their time and energy not only to learn but also to do everything they could do to serve their master with devotion and dedication. Thus the *gurukul* system was hailed as a model for imparting knowledge and a place to acquire respect for values.

Once the master realized that he had imparted all knowledge that he could, he would tell the pupils, "My sons, you are now ready to leave my *gurukul*. I have no more to teach you. May God be with you in whatever you do. You may pursue higher studies under any master you wish." In return the *shisyas* (pupils) presented humbly *gurudakshina* (offering) according to their means and there was no compulsion about it. In course of time these *gurukulas* were recognized as centres of excellence. Later on such a practice was followed in the *gharana* system of imparting classical Indian art, dance and music. In such schools, under the patronage of a well-known *guru*, the tradition specific to that *gharana* was maintained without deviations. However, there was scope for innovation but strictly within the broad structure of that *gharana*. Anyone who dared to violate the time-honoured tradition of that *gharana* was looked upon as a rebel and shunned for his/her deviant behaviour for tinkering with the system that was laid down for generations by revered masters.

To sum up, in ancient India, the creed of excellence was maintained through time-honoured and tested systems:

Gurukuia
Gharana

Great civilizations all over the world have built monuments that have stood the test of time. It is well to remember that, "*Excellence is not a skill. It is an attitude.*" It is remarkable that those civilizations, with such low technology, could fashion out great structures like the Pyramids, Great Wall of China, and Taj Mahal.

Taj Mahal, a poem in marble

For instance, the Pyramids were built about 3000–5000 years ago but have weathered the intense heat and the dust of the desert storms raging around these for centuries. The Cheops Pyramid at Giza, near Cairo, which is one of the seven wonders of the ancient world was so carefully built during 3000 B.C. with a height of 481 feet 4 inches and the sides of its square base 775 feet 9 inches vary by no more than an inch. A great deal of thinking and planning must have gone into the design of the pyramid and the chief designer must have been a genius. One is awe-struck even to think of the tremendous efforts that must have gone into the planning and execution of the Pyramid. Contrary to what was thought to be cruel employment of slave labour, research indicates that the workers were devoted to their task, were supplied tools, food and drinks and put up in housing colonies near the construction site. They took pride in their work and wanted to make the final resting place of their Pharaoh memorable so that he can have an easy passage to the next world.

A few countries like France, Germany, Switzerland, UK and USA, have a high reputation for quality. They dominated the global market for a number of years till China, Japan and Korea, and India too in some fields like IT, are posing serious challenge to the dominance of the western countries. Post-war Japan transformed itself to become an International producer of high quality and low cost products and services. It rose like a Phoenix from the ashes of two atomic devices unleashed during the fag end of World War II. Japan became known for its quality of goods like automobiles, cameras, photo-copiers, video-cameras, low cost watches and audio and video electronic goods like two-in-one radio/recorder and TV sets of high definition. Not to be left behind, Asian Tigers like Singapore, South Korea and Taiwan challenged Japan and have now won a slice of the global pie.

Thanks to the WTO regime, national boundaries to free trade are coming down with a result the customers all over the world are able to enjoy world class goods and services at affordable prices, due to competition. Thanks to such liberalization and globalization, Indian customers are now able to have access to quality goods of various International brands within the country on competitive prices. However, there is still some protectionism to safeguard domestic producers, though such artificial safeguards to protect domestic producers will have to go in the long run. In other words, customers are likely to have freer access to quality goods and services as never before. No one needs to bring in any item from overseas, as most of the items would be readily available locally. Long waiting periods and premiums on goods and services are now things of the past when protectionism of a close market reigned.

ANCIENT INDIANS

We have in our ancient times, a few fine examples of creed of excellence as could be seen from the above discussions concerning *gurukula* and *gharana* system of learning—generally, a master-pupil dedication spread over a number of years. It should also be noted that our people had gone ahead of the world in several disciplines. Some of them were famous astronomers and astrologers. They calculated the occurrence of solar and lunar eclipses accurately. With an expert knowledge of human body, our ancient doctors like *Aryavarta* and *Susruta* had mastered the methods of healing and curing diseases with their mastery over *ayurveda*, an ancient Indian system of medicine. Ancient sages practiced and taught *Yoga*, a system of philosophic meditation, controlled breathing and physical postures and exercises to achieve a higher plane of consciousness, which helped them to lead a life free from stress and also to overcome many chronic ailments.

Indian mathematicians were the first to postulate the 'Zero' (*shuyna*) concept, one of the significant contributions to the world of mathematics ever. Other examples of the exquisite examples of construction and paintings seen are: The Rock temple of Ellora, the cave paintings of Ajanta, the Iron pillar near Kutub Minar, the wonderful monument of Taj Mahal, described as a 'poem in marble'. Some of the structures to store water and lead water to parched lands are good examples of the skills of our ancient people. These structures were not only sturdy but also pleasing lasting hundreds of years; a true testimony to the meaning of quality as demonstrated by the ancients who believed in the creed of excellence.

Unfortunately, such a creed of excellence gave place, slowly, over the years to shoddy and indifferent work in every sphere. The industrial revolution in UK, and Europe in the mid 1700s transformed those countries from agricultural economies to production-based economies by adding value to the finished goods. For instance, cheap cotton from India, Egypt and other countries were imported into U.K., which in turn exported finished textiles at.much higher price, due to add-on value, to other countries, thus earning foreign exchange, with high profits in the bargain

Import low cost raw material → Added value for export → High profit

Another example is India used to export pig iron (even now to some extent) and import high quality steel from Germany, Japan and UK.

Slowly, our craftsmen lost out to finished goods from abroad and their skills deteriorated over the years due to poor patronage.

The colonial rulers stifled local industries in the country they had colonized, including India. They saw to it that their finished goods were accepted in their colonies by charging high costs. Obviously, they brooked no domestic competition, which could hurt their exports. Thus, UK prospered at the expense of their colonies.

A NEW DAWN

After Independence, priority was given to setting up several Public Sector Undertakings (PSUs) in core sectors like steel, heavy machinery, heavy electrical, machine tools, electronics, telecommunications, power generation and so on. But over the years, these PSUs diversified into low technology sectors like bread making. Moreover, the politicians and bureaucrats, with their own vested interests, saw these PSUs as employment generating devices and began to dish out favours to one and all at taxpayers' expense. Described as the 'modern temples' by Jawaharlal Nehru, the architect of the PSUs and India's great prime minister, the very same PSUs over the years became white elephants with no infusion of funds or technology. Many of them became 'sick' and employees had to be offered the Voluntary Retirement Scheme (VRS), euphemistically termed the 'golden handshake'. Disinvestment is not a pleasant subject with the employees, their unions and the left parties opposing the move to hive off the PSUs, loss-making notwithstanding. It needs great debate and persuasion to make people understand that we cannot go on subsiding a loss-making unit. Privatization, done through a proper and transparent route, is good for the country with adequate checks and balances.

In the earlier days, with little technology upgradation, and no competition, quality was accorded the last priority by both the public sector and the private sector. The customer was taken for granted. He had to wait for years to get an automobile, a two-wheeler or even a telephone connection. When he got what he wanted, there were many glitches, which the manufacturers and the service-providers were least worried about rectifying. 'Self-reliance' (*Swadeshi*) was the mantra, which oiled the industry. While rapid changes in technology, processes and materials were going round us, we blithely ignored all these in a sheltered market insulated from outside influences. High import duties kept many goods away. Moreover, the government refused to allow many goods to be imported, which resulted in rampant smuggling and black-marketing. Local goods and services were shoddy and expensive compared to the imported items.

Our development was based upon the erstwhile USSR's centralized planning model. That meant strict control from the government from planning to execution and marketing. There was no free hand to anyone within the PSUs to take decisions unless approved by the concerned ministry. The break-up of the USSR was the signal for winds of change to blow in with adoption of alternate models of development. It was under our ex-prime minister P.V. Narasimha Rao that liberalization and globalization took root. Thanks to the dynamic Dr. Manmohan Singh who was the then finance minister, the market was open to competition with liberal licensing for manufacture. A fair degree of customs duty was slashed to allow imports of goods and services. A cautious welcome was given to the foreign companies to open their offices and manufacturing units, often in collaboration with local Indian partners.

Even China has opened its market for foreign direct investment and now 'Made in China' label products are flooding the market, including the USA. Liberalization and globalization are yet to be accepted by some politicians and union leaders due to mind-set. This, hopefully, will change for the benefit of the Indian customers who would have plenty of choices for his hard earned money. However, a point that needs to be stressed is that such liberalization and globalization should have a *human face* with considerations for those who have to be sacked or those who need to be relocated. That's why the idea that every employer has to see that his employees are employable elsewhere should be stressed. That would make the pain of separation or loss of job less traumatic. 21st century promises greater emphasis on quality with many brands, some of International standards, competing with Indian brands.

The cycle of ups and downs in quality of goods and services in India may be summed up as in Table 1.1 below:

Table 1.1

Ancient times	—	High quality
Middle ages	—	Declining quality
Colonial rule	—	Poor quality
Independent India	—	Poor quality
Under liberalization from 1991	—	Upswing in quality

In the past most of the private sector companies did not pay much attention to quality as these were operating in a sheltered market. There was hardly any customer focus in their sales and marketing. "We do not need any advertisement," boasted a marketing director of a well-known MNC. It was a fact that company had the monopoly in the market and there was hardly any competition. Henry Ford is believed to have stated that a customer can have a car of any colour, as long it was black! That was his offer of a 'choice'!

However, the situation has changed dramatically over the years where the manufacturers have no option but to bend backwards to please the customer who has a wide choice now. The organizations are now forced to put customer first because without him there is no sale and hence no company. This realization has come out late though a few organizations still have not embraced such a concept wholeheartedly as it has become difficult for them to change their mindset. Long waiting periods are a distant bad dream. Customers earlier could choose one or two brands at the most, if they had a choice that's! Hoarding, black-marketing, selling at a premium have all but disappeared when it comes to buying consumer durables. It is clear:

Sheltered market = Poor quality

A few nations have prided themselves on their culture of excellence. That kind of culture has yet to seep in our business milieu, though we have inherited a rich culture of excellence as discussed in the earlier paragraphs. People do not take pride in what they do. It's the *chalta hai* philosophy at work, accepting poor quality and tolerating it when such a poor quality work is offered. Customers rarely complain about poor quality due to sheer laziness, apathy and indifference and stoicism. Another factor is the customers' fatalistic approach, 'nothing-ever-happens-even-if-we-complain' theme.

The ethos of dignity of labour is missing in our country. We believe in getting the most trivial jobs done by others — jobs that can be very well done by ourselves. Helper, mazdoor and class IV employees are found only in our country. On the contrary, in most other countries, each one is expected to do his/her own work without outside help. That includes cleaning and moving papers and files from place to place. With such an attitude and arrangement, delays are inevitable with consequent built-in inefficiency. Just keeping files pending is for a show off to tell others how busy that person is. There is no incentive for efficiency or punishment for lack of it. Thus, a customer wanting his work to be done by others is often at a dead end trying to break such a barrier of inefficiency. It takes Herculean efforts to get even a normal work done, unless some bribe is offered for speeding up even a legitimate routine job. Whether it is the public, semi-public or private sector the concept of being customer-friendly is yet to seep in despite winds of change. Hence a poor quality service means the customer is dissatisfied and would look elsewhere to get better service. In future, quality of service could play a vital role in decision-making as far as the customer's choice is concerned.

There can be no better way to express the importance of dignity of labour that is taking pride in whatever we do, than to quote the words of John Gardner:

"Good plumbing:
An excellent plumber is infinitely more admirable than an incomplete philosopher. The society, which scorns excellence in plumbing because plumbing is a humble activity and tolerates shoddiness in philosophy because it is an exalted activity, will have neither good plumbing nor good philosophy. Neither its pipes nor its thoughts will hold water."

LIBERALIZATION AND GLOBALIZATION

With the dawn of the era of liberalization followed by globalization in 1991, there emerged a totally new concept — that competition is good for the economy and is a better way to deliver quality goods and services to the customer more efficiently. We have seen how in the post-1991 period has seen a sea change in the availability of goods and services. Long waiting periods are a thing of the past. Now the consumer has a wide range of choices — for example, he can choose shiny cars in a variety of colours, various capacity engines, shapes, sizes, with additional fittings, with no waiting period. He also has a choice of loans with a small down payment, the rest in easy instalments at low interest rates. There is also an exchange programme to trade in an old car for a brand new one.

New advertisements and marketing strategies are being evolved to woo customers. For instance, 'scratch and win a car' or a 'free ticket to Singapore' and so on. There are offers of attractive prizes including overseas trips for one or two persons after buying a car and if lucky to win a prize in a draw held at random. Gifts and freebies are offered if one chooses to a buy a car during festival seasons when the manufacturers would like to increase their sales. Other consumer durables, 'white goods' are also offered for sales, of international brands at competitive rates by promising gifts, freebies, lottery *et al.* It is now possible to buy most of the foreign label goods within the country without having to step out of it, such is the choice before a consumer of today. Even there is an incentive for subscription to some of the popular journals and magazines by offer of prizes and free gifts with a chance to win a mega prize like a car in a lottery.

The present-day consumer had never had it so good. He is often confused about the choice that he has to make. He has come a long way from the problem of scarcity and no choice. Obviously, some of these consumers have a problem with a plethora of choices. "Market-driven quality starts with making customer satisfaction an obsession and empowering people to use their creative energy to satisfy and delight customers," so stated John F. Akers, Chairman and CEO, IBM some years ago. Companies will be forced to focus on quality, which will be dictated by the likes and dislikes of consumers. The strategy for companies in such a business milieu is to try to understand customers' perception of quality, monitor it regularly, measure it and use the data for enhancement of performance to retain the competitive edge over others. Thus, customer focus is the new strategy for the success of a business.

POOR CULTURE OF SERVICE

While there is good news on the number of products offered for sale, where there is plenty of choice, the service sector has yet to absorb the culture of service, which is needed to make customers happy and delighted. Unfortunately, the customer is not always right as far as a dealer/serviceperson is concerned. 'Customer is King', 'Customer Focus', and 'Customer-friendly' are mere slogans left behind in the management/business school. Hardly any service organization is putting into practice what it has learnt. On the other hand, such slogans are just part of overused corporate parlance. Every time one encounters pathetic demonstrations of these values, more from the private sector, one has reason to conclude that these are terms just to lure the customers. Some instances where the private sector fares badly:

(1) A private sector ATM is not working and the other machine runs out of cash.

(2) Set-up box on the TV malfunctioning.

(3) Cable operation faulty.

It takes a long time to get the complaints redressed and that too after follow up.

Surprisingly, the public sector is becoming more responsive and accountable like never before. They have realized that if they were not responsive they would lose business and may have to be shut down. Thus, the employees of such organizations are realizing with all seriousness that unless they try to make peace with their customers there is a good chance of losing business to the private sector. Such a healthy change in outlook is welcome. For instance, the time taken to attend to complaints has been much reduced. In India we have transitioned from an era of face-to-face communication to faceless communication and in this bargain have lost the meaning of customer service. Call centres are welcome but they are too impersonal and it takes a long time before we can communicate with a human operator. Most of the time it's frustrating to be put 'on hold' listening to some music.

It is clear we need a proactive ombudsman for each organization whose main function would be look into complaint redress mechanism and see that matters are speeded up. It may appear simple that when companies have more than a million customers, losing one does not matter. But then again, there is something called 'word-of-mouth' publicity. And if you were not careful, that negative word would will soon spread to all the million. Dealers take on an entirely different stance from their usual courteous self when the product they have sold to you shows a defect after sales. Even if the product is within the warranty period, they shift the onus of repair or replacement onto the manufacturer, who may be a company in some other part of the country or world. However, the fact remains that in several consumer court decisions, it has been made amply clear that both the dealer and the manufacturer are jointly and severally liable in case of a problem.

There is a ray of hope for the harassed Indian consumers. Politicians have slowly realized that the voter, the common man, is voting as per his judgment whether a particular government is responsive to his needs or not. He is no longer fooled by tall promises or inducements like cash, sari, cloth, freebies, liquor on the eve of elections. The common man, thanks to the information revolution spawned by satellite TV channels, e-mail, magazines and newspapers, is increasingly becoming aware of his duties and responsibilities. He has access to information that is often instantaneous and knows what is happening in some corner of the world. He is definitely influenced by global trends while keeping his feet firmly on the local soil. So manufacturers/producers/retailers are beginning to realize that customers can longer be taken for granted despite inducements and low prices. He wants value for his hard earned money. The more value he gets for his money the better. Thanks to the availability of foreign goods/ services, he has set his benchmark on international standards which he expects at domestic prices. However, he has a problem while choosing a particular TV channel to view inspite of showing popular soaps. Though each channel touts its own popularity rating, he has no independent authority like the 'Nielsen' in the USA for a TV show guide. This is expected to change in the future, if the government takes interest in setting up such an independent TV channel viewership rating authority.

COMPETITION

Everyone is realizing, barring diehard manufacturers who have yet to change their mindset, that competition is good for everyone, customer as well as producer. This means the production is cost-effective and benefits the producer as well as customer with better quality and that too with quicker delivery. Survival of the fittest is becoming truer and truer. Just look at the open sky policy of the government that has opened the sky to competition. A number of airlines in the private sector are giving a run for the money for the nationalized carrier Indian and Air India, which is now forced to upgrade its service to survive the challenge of the many private carriers. However, 'survival of the fittest', the law of the jungle, is true even in the business world and there will be consolidation to stay competitive.

Sometimes a customer is enticed with half prices, and 'take one and the other free' type of offers which are hard to resist. In the end, it is possible that the customer is led up the garden path and would regret his decision to go in for a certain product or service which he could do without. It is possible that at the first glance, an offer might look very attractive but it could also prove in the long run to be 'too good to be true'. Deals which claim: 'Export rejects', 'seconds', 'half prices', 'every day low prices', 'lottery', 'freebies', 'no interest or no deposit' need to be examined carefully and not fall into a trap unwittingly by the spur of the moment decision which one might regret later on.

It is possible for a customer in certain instances that he could be the judge to decide the quality of a product/service. At other times, the product features could be too complicated for the uninitiated to make a considered judgment about the product. In such cases, the customer would refer to the catalogue, ask friends and relatives about their experiences vis-à-vis a product and its performance. The 'word-of-mouth' publicity, both good and bad, plays an important role in decision-making. Another factor is the brand loyalty. You tend to purchase products from the same company (brand) unless you have come across something else, which is equally good. While it takes several good measures to get the seal of approval of a customer, one bad experience can ruin the brand name forever. And it is a difficult job regaining that trust and confidence.

The trend of multiple choices will continue and the regime of liberalization and globalization cannot be reversed as the customers are used to it by now. They know it is good for them as well as the nation. However, a problem faced by customers is the lack of reliable ratings for products/services though a few consumer organizations like the *consumer voice* are trying to fill the gap. That is the problem in a situation of multiple choices compared to zero choice of the past.

Liberalized/Globalized market → Multiple choice for customers.

MULTIPLE CHOICE

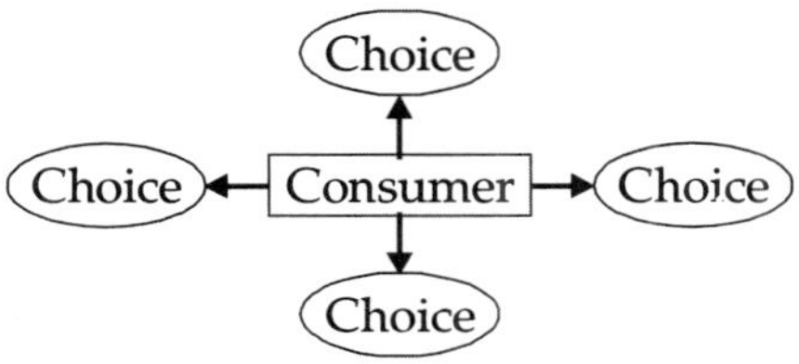

MEANINGFUL CHOICE

The 21st century has been a bonanza for Indian consumers who never had it so good with a bewildering array of choices — domestic as well as International brands. With the W.T.O. regime in place, we can expect more tariff barriers and protectionism to come down for the benefit of the consumers all over the world. We have no escape from such a situation. Some Indian companies still work with a mindset to the 'bad old days' of protectionism. However, the point that everyone should get a level playing field is well taken. They have to realize that the consumers have a choice and they have no alternative but to keep pace with the global trends of improved quality. The list of items that could be imported, with reasonable import duties, is getting longer. The Indian consumers have now a taste of American, Australian and Chinese apples besides our own. We can now get Kiwi fruit imported from New Zealand. We have a choice of fruit juices from Australia, VCRs from Japan, Tea from Sri Lanka, preserves from Thailand and so on. That the prices of some of these items are too high and beyond the reach of most Indians is a different point to consider. Over the course of years, these prices are going to come down and become competitive to local produce. No doubt, this is an opportunity for our own producers to go global and be competitive to earn valuable foreign exchange. For instance, go to any stores in the USA and you will find most of the items are imported.

The book is an attempt to provide information and the tools needed for consumers before they make the buying decision. One can easily be confused by the proliferation of goods and services all looking more or less the same, with the same attractive features nicely packaged and competitively priced. A word of caution is advisable when the market is full of aggressive sellers each trying to improve their sales and thus their bottom line. In principle the consumer should buy a product that is needed by him and not because someone else wants to force him to buy because of freebies and low prices. With a little caution, he can avoid the pitfalls of misleading advertisements by seeing the fine print and asking searching questions to make matters clear. 'Do not presume anything,' is a good piece of advice. Often, though the price of a particular brand is higher, in the longer this could prove economical by way of 'life cycle costs', which could be cheaper ultimately. Another factor is the quality of service in the neighbourhood. If you have to send the product, when needed for service/ repair, to a distant city by spending your money, then it is better to look for an alternate product where the service facilities are available in the same town or nearby. Do not be fooled by price tags such as Rs. 99, 499,

1999, 14,999 that are more to convince the gullible consumer that the price appears less than what the eye meets!

A factor that should be borne by present day consumers is the need to be technically savvy. There is no reason to fear adapting to latest techniques. For instance, 24-hour banking through an ATM card is almost becoming commonplace in our country. This is convenient, which avoids the hassles of going to a bank at certain hours only to draw cash. However, it is in the customers' interest that they keep a regular tab on the transactions, by way of either on-line or through pass books that are updated regularly. Another example that could be cited is the purchase/sale of stocks and shares. Trading in shares earlier was easy—go to a stockbroker with your paper share certificate and get cash soon or after some time. Now most companies insist on *demat* account, which is an electronic method of keeping a registry of stocks and shares. It would be advisable to convert all paper shares and stocks to *demat* format to avoid problems of trading, if and when needed. For sheer convenience, there is nothing like the ECS scheme which is 'Electronic Clearing Scheme' to settle bills for water, electricity, telephone bills and so on. However, as a matter of caution, check if the transactions from month to month are in order. It is better to note: *Computers do not make mistakes but human beings do.* Thus, regular updating of your pass book or transactions via on-line or by the bank would be good to prevent surprises. Those who had earlier apprehensions about introduction of computers and related change in methods are now clamouring for more such changes that are beneficial to consumers.

TECHNOLOGY ADVANCES

As technology develops more, the consumers are likely to face a barrage of new features, which appear to them bewildering and bordering on sci-fi stuff. No doubt some of these are improvements while the others are new inventions to make products/services of better quality with newer add-on features. An ordinary consumer is likely to be confused with jargon like: 'Quadra', 'Dolby', 'Kirara Basso', 'Bazooka', 'Golden Eye', 'Demat', 'ECS' which might sound like Greek and Latin to him. Unfortunately, he has no option but become knowledgeable if he has to make a meaningful decision about buying a product with so many features.

At the present rate of technology advance, we are likely to hear and more and more of newer technologies like 'Nano-technology'. Another problem a customer is likely to face is the unscrupulous dealers/sales persons who want to palm off an inferior product claiming, by using high flown jargon, that particular product is better than a standard one. He might even persuade a customer that it is brand new technology and so sure to be better than a standard brand. It is likely that dealer/salesperson is getting a better discount by selling that not-so-great product to gullible customers. He might offer a discount to make the offer even more attractive since he has a better margin of profit. Such tactics are not ethical but what can we do if there are greedy and not so ethical persons who want to make a fast buck at the expense of someone else.

The availability of many brands of products/services might be outpacing the culture of customer service. There is more incentive to sell than redress customer complaints, which are 'non-productive'. The customer is likely to face a stonewall when it comes to repair/replace/refund a defective product. The customer unfriendly motto of today, despite winds of change: "Goods once sold cannot be returned, replaced, exchanged or refunded." Despite competition, manufacturers/dealers/salespersons are behaving the same old way and there is hardly any difference between one company and another. Effectively, it means there is no competition when it comes to after sales service. However, this might change if the customers start demanding their rights aggressively instead of being apathetic to problems or being stoic about a defect. That culture of 'will do', 'what can we do?' should be abolished, the sooner the better.

Being aware about customer's right is one thing and getting redress is another matter. One might have to run from pillar to post to get quick redress. A responsible customer will not take 'no' for an answer from anyone. He would fight for his rights with conviction but without anger or rancour. It is a comforting thought that an aggrieved customer can get redress from a Consumer Court, which will be discussed in the forthcoming chapters. However, self-help is still the best help as this gets a complaint redressed faster. Moreover, one has the satisfaction of getting something done on one's own efforts. It would be necessary, in view of advances in various fields, that a customer keeps in touch with these developments that would give him the necessary wherewithal to fight his own consumer battles, when needed. That would also give him that edge to get value for his purchase.

'Shopping' for a good deal is common in USA. The Internet is a powerful tool where one can search the websites of various manufacturers as well as service providers. For instance, if a person wants to fly from one place to another, he would check up competing airlines and choose the one that is cheapest and at the same time reliable. That applies to booking a hotel room in a distant place where it is possible to check the rates, the location, the various facilities and so on. All that would be necessary then would be pay by a credit card to hold the reservation or settle in full the amount due. Most of the service sectors, including banks, insurance, hospitality industry, entertainment centres like theme parks, theatres and cinemas have the facility to check the availability of tickets and book the same on the Internet. Now facilities in hospitals and educational institutions too could be surfed without going all the way to find out details.

It is not far-off before we too could make use of the Internet more effectively that would save time, energy and costs. Personal Computers (PCs) and laptop computers are becoming a feature in most middle class homes. Moreover, Internet cafes are mushrooming that could access any website one likes for a charge per hour. In our business milieu, already a few companies have started their own websites to provide all the information needed for a customer to take a meaningful decision. Indian Railways, most airlines, big manufacturers and service providers are all geared up to meet the challenges of the Internet and provide customer-friendly service to satisfy customers. They have realized that the best and easy way is to reach the customer is through the Internet so that the customer can take a decision by a simple click of the mouse. In fact, by eliminating the reservation/booking staff and related infrastructure, companies are saving cost, some of which is passed on to consumers.

Tele-shopping, tele-marketing, and tele-banking are all catching up. Tele-conferencing is another feature that is getting more attention as it has several advantages. E-commerce has made a good beginning with Internet proving to be a useful tool for delivering information to millions of consumers instantly and cheaply. The 21st century will be the era of dot.coms and websites where information is there for the asking without having to pay for it, at least not at present. IT revolution is becoming customer-friendly by giving the customer a meaningful tool for better decision-making.

CHAPTER 2

CONSUMER RIGHTS AND RESPONSIBILITIES

You succeed only by continually surpassing expectations
—Anonymous

In a sense everyone is a consumer—the buyer, seller, manufacturer, dealer, retailer, service provider. If a seller sells something, he is a consumer of something else, such is the interdependence in a society. No one can claim to be totally self-sufficient. Thus, we are all consumers of something or the other, and so, theoretically there is a commonality of objectives among one and all. But in reality there is a dichotomy—a seller thinks only of selling and does not at that moment think he is a consumer too. He has no interest, at least that moment, in safeguarding the interests of consumers against fraudulent transactions, and may even go the extent of palming off substandard goods just to make a profit—at the expense of the buyer. Such an attitude is true of a consumer as he acts as if he is only a consumer and not a seller though he could be selling some goods or services. In that position he tries his best to safeguard his (consumer) interests by every means.

We might be thinking that with the free availability of goods and services the market is fair while dealing with consumers. On the contrary, there are unscrupulous traders/dealers/manufacturers who think of making money—at the expense of hapless and gullible consumers. In a vast country like ours, there are millions of illiterate/semi-literate persons who are easy prey to those who want to sell less than good quality to consumers. The reason is the level of awareness among such people is low and no one is educating them to impress upon such people that they have consumer rights as well as responsibilities.

Also, in such a diverse country like ours, there are educated and knowledgeable persons who fall a prey to tall advertisements and taller promises. For instance, a blade company might declare, "We will give you double the interest rate than banks. We will guarantee that your money will double in three years." We can be sure there are a few hundreds of people who will bite the bait and invest their hard earned money. For sure, the dubious company operators are clever. They will see to it that interests are paid regularly to depositors for a few months so that more persons are wooed to join such 'attractive' schemes. Then one fine day, when their nest is full, the company downs its shutters with no sign of the directors of the company. The depositors are heart broken as some of them had invested all their life's earning to increase their net-worth. Complaints are filed with the police and if lucky some of the absconders are arrested. But the damage is already done because to recover the lost money is a Herculean task.

This chapter is an attempt to guide the consumers about their rights and responsibilities that could help them to make meaningful decisions. Some of the material presented here could help a consumer in dealing with dealers/salespersons/retailers. It is important to know consumer rights as well as responsibilities that could help consumers to use better judgment while buying goods and services. These are basic facts but real world matters could be more complex. There are a few gray areas where the difference between a dealer/manufacturer could be blurred. If a dealer states that he is not fully responsible for what he sells but that he is acting, as an agent for the manufacturer, he might be right. But a consumer knowing his rights would not give up easily with such an explanation. He would argue convincingly that he is transacting business with the dealer only and there is no reason why he should approach a manufacturer directly. However, he could help the dealer in taking up the matter with the manufacturer by providing useful inputs that would clarify matters.

CONSUMER RIGHTS

A consumer has the rights as depicted below:

- Right to education
- Right to safety
- Right to information
- Right to choose
- Right to be heard
- Right to enjoy the goods/services as consumers

We shall discuss these consumer rights in the context of the present situation, which is far better than earlier years where consumers got a raw deal due to a closed market condition. Now there is a vibrant consumer market that caters to a variety of goods and services, often of International Standards. The passage of Consumer Protection Act [COPRA] in 1986 (which will be discussed in another chapter) was a landmark Act in the Indian context. Unfortunately, a feeling has crept in that this Act is a panacea for all the ills affecting Indian consumers. Far from it, this Act can provide some relief but many a battle, at all levels, have to be fought by individual consumers to get their rights protected. Moreover, COPRA is one more tool to guarantee rights of consumers and nothing more.

The NGOs working in the past, trying to redress consumers problems, are overcome by a feeling of redundancy after the Act came into force. They feel that their work is now over as the courts are vested with powers to settle consumer complaints. Slowly, the NGOs in the consumer field are regaining confidence that they still have a useful role to play in helping the consumers to make the right choice, by educating them, as well as help them to get their complaints redressed. Their role in educating consumers about their rights and responsibilities cannot be overstressed. They can guide consumers make informed choice in a multiple-choice environment. Moreover, some of the consumer organizations are now working on testing and rating goods and services that serve to enlighten the consumers in making the right choice. Their *raison d'etre* is more important than ever before in helping the consumers to make the right choice in a multi-choice market milieu, take up their cases when needed and more important of all to educate them about their rights and responsibilities.

We shall now discuss the various consumer rights and responsibilities in the following paragraphs:

Right to consumer education

Unfortunately, this is one of the most important rights of a consumer, which is neglected. In our country this aspect has been more or less neglected by the government (State as well as Centre), industry, business, educational institutions as well as the NGOs. Educating a consumer is a pro-active measure to help fight for his rights. However, in reality this comes last when everything else fails! Very few organizations are involved in educating the consumers about their rights and responsibilities. This means practically every one in the country is neglected as far as consumer education is concerned. It is a fact that even after so many years of independence the overall literacy rate in the country is about fifty per cent, though there are islands of excellence like Kerala where it is over

90 per cent. Women, tribals and villagers are those with low-level literacy especially in states like Bihar, Madhya Pradesh, Rajasthan and Uttar Pradesh. There is a big gap in the level of literacy and awareness between the urbanites and the rural people. Another factor is the gender gap in literacy with the women being less literate than men in general. Those states where the literacy rate is high have shown improvement in various fields such as better sanitation, adherence to small family norm, improved awareness about educating the girl child, increased participation in elections, including local body elections, and enthusiastic participation in community development activities.

The fact is, a literate consumer is in a better position to think for himself about his rights and responsibilities. He would then take measures to protect these. For example, a gullible consumer would fall a prey to sweet talk, offer of freebies, prizes, and lotteries when a dealer is trying to sell an inferior quality low-priced item. He is in no position to see through the dubious means used to sell something, which is going to be troublesome once it is bought. This is where judgment, awareness and education are important in decision-making. A better-informed consumer would be able to differentiate between genuine stuff and which is mere hype. Thus, a knowledgeable consumer has insured himself against cheating and deception. Take for example, a dealer who is keen to sell a TV of a less than standard brand because he gets a better commission if he sells it. The dealer could adopt unethical measures, for instance using a booster to get a better picture, to convince the consumer that the TV brand is 'superior' and of a better picture quality than a standard brand which is also demonstrated alongside. A smart consumer is likely to figure out why that particular brand, which the dealer is keen to sell, is not so good after all as compared to a standard brand. By a few intelligent questions by a consumer, the dealer could be exposed about the devious methods he had adopted in the demonstration.

In the advanced countries where both the literacy and awareness are high like France, Germany, Japan, UK and USA, the consumer makes an informed decision. Consequently, the dealer dare not fool the consumer lest he be blacklisted. When a potential customer enters a showroom, he is already armed with knowledge and information about a particular brand. A few searching questions are all that are needed to clinch the deal. Since the consumer is knowledgeable, the dealer cannot hoodwink him by making tall claims. However, a customer should never let his guard down when he is making an important decision about buying a product or service. The more data he has about the product/service the better for sound decision-making. That is the reason why impulse buying should be avoided as far as possible, in view of the risks involved in any hasty buying. Obviously, a customer expects the dealer to have done his homework too as far as goods he has stocked is concerned. In general, a customer would like to get a feel of the product by hands-on-experience before deciding to purchase it. For example, a car buyer would like to test drive a new model car before making up his mind about that particular model. That is the reason why shopping on-line is not yet become so popular.

In view of TV and Internet, consumers are swayed by advertisements and endorsements by celebrities. Print medium is still widely read and still has influence over a large population. Periodic publication of ratings of products and services in newspapers and magazines would go a long way in educating consumers before they part with their money. Take for instance, mutual fund companies. This is one area where an unwary customer can get into trouble. Regular, say weekly/fortnightly, ratings of various mutual fund schemes of several companies could aid the investor to a better portfolio for investment. That would keep wise investors away from dubious companies, which promise a lot but fail to deliver after a while. A study of the ratings would warn a potential investor to be careful about investing in a particular company that has poor ratings. It would be in his interest to keep away from such companies. We need a strong consumer organization, on the lines of Consumer Union (CU), USA, which is providing ratings that are acceptable to one and all. The ratings of products/services that appear regularly in their monthly magazine is a guide for any potential buyer as these ratings are respected and relied upon by consumers. Consequently, no wise buyer in USA would invest in a product/service, be it a car, fridge, telephone service company, banking, or insurance, without checking its ratings as published by CU.

As mentioned earlier, Consumer Magazines like the *Consumer Voice* published from New Delhi try to provide rating information on products/services. However, it would take quite some time before every one, including manufacturer, dealer, consumer, accepts these ratings as guides for decision-making. It would be better if more NGOs and organizations concentrate on product/service ratings so that consumers can rely upon these before taking purchase decisions. It is possible that the government's consumer affairs department could find independent organizations that could work on product/service ratings. It would be better if no private or government organization gets involved in such independent test-house to prevent any bias. That is why CU does not accept any advertisement or sponsorship either by private companies or government.

We have yet to take consumer education more seriously. Part of the apathy may be attributed to consumer indifference. But the government cannot absolve of its share of the blame for not doing more in the field of consumer education that is a fundamental right of any consumer. The industry and business have not shown much interest either in consumer education and making consumers better aware of their rights and responsibilities. There is a possibility that some of the private organizations would like to keep the customers in the dark to further their ends. However, this is a shortsighted policy that does not improve the quality awareness in the country.

The Industrial/Business Associations like FICCI, CEC should take the lead in organizing seminars/workshops/training programmes inviting consumers to participate so as to increase their decision-making capability. A small fee might be charged to make these sessions purposeful. Organizations should issue regular newsletters that have a wide circulation to increase awareness of consumers about their rights and giving them an idea of what is happening inside as well as outside our country on consumer matters. Some of the organizations like ICICI bring out a series of informative reports on various matters like fixed deposits, car loans, and house loans that highlight the finer aspects. Such informative reports act as good guides for those who are interested in taking advantage of facilities offered by banks and other financial institutions. The questions consumers should ask [frequently asked questions (FAQ)] before making a purchase decision, the precautions to be taken while talking to dealers/sellers and the tips that come in handy while making any decision should be discussed in any seminar/workshop/training programme.

Here is an example how a car battery manufacturer educates the customers on the right way of using/disposal of the product:

- The battery should be firmly secured in the cradle. Please ensure that the cable clamps fit tightly and properly on the terminals. A loosely held battery vibrates and bounces, causing damage to the container and the plates.
- The top of the battery must be kept clean and dry. Petroleum jelly (Vaseline) should be applied to cable clamps and terminals. Never apply grease. Terminal corrosion, dirt and moisture cause loss of power and make the battery weak.
- Get your fan belt, electrical wiring, dynamo/alternator and regulator settings checked regularly. A faulty electrical system will immediately damage the battery.

- The regulator setting should be such that the charging voltage across the battery terminals should be 14.2–14.4 volts.
- Vent plugs of maintenance-free batteries should be opened with a rupee coin. Do not use a screwdriver.
- The electrolyte level should be up to the bottom of the filling hole.
- Use only distilled water for topping. Do not top up with acid/ electrolyte/mineral water or tap water.

Caution

- Keep away from sparks, cigarettes, and open flame. These can cause explosion.
- Avoid metallic contact across terminals, as this can result in short circuits and sparking.

Important notice

This is to make you aware that your battery requires careful handling because of the following:

- Lead acid batteries contain lead and sulphur, which are highly toxic and extremely hazardous for health and environment.
- Lead poisoning affects the central nervous system causing irreversible retardation and subsequent death.
- Unauthorized smelters tend to pollute the air and ground water with these toxic substances during smelting.

To safeguard society, the Government of India has notified as under:

"It shall be the responsibility of the consumer to ensure that used batteries are not disposed of in any manner other than depositing with the dealer, manufacturer, re-conditioner or at the designated collection centres."

Hence, please do not discard the battery in a trash bin or sell to a non-authorized person. It is mandatory for our authorized dealers to accept a used battery and provide corresponding rebate on purchase of a new battery. Please note that violations of these guidelines may lead to legal action/prosecution by Government authorities.

However, it should be noted that the consumers too have to get over the mind-set of the past. They should realize they are in a dynamic market with so many choices. That is why they should willingly take part in consumer education because that benefits the consumers. While consumer goods exhibition, seconds sales, reject goods sale, discount sales and so on attract a large number of people, there is indifference to attend any training programme/seminar/workshop that would help consumers to help themselves. Even though such programmes are free, or with minor fee, hardly any one attends such programmes such is the indifference.

The relation between level of awareness and quality of decision-making is depicted in Fig. 2.1 below:

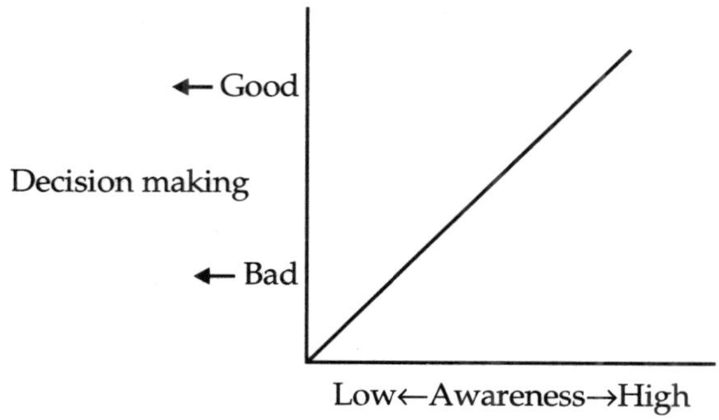

Fig. 2.1: Decision-making and level of awareness

Right to safety

Safety of equipment is paramount in a buying decision. The risks involved in buying something cheap, and not so safe, is horrendous. Life and property are involved when some equipment malfunctions and catches fire. Worse still is the case of electrical equipment, which is unsafe to touch, and could result in serious injury or even a fatality. For example, when a customer buys a toaster he would like to have crisp toast every time he uses it. He would be in a nasty surprise, if instead he gets a severe shock while inserting a bread slice. A few instances are there where a customer makes a compromise with safety by buying sub-standard equipment. For example, an immersion heater is used to heat water for bathing. This is an unsafe practice as it could result in a shock. It would be advisable that the customer instead buys a standard water heater certified with an ISI mark. That is the reason why safety should be given the topmost priority while purchasing electrical equipment. 'Safety first' should be the motto. There is no question of compromising on safety by buying cheap and nasty electrical goods that could prove very costly. Thus the onus is on the buyer to go in for a standard product, which is safe and economical by way of power consumption.

The assurance for product safety starts with the choice of a product, which carries a certification from India's premier standards organization, the Bureau of Indian Standards (BIS), formerly known as the Indian Standards Institution (ISI). However, there are a few reputed product manufacturers claim that their product meets, and often exceeds, the minimum standards for quality and safety as laid by the BIS guidelines. Their plea is that they do not want to be equated with those who meet just 'minimum' standards but they would like to be known as producers of superior products that exceed the minimum standards. This argument is convincing but for the uninitiated it could pose a problem. They would rather see that ISI mark on the product they buy and not depend only on the manufacturer's words and claims of superior products. In course of time even such manufacturers will have to fall in line and have the ISI seal of approval as that carries weight in the market and influences a buying decision. The customer should make sure the electrical items he buys are of reputed brands, with ISI or other international certifications, and not any other manufacturer because it is cheap or because he gives discounts.

Safety of items is not exclusive to electrical goods. For instance, the toy meant for a toddler should be safe to use even mishandled. It should not be toxic as the child could chew the toy. There should not be any sharp edges or projections that could hurt a child. In other words, toys should be 'childproof' and safe to use under any condition. In homes, the parents take care to make the house childproof by covering electrical sockets with dummy plugs, see that no dangerous medicine or substance is accessible, the drawers are locked that prevents a child from opening it, the stair cases are railed and barrier put up to see that the child does not fall down inadvertently and so on. Factory settings on products should not be easily accessible to a customer so that he does not fiddle with these controls. Trained technicians should operate these controls only.

Safety is not limited to product and service alone. In fact, it is important in every walk of ordinary life. But the level of safety consciousness in the advanced countries is much higher than countries like India. Though modern cars, even in our country, are equipped with safety belts, very few, including the drivers use them. In advanced countries, car seats are mandatory. Here we find drivers putting small children on their lap while driving! Those at the back rarely wear seat belts though provided. Helmets are meant to protect two-wheeler drivers in case of accident. Though it is compulsory to wear helmets while driving in some States, there is reluctance on the part of the drivers and the pillion riders to wear helmets meant to protect their heads. Some think it is just a piece of equipment to fool the police. They forget that a helmet has to be properly buckled up if it has to protect a person in an accident. On the contrary, in the advanced countries, even a child while riding a bicycle wears a helmet without anyone telling him/her or ordering to do so.

Thus, safety considerations in every walk of life in India need to be stressed from a young age. Safety is meant to save a life and no one need to tell about an individual about it. There are horror stories about overloading, over-speeding, rushing headlong into an unmanned level crossing when a train is passing through, shoddy electrical wiring, dangerous constructions that are patently unsafe and many other hazardous instances are mere tip of the iceberg when we think about safety in our society.

Safety should be a way of life rather than an imposition from the government.

Safety features

Just imagine a few safety aspects that are designed to prevent accidents. Safety guards in fans at homes have close mesh so that children do not poke their fingers inside a rotating fan and hurt themselves. Containers with medicines and toxic substances should have tamper-proof lids so that children cannot open these easily. The blades of a lawn mower are safely encased in a mesh to avoid accidental contact with the person who is using it. Safety-guards on running machines are so designed that unless the machine stops, one cannot open the lid. A safety device in a rotating washing machine makes it stop automatically if a person tries to open the top lid. Provision of a safety plug in a pressure cooker is meant to blow up if an abnormal pressure builds up due to some fault within. In a few modern cars, there is constant buzzer sound till the driver buckles up.

The more the safety features in a product/service the better to prevent accidents while using them. Merely buying a product because it is cheap could turn out to be a case of 'save a rupee and risk a life.' It is important that a product/service should be designed with the safety aspect being paramount. During manufacture, handling, packing, transporting and installing the safety aspect is equally important. Some electrical/electronic products require good earthing to prevent shocks when someone touches it. The impression of a product is the external appearance, which the customer can see and judge. He might not be able to open the case and see how the wiring is. Naked wires protruding, shabby appearance that includes poor painting, rust spots, sharp corners and other could dissuade a customer from buying that product as the first impression of safety and quality is poor. It is equally important that a customer heeds the warning printed on the product. For instance, there is a warning about opening the cover of a TV while in use. High voltage can cause fatality and that is why the TV should be switching off and power chord removed from the socket before attempting to open the cover for repair.

Buying a standard well-known brand of any product, with ISI marking, is a guarantee of safety and quality, though more expensive than an unknown but cheap brand.

In brief, safety is built in design and carefully executed at each and every phase of activity till it is installed at the customer. Buying a cheap unknown unsafe product is an invitation to disaster.

Right to be informed

A consumer has every right to be informed on the merits and demerits of a product/service which he would like to buy. However, a dealer, often, has his own interest while offering a product to a consumer. He would like to maximize his profit (commission) by selling a product/service that fetches just that. A prospective customer needs to be informed about any precaution needed to use the product/service without problems. A few examples are:

1. A TV may need special earthing.
2. A motor car a special grade oil.
3. An electronic device (like a computer) special protection like 'spike-buster'.
4. A refrigerator a voltage stabilizer.
5. An acid-battery cell special distilled water.
6. A car coolant, not water, but a special fluid.

The idea is to equip the customer with all the information and inputs that are necessary to have a trouble-free service. It is possible without these special precautions the customer might run into serious problems. The dealer might point a finger at the customer for 'mis-use' and refuse any guarantee period service/replacement. An ordinary customer could be ignorant of the precautions and could be a victim due to faulty use.

Thus, an important aspect of customer-dealer interface is information/communication/dialogue to make the product/service with the customer trouble-free. The more information a customer gets the better it is in his task of looking after his product/service carefully. Unfortunately, often a customer fiddles with his product/service until he gives up in despair. Then only as a last resort, he reads the handbook/instructions/literature associated with the product/service. In fact, it should be the other way—first read the instructions carefully then only operate a product/service.

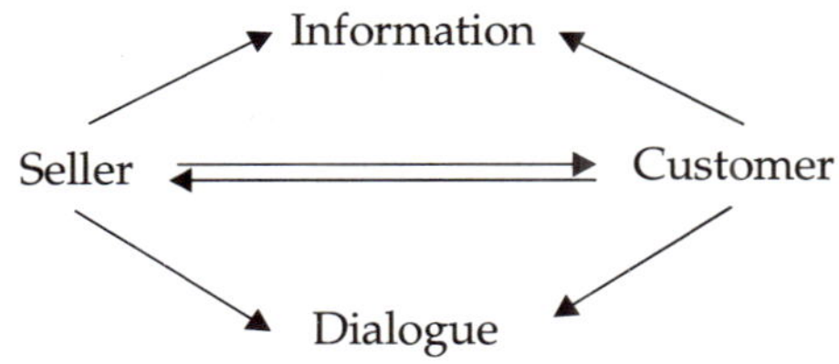

Fig. 2.2: A two-way communication

The two-way communication is equally, if not more, important in a service environment. For instance, the doctor-patient dialogue is critical for the wellbeing of the patient. A doctor has to give all the facts about a patient's condition, the prognosis—good and bad. In our social milieu, a doctor tends to be positive about a patient's condition and progress; whereas in the advanced countries, the doctor plays safe and often paints a not-so-rosy picture of the patient's chances of recovery. A doctor, caring for the welfare of a patient, would advise him about alternative treatments, as also the risks involved. For instance, a MRI has become routine but yet in the advanced countries, the doctors spell out the risks involved with such a procedure. It might appear as if the doctors in the advanced countries are trying to play safe. There is nothing wrong if a doctor briefs the patient or his family about the special surgical procedure and the consequences if any. Such a culture of a frank discussion/dialogue between the patient/family/doctor is limited and often missing in our set up.

In a few cases, the doctor concerned is either silent or gets annoyed if a patient or his family member makes enquires. It is difficult under such conditions for the patient or his family to make an informed choice. There is a tendency to rush a patient/family to take an on-the-spot decision, like in case of an emergency operation, without having the full background information. Those who render service of any kind should be open and frank about informing the customer (patient) of all the risks involved and precautions to be taken as well as alternative treatment, if available.

In these days of Internet, a number of useful websites have come up which give all relevant information on various matters of interest. For example, if a patient wants to know whether he should undergo a knee-joint operation as he is suffering from knee-joint pain, he would be advised to check up with the website (example: webmd.com) and get all the information. Such knowledge about any medical or any other could prove useful in having a meaningful dialogue with the doctor or service-provider. The tendency to hide unpleasant facts or negative aspects of a service/product is dangerous but is going on in our social milieu. This is unethical, a wrong way of increasing business at the cost of the customer/patient.

This also applies to legal advice where a lawyer/attorney tries to make a case that his client has a good chance of winning, though the facts could be otherwise. Ideally, a lawyer should lay all the cards on the table and be honest about the case he is about to take up. When the lawyer—client relation is based on sound principle of honesty and trust, there is goodwill all around and the chances of being misunderstood are less. That is also true of a house-owner and a builder relationship where there is so much of mistrust because the relation is not based upon facts, openness, honesty and trust. The client should invariably be informed about the fee/charges which should be realistic and not mere speculation just to play safe.

It should be clear by now a customer himself is to blame if he does not ask the right questions while buying a product or service of any type (medical, legal, construction, education or any other). He should assume that dealers and service-providers are busy and more motivated to sell and get business. However, some of them could be helpful but, by and large, the customer alone has to safeguard his own interest rather than depend upon the goodwill of someone else. A well-informed customer does enough homework before venturing out into the wide world in search of that elusive product/service which he wants so much. He should be prepared for all sorts of hurdles in the way though he is eager to spend his hard-earned money. If, for example, he wants a home loan, to build or renovate his own dwelling into a dream home, he should be knowledgeable about:

(a) the rates of interest for loans offered by various agencies,
(b) the conditions; like documents and proof of income, PAN number, bank statement,
(c) flexible *vs* fixed monthly outgo,
(d) early payment option, if any,
(e) penalty for delayed payment of instalment, and
(f) any other legal conditions in fine print.

Obviously, he has to shop around to get the best deal possible at that point of time.

Sometimes the conditions laid down by the dealer might not be clear or understood by a customer. Suppose, the customer is lucky and he wins a car in a lottery as a prize. He should know whether he has to pay tax, handling charges, transport costs for delivery to the customer, and whether he has to provide insurance and so on. That is the reason, it is stressed in this book that a knowledgeable customer is the best guarantee for avoiding traps set by the dealers and others. To state, "Oh, I didn't know before," does not help the customer since ignorance of a rule or condition is no excuse. A well armed customer, with information on all relevant matters of an item he is about to invest will go a long way in minimizing surprises later on. The customer should be able to exercise his judgment regarding pros and cons of any deal, be it product or service, he is about to invest.

Right to choose

There is hardly any waiting time or black market in the availability of goods and services, thanks to the regime of liberalization and globalization, which was adopted in our country about ten years back. Unlike a choice of one or two models in scooters and automobiles, we have now a wide choice of models that are being added regularly. We have automobiles, which are of the state of the art technology. In fact, some models are being exported to advanced countries. Our country has become a hub for some automobile manufacturers, especially for some auto parts. Gone are the days when a dealer used to dismiss a customer haughtily, "If you don't like our model, you need not buy." Now manufacturers/dealers/sales-persons are wooing potential customers with offers they cannot resist. There are attractive schemes like minimum down payment, easy loans without hassles or elaborate documentation, prize/lottery/lucky draw schemes and so on.

Sheltered market→Customer has no choice→Poor quality→High price→Delays

We have come a long way from those days of shortage and absence of choice. Now we have begun the journey from poverty to plenty as far as availability of goods and services are concerned. It might sound strange that we have a problem of multi-choice on our hands! Now the problem is what and how to choose among a plethora of models and brands in the market, each of which appear to a layperson as equally good and at a competitive price. A wise customer wants to invest his money on a brand that gives him long-time continued satisfaction, which is trouble-free as well as economical in the long run. However, there are fussy customers who think of quality and not the price or other freebies associated with the product/service.

A plethora of goods

The mark of a good business environment is when the customer can exercise his right to choose, which means the market is competitive. The final say in such decisions is when a customer exercises his likes and dislikes freely. Those dealers who believe in pushing a product aggressively through a blitz of an ad campaign could at best have a short-term gain as it catches the attention of customers. A choosy customer looks for value for his investment as well as long-term sustained satisfaction.

In advanced countries the 'throw-away-culture' dominates. This means customers are constantly changing their models. The attraction of 'trade-in' old models for new is also catching up in our country. In fact there are '*melas*' where cars are on show and a customer could not only sell his old car but also could buy a newer model or a brand new car. There is a simple paper work to be completed either to sell your car or get a loan for a new car. The interest on car loan is competitive. This also applies for getting home loans either to buy an old home, buy a new home or renovate your old home.

Our society by and large believes in the tradition of keeping goods and services as long as possible contrary to the advanced countries practice of changing models regularly. Hence repair and maintenance play an important part in the choice of a product or service in our business environment. A customer would like to have a product/service that provides reliable performance as long as it is with him in use. He might not mind minor repairs or periodical maintenance to keep the product/service going economically. Only when it gives him endless trouble he thinks of going for a brand new one that fits his budget. People develop a sort of sentimental attachment to an old product/service that is beyond any logic! This only means organizations in our country have to keep their repair/service departments in top conditions with adequate spares and qualified technicians who can repair old products quickly and cheaply.

However, winds of change are blowing in from the west and the east. There is now a realization, especially among the youth, the affluent sections of the society, businessmen and executives that they could afford to go in for newer models every two to three years and write off the balance of what they have to pay extra as business loss or get income-tax rebate for business purposes.

Throw away culture→Replace old products with new→Demand for newer brands

Due to prohibitive cost of repair of older products or sometimes even newer products, it has become cheaper to buy newer products than try to repair the old defective ones. At one end is the desire to buy newer and better gadgets while on the other hand the high cost of repair, which has given rise to the 'throw-away-culture' that is slowly catching up in our country too. So trading in old cars with brand new ones has become common which means there is a boost to the automobile sector that has never had it so good. This is the trend in other products and services too:

(a) old fridges are exchanged for new;

(b) an outdated lawn-mower/dishwasher is replaced with better and with more energy saving features;

(c) the telephone service-provider who is expensive is cast aside and the consumer goes in for a cheaper and better service-provider;

(d) old furniture is traded in for a brand new better designed and long-lasting furniture; and

(e) a credit card company whose service is poor is cast away and a better and quality minded credit card company is chosen and so on.

In general newer products/services are better in every aspect without costing too much or they could be even cheaper. They are designed with customer in mind and ergonomically sound. There are more safety features than earlier. The emphasis on energy saving/efficiency too. For example, customers are considering the kmpl (kilometre per litre) aspect in a car than mere features. They also demand compliance to the latest pollution control level like Euro III or Bharat II. However, a word of caution is in order. A few products do not enhance the quality of life as claimed by manufacturers. For instance, who needs an electronic back-scratcher or a powered toothbrush? This is nothing but technology gone haywire, also a waste of valuable resources, which could have been put to better use than some fancy, but useless product. We have to guard against those claims where there are only cosmetic changes without improving the performance of the product/service. This does not mean we should not patronize technologically improved products/services that are better in most aspects compared to older and less efficient designs. Such products and services are certainly worth investing. For example, an energy efficient light-bulb saves energy, and uses the resources of the earth better than an energy-inefficient light bulb.

The problems of plenty

During the early years of 1960–70s the choice before a consumer was very simple. For example, if he wanted to buy a car he had only two models to choose from. That applied to most of the consumer durables and even items like cement and steel. Those who faced that kind of 'choice' would recall that to get a bag of cement, at the controlled price, was very difficult because there was acute shortage of these vital building materials. Many a housing complex had to be stopped until the builders could procure these in the flourishing black market. The waiting period of items like two-wheelers was anywhere from five to ten years. To get a telephone connection was a Herculean task with a waiting period of three to five years.

We have come a long way from the bad old days where the market was 'sheltered' with the belief that what we produced in the country was good enough for Indian consumers, if they had to wait, that's their problem! The Indian producers and sellers were making hay while the sun was shining. They were not bothered about quality or timely delivery. The consumers were prepared to wait for any length of time and take whatever the producers had to offer. Consumers of those days would have understood the problems of getting milk from government or private sources. The quantity was always limited and the quality suspect. Rice too was in short supply and a permit was needed to take rice to other states even for personal consumption.

Liberalization

The opening up of the market has spawned a new consumer culture. In these days, with a worldwide market, consumers have a choice—they can buy, if they want, apples from Australia or USA besides our own homegrown apples. That the price of some of the imported goods is beyond the reach of the common man is another matter. However, competition is likely to bring prices down over the years. The WTO regime of liberalized imports has broken down the trade and tariff barriers. EU, NAFTA, ASEAN group of countries have established their own block of nations where there are no barriers for each other nations products/ services. This trend is likely to continue given the advantages to the consumers who have a choice as never before. SAARC has yet to make a beginning.

Let us take the Indian automobile sector, a few of the sectors, which are bucking the slow growth. The major players like Maruti, Tata, Hyundai, GM, Ford, Fiat are getting into the act with a variety of models with newer models being added to increase the choice before a customer. From the ubiquitous people's car, the workhorse of Maruti Udyog's, Maruti 800 basic model, the super luxury Mercedes Benz limousine is available. Companies are wooing consumers as never before—with choice of fittings, freebies, trade-in facilities for used cars, 'zero' interest instalment, free insurance, lotteries, gifts.

Meaningful choice

It might appear strange that there is a problem of plenty before the consumers. Unlike in the advanced countries where there is a comparative rating of various models available from consumer-oriented journals like the '*Consumer Report*', Indian consumers are in a difficult situation. However, of late one or two consumer organizations have taken small steps to rate some of the consumer durables like domestic refrigerators and fans, though these have yet to gain widespread consumer/trade acceptance. Ratings are being published by the manufacturers themselves, regarding various performance parameters, which could guide a potential consumer.

It is but natural that a consumer, given a wide choice, has to make an intelligent choice to make his rupee stretch. He should look for 'value for money', the more features the product has the better for the same price. For example, if a car has leather seats, stereo music system, air-conditioning, 'zip drive', good fuel efficiency and a sound warranty, he might go in for a model of his choice. A brand loyalty is an important feature when a person wants to buy a product/service. He might not be unduly influenced by attractive gifts, freebies and lottery when he is investing so much of his hard earned money.

Brand loyalty might be seen as:

- Personal preference
- Familiarity
- Confidence
- Guarantee of safety, quality and reliability.

Airlines try to woo their passengers by attractive schemes like 'frequent flyer' programmes, which is a reward for flying with one airliner. This could result in accumulating miles, which could be converted either into an upgrade, companion ticket or free ticket to either self or companion. Such airlines could provide add-on services like planning trips overseas, hotel accommodation, conducted tours, discount for purchase of well-known brands and so on. A few brands like ADDIDAS, AIWA, ARMANI, BAJAJ, CARLSBERG, GM, HIENEKEN, KONIKA, L'OREAL, MERCEDES BENZ, OMEGA, PHILIPS, ROLEX, SAMSUNG, SHARP, SONY, TATA, TISSOT, TOYOTA and so on are on the hoardings, advertisements and are well known throughout the world. This is how they create the image for a brand that is very visible and seen as a prestigious one to be owned. Even successful, the high profile international brands will have to maintain their high visibility and profile through advertisements. The idea is to retain their loyal clientele and gain new ones.

Word-of-mouth publicity, strangely, is an important aspect of a person's buying decision. If his relative, friend or colleague has a certain brand and he has heard glowing reports about that particular brand/model, then he is more likely to go in for that similar brand rather than try anything new, however, attractive it might sound on paper. However, if he has personally verified the claims of the manufacturer and has a hands-on experience of, say, driving a vehicle, he would be tempted to buy that brand although none of his friends and relatives has it. A favourable report tempts a potential buyer whereas a negative report is likely to keep him away from investment in that brand.

The Indian consumer has plenty to learn and unlearn. Everyday newer products/services are entering the market, some of international quality. A consumer is likely to be confused about terms like 'Karaoke', 'Qudrasound', 'Flat screen', 'Plasma TV', 'Internet access', 'Multimedia', 'Internet banking'. Computers have made inroads into human related activity and those not yet 'computer-literate' are in big trouble. Some of the jargons appear Greek and Latin to them and they feel left out of the consumer revolution. It is but natural that they are a bit apprehensive about accessing their accounts through the Internet and the ATM. Some of them are more comfortable with bank passbooks rather than paperless transactions. However, matters are slowly, but surely, changing. Consumers who had refused to use facilities like ECS transactions for paying bills are now more confident about the security of such payments after gaining experience.

Trends

The pace of liberalization and globalization may not slow down given the fact that the consumers, once used to a certain standard of quality, are unlikely to accept anything less. The WTO has opened many opportunities for the nations to produce cheaply and of a better quality as they gain a slice of the world market that is huge and is growing steadily. The consumers of tomorrow will have a bewildering array of choices before them. What a consumer in the advanced countries like the USA, UK, Japan could buy, an Indian consumer too would have a similar choice. With the international production centres spread geographically across the globe the supply of goods and services will be easier than before. Gone are the days when Indian visitors to the Gulf countries used to return home with many consumer durables paying a high import duty.

Products/services of the future are likely to have more features, and so more complicated, giving better return on investment. Hence it is necessary that a serious effort is made by the government/trade/NGOs to upgrade knowledge and expertise of the public, the potential consumers, in the age where many sophisticated consumer products/services are flooding the market. Without the right information, a consumer is likely to be confused and his choice may not be an informed choice but based on hype and trappings like gifts, freebies and lotteries. The consumers too should make efforts to upgrade their knowledge and expertise constantly through journals, newspapers and Internet. Only then they can expect to stretch their rupee by intelligent choice based on facts, and not hype.

A customer must try to maximize the return on investment (ROI). The market is being flooded by products/services that are sophisticated and technically more complicated than before. An easy way out is to ask the dealer which is the standard brand 'popular' that is selling like hot cake. Then the customer can see and try that brand for himself before investing. There are those who take brand loyalty seriously because they are happy with the product. For instance, those Maruti car owners who were happy with their earlier models like Maruti 800, Alto, Esteem, and Zen waited a bit longer to buy Maruti Suzuki's latest model SWIFT when they were brought into the market. Even when a customer is forced to buy a product/service that was not in the range of manufacture of a particular company, he would first check if any suitable model was available before turning his attention to some other company's brand. However, given the behavioural pattern, sometimes, a customer can become adventurous and would like to buy an altogether newer brand from a newly introduced company. That decision could turn out to be good or it could be a flop.

Right to be heard

Without consumers there won't be any business. In other words, customers are the mainstay of any business worth its name. This fundamental principle is forgotten by some businesses, which think it's their job to make money and nothing else. Such a shortsighted policy is bound to recoil sooner or later when it's too late to rectify the situation. That's the reason why the customer's right to be heard should be respected in letter and spirit. All businesses should have the customer-focus so essential to success. Efforts should be continuous to establish a strong bond between a business and its customer base by all means possible.

Certain dealers/manufacturers/sales-persons still work on a mindset of a 'captive' customer. That means they are right and the customer in general is wrong. This results in ignoring customer's opinion, suggestion and complaint. The 'take-it or leave-it' arrogance still dominates in certain sectors of the economy. Fortunately, that 'culture' is slowly changing for the better. More dealers/sales-persons have come to realize the customers' have a choice and so they could take the business away from them. This has forced them to rethink vis-à-vis customer relations, including giving a patient hearing to what customers have to say. For some dealers, every single customer is important and so they would go out of the way to accommodate that customer's wish and suggestion, as far as practical since they would like customers to come back and buy from them as loyal customers. Repeat business is what some dealers prefer. It takes a few minutes to annoy and lose a customer but it takes five times longer to make a customer return and do business once again.

Organizations have established a forum where customers and their representatives meet and discuss issues and suggestions. They have realized that their customers have a right to be heard and action taken on genuine suggestions and complaints and to improve the overall performance. It could be a regular structured meeting or as and when needed by either the organization or a group of customers. The dialogue should be two-way to exchange valuable information that could help in setting matters straight or improve the product/service features. There could be an 'open house' on a certain day on which any one could walk into a factory/business/bank and see for himself how it works and make any suggestion or complaint about its product or service. This applies to technical or non-technical customers of an organization. Thus, a feedback system from the customers could go a long way in smoothening the working relations so that both the parties can work together harmoniously.

Customer feedback is important as can be seen from the following:

Products→Use→Feedback→Actions→Improvement→Better quality products/Services

An aggrieved customer, that includes who is upset that the organization failed to listen to his complaint, could be a source of trouble for any business-house. Even one vocal customer can raise his voice and bring problems to the organization. For instance, that customer's word of mouth adverse publicity could damage the reputation of the company. Bad news travels faster than good news and it could snowball into something big for the organization. It could be a case of too little too late for the organization that reacts after a while to a complaint. That's the reason why a customer should be heard early and action taken quickly to defuse a potentially dangerous situation. It's also possible that the spurned customer might not complain but decide never to do any business with that organization which could be worse for the organization in the long run. Hence it's better that a customer complains loudly rather than not complain at all. An unresponsive company could be the proverbial last straw that could make the customer stop doing business.

Recording of customers' complaints/suggestions is fairly routine in any reputed organization. However, it should not be done for just show but for taking action quickly and to the satisfaction of the customers as far as possible. Even if a customer has some trivial complaint, it should be treated with sincerity and efforts made to convince the customer. Often, due to sheer ignorance or lack of knowledge a product/service is misused/mishandled. However, the organization should be large-hearted and address that issue with understanding instead of humiliating the customer who has made that trivial complaint.

A responsive organization reacts positively to customers' complaints as can be seen from the following:

Customer→Complaint→Business→Redress→Satisfied customer

There is a distinct possibility that a dissatisfied customer could drag an organization to court to get his complaint redressed. This is an adverse publicity, which an organization could do without. The fact is the courts are usually 'customer-friendly' which means the courts take a dim view of an organization while believing the customer who has suffered because of an organization's defective product or deficient service. Though punitive fines are not much, the adverse type of publicity would show the organization in the wrong light and could influence potential customers not to have any business dealings with that organization of ill repute. A lesson any organization should learn is that no customer can be taken for granted and his voice should be heard with respect and understanding.

Contrary to our customer-business relations, in the advanced countries like the USA, customer complaints are treated with attention and as a matter of fact. No offence is taken if a customer wants to exchange his goods/ services, seek a refund or simply return the item for money paid. So the customer service department in every big store handles routinely: (a) refund (b) exchange (c) return. Normally the customer is expected to produce the receipt as proof of purchase. However, even this could be waived if the counter-person concerned believes the item is from that stores only. It is also possible to exchange goods bought in store with another one, if it is belonging to a chain stores with different outlets spread across the city or town. Such an easy and hassle free customer service is yet to seep into our business milieu despite liberalization and globalization. It is hoped it would arrive in the near future, if customers have to be given their dues. The time has come for the manufacturer/dealer/service personnel/retailer to start believing the customer and repose trust in him, though a few black sheep of customers could take undue advantage of a liberal 'open door' policy of customer exchange/refund/return.

Right to enjoy as customers

We have not yet reached the level of consumerism of the advanced countries, though much has changed in an open market economy with the free availability of products and services of international reputation. When a customer invests money in a product/service of his liking, the least he expects is that he would be happy and pleased with his investment and so he expects a right to enjoy his newly acquired possession.

For example, a passenger after paying a high fare expects comforts in an AC car free from noise, dust, insects and over-crowding. If he finds the AC not working properly (either too cold or too hot or not working at all), there are unauthorized passengers travelling in the compartment who block the passages, toilets are not clean or there are rats, cockroaches and mosquitoes, his enjoyment of the travel would be curtailed drastically and he would even regret travelling by train by spending so much money. A mere monetary compensation is likely to reduce that unhappiness slightly but is no substitute to a comfortable travel in the first instance. The misery of travelling in a bad compartment is not what he bargained for when he bought the higher-class ticket. He could even think of an alternative like cheap air travel by advance booking on-line next time he travels.

Customer expectation is tempered by the money he invests in a product/service.

Value for money→Customer expects a certain grade of quality of product/service.

For example, if a well-heeled customer invests Rs. 50 lakhs on a brand new Mercedes Benz super-luxury limousine with all the latest gadgets, he expects to enjoy the ride. He does not expect a bumpy ride with some humming sound all the time. He would be very annoyed if such 'minor' flaws occur. On the contrary, a person who pays Rs. 2.8 lakhs for a standard Maruti 800 with AC and stereo, he still expects a trouble-free service but he won't demand a Mercedes Benz comfort or smooth ride. Hence a person's expectations are tempered by the amount of money, he invests when he bought a product or service. That applies to a hotel customer who has paid Rs. 6000 per night for a stay in a luxury room in a starred hotel. The least he expects is that his room is clean, the linen is spotless, the central AC is working without too much noise, and the mini-bar is well stocked.

If a music lover has invested Rs. 20,000 on a stereo music system with DVD player, he expects a pleasing music not screeches or hisses when playing a record. The eager music lover would get everything ready, put his feet up with his favourite drink and insert that famous music cassette which is the talk of the town. The moment he switches on the equipment, a loud noise is heard and the player stops. He would be very annoyed, as he would blast the dealer who has sold that bad piece. He demands, justifiably, replacement of the offending music system immediately.

We are so used to certain conveniences that the moment something goes wrong we are annoyed and feel like tearing our hair in sheer frustration. For example, if an important cricket or tennis match is in progress, we expect the electricity to be on and the TV working properly. Any deficiency would mean that we are not enjoying what we are entitled to. No one likes frequent service calls or taking the faulty product for repair endlessly. The frequent trips and service calls means the customer is not enjoying the product he has paid for. Such deficient service means he has strong feelings of disappointment, frustration, anger and anxiety all rolled into one. If, on the contrary, the dealer rushes immediately with alternate working equipment, then his anger and frustration could be less. That is why some dealers give service batteries and even spare cars to tide over an immediate crisis. But that is only a temporary reprieve the dealer is getting. At one point of time one would complain bitterly, "Enough is enough. I will junk the product and buy a new one."

That dealer who has palmed off the sub-standard product is blacklisted and the word-of-mouth adverse publicity would spread about the dealer as well as the brand of product, he is selling. Manufacturers/dealers/retailers/sales-persons should try to understand and appreciate the sheer frustration of a customer holding on to a defective product/service that is a constant source of trouble and irritation at the customer's end. The sooner a permanent relief is provided to the harassed customer the better for a sound customer-dealer relationship.

Some manufacturers are coming out with products/services which do not need much servicing or maintenance. This is a boon to the consumers who are assured that the product/service they have bought would work well for a number of years without any problem. Such a sales guarantee is an important advantage for that brand compared to the one that needs regular service. We have example like long-life car batteries, which work for five years or more with little attention. Most of the TV brands do not need any maintenance and they work well within a wide range of mains voltage. This is one sure way of retaining brand loyalty instead of tall promises or freebies.

Some service organizations, like the hospitality and airlines industry where there is stiff competition, go out of the way to retain customers' loyalty. They offer free vouchers, upgrade room to better class, provide complimentary drinks and breakfast, leave flowers and fruit baskets in the guest room, provide free shuttles for pick up and drop off, give small gifts and award points for frequent stay in their chain of hotels. This would make the customers happy too as they are being treated well by the service providers. That too applies to airlines where the brand loyalty is eagerly sought after. In case a passenger/client is unhappy about deficient service, he is immediately compensated by vouchers which he could use whenever he wants. Often refunds, in case of cancellation of booking is done without fuss so that clients could have a choice.

> Unhappy customer→Word-of-mouth adverse publicity→Refuses to buy that brand
>
> Happy customer→Praise for the brand for good quality/service→He is the best sales-person

Let's see how a few service-providers are innovative in pleasing their clients. Suppose you have hired an event manager who arranges everything for your child's birthday in a hotel. You hope everything would work out fine without any hitch. You are more concerned that your child and his young friends have a great time and enjoy themselves in the birthday party where you have invested so much money. The first impression appears good with the hall decorated nicely with balloons, coloured flags, and twinkling lights. You are pleasantly surprised that the service-provider has hired two comic characters to greet the little guests and hand them over balloons, gift items and a packet of chocolate. But the pleasure is shortlived. Due to some strange reason, the catering department has failed to deliver your son's favourite ice-cream and the birthday boy is inconsolable. All the efforts and money have gone waste by one simple lapse.

A consumer, with a wide range of choice now available, will think of changing the product/service-provider at the first opportunity in case he finds that brand/organization is not giving him any happiness but plenty of headaches. He would then decide to junk the product/service provider and go in for someone who has a better quality and service reputation at the first opportunity. He doesn't mind trading in the product for a better product or even donate or give away the existing troublesome-product to some one else. He then hopes that his fortunes would change for the better with the new deal.

In the service sector, now with a wide range of choice, changing the service-provider is easier than before. If you are not happy with the catering service, you opt for a better one by investing more money, if need be. If your experience with a particular airlines is bad, because you got a raw deal or were treated with scant respect, you will go out to teach a lesson by adverse word of mouth publicity as well as by boycotting that airlines once for all. Even doctors and lawyers have to ensure that their clientele are happy because their customers have a choice and could easily change the service-provider. It would be better to build a strong bond of friendship and loyalty so that you have repeat customers who won't even think of changing your services.

A competent friendly service is all that a customer wants at a reasonable fee. In the hospitality and tourist industry, a personalized friendly prompt service is sure to retain loyalty of clients despite offers of cheaper prices and attraction of freebies by competing organizations. Where a customer feels happy and satisfied due to prompt and courteous service, continued patronage is assured. That's why a consumer's right to enjoy the use of a product/service, he has invested in, must be enhanced if a business has to succeed in retaining the loyalty of that customer. This could mean attracting more patrons due to good word-of-mouth publicity of your satisfied customers.

Gone are the days where a good product/service could sell by itself. We need to put more stress on customer-focus. Efforts to satisfy customers should be intensified due to stiff competition spurred by open market economy. No organization could rest on its laurels as there is always someone else waiting in the wings to spring a surprise.

CONSUMER RESPONSIBILITIES

We have discussed so far what a manufacturer/dealer/sales-person/service-provider should do to win a customer's confidence. The subsequent paragraphs would focus on customer's responsibilities too that could make a difference to the customer-business relationship.

For example, while enjoying a product/service, a customer cannot be irresponsible and throw the packing/wrapper/product when it's life is over, wherever he wants. That would cause pollution and a hazard to others. With the increasing range of products, with newer features, and newer inventions, our earth's resources are being depleted fast. Some of them are irreplaceable which means they could become unavailable in future. For instance, fossil fuels like crude oil and its derivatives like diesel, kerosene and petrol are limited in supply and one day or the other we will have to face a bleak future without these. A few items like gold, silver and iron ore are mined from beneath earth's surface. These cannot last forever looking at the speed by which these are being used up.

An affluent society, where there is a plethora of products/services, is a wasteful society as far as natural resources and energy are concerned.

We cannot go on plundering our planet's resources with gay abandon, assuming these would be available in plenty all the time. That's the reason why consumerism has to be more responsible to the environment in which we operate. There is already pressure on the environment due to human related activities, which have increased the emission of 'greenhouse gases' that have played havoc with the climate change. There is evidence of increasing global temperatures resulting in unseasonal rains, floods, droughts, cyclones, tornadoes and other natural disasters.

At the micro level too much needs to be done by individuals. For instance, a music lover who has brought a fancy high-power stereo system should not play the music that disturbs the neighbour. Obviously, one man's enjoyment cannot become another man's misery. While we might keep our inside premises clean, we cannot dump our garbage out in the open and cause annoyance to others. Thus, discipline is needed in whatever a customer does that does not affect adversely the other fellow beings. Responsibility means concern for others too.

Let us take warranty/guarantee of a product/service, assurance that it work well for a certain period, at least, without problems. A responsible customer does not misuse this warranty/guarantee and misuse the product/service because someone else will repair or replace it. That would be unethical and a bad example to set. Suppose a product is dropped inadvertently. That person has to reveal honestly what happened and hope that the dealer would listen to his complaint and redress it. However, that dealer might refuse a free repair/replacement since the product has been dropped by the customer. That customer has to accept the dealer's verdict instead of fighting with him or telling lies that the product went defective while using it in a normal way. A customer/or some inexperienced person cannot repair himself a product that has gone defective. Tampering of controls by the customer means the factory settings have been altered and the dealer can refuse to do any free repair or replacement.

Technology sometimes goes wild. One might wonder why we need to have powered windows in a car that work by the touch of a button. Is it so difficult to wind the window up or down when needed? Surely, such gadgets consume extra resources that could have been utilized elsewhere better. That applies to a number of products that are luxuries which we can do without—powered backscratcher, powered toothbrush, remote control in a car that locks or unlocks the car from a distance, robots that walk and talk and so on. Unfortunately only market forces can decide whether such products have consumers' preferences or not. However, an environmentally concerned individual will shun such products as they do not add to the quality of life but deplete the scarce resources, which could have been put to better use when really needed. But the diehard consumerists might think differently and still go on patronizing these.

As a responsible consumer, you would like to patronize products/services that are ethical, do not waste resources, environmentally friendly and improve the quality of life. That is why products/services as well as packaging that use as much recycled material as practical, thus saving 'virgin' materials, are labelled 'green'. There are special racks in stores where these are kept. Environmentally concerned individuals patronize these though often these are more expensive than the regular items. For instance, glossy pages in a magazine use good quality paper but which are often simply junked after glancing at it. As a corollary, products/services, and packaging which waste virgin material and which have disposal problem and cause pollution in addition, should be shunned by responsible consumers.

Green products

Produced with least input costs→Use recycled material to the maximum→Consume less energy to produce and operate during their life-cycle→Environmentally friendly—easy to use→Easy to dispose off product/packaging

Life cycle cost

An important aspect of a product/service is the 'cradle-to-grave' cost—total cost of acquisition, running cost and disposal cost. Normally, a customer is concerned with initial down payment and not the total cost. If a refrigerator costs Rs. 10,000 (Model A) he would choose it rather than the one that costs Rs. 15,000 (Model B) with the same capacity and with the same features as the one that costs Rs. 10,000. A careful calculation could be like this:

Model A:

Initial cost (Rs. 10,000) + Running cost per year Rs. 2000 and for 5 years Rs. 10,000 = Rs. 10,000 + Rs. 10,000 = Rs. 20,000.

Model B:

Initial cost (Rs. 15,000) + Running cost per year Rs. 1000 and for 5 years Rs. 5000 = Rs. 15,000 + Rs. 5000 = Rs. 20,000.

Apparently, both models over a period of 5 years cost the same to the customer. In fact, it's possible that an initially higher cost equipment could save the customer and work out more economical over the years. A customer should keep this aspect in mind when he is investing on domestic equipment. Another example is a car, though of higher purchase cost, could be more economical in the long run if the running cost, that's km/ph cost per litre, is cheaper and the maintenance cost is lower. This is the life cycle cost concept that a customer should keep in mind while investing in any equipment. Energy efficient and fuel-efficient equipment should be preferred rather than one with lower initial investment. A more reliable product/service with less maintenance cost might score over another which is less reliable due to the fact the product/service is available on demand without waiting too much about repair/service/spares.

Life cycle cost

Life cycle cost = Initial purchase cost + Cost of running + Cost of repair and maintenance + Cost of disposal

Inducements

Freebies, prizes, lotteries, lucky-draws, price discounts, gifts, free overseas trips *et al.* are inducements to lure the customers to invest in a particular product/service. A responsible customer will not be easily lured into buying that brand provided all other things are in order. For example, an investment company with a poor track would do its best to rope in investors by offering all kinds of inducements, apart from promise of high interest rate. A few persons would fall a prey to such a ploy and part with their money to regret later on when the investment company defaults on interest or, worse, return of capital. Some of them are 'blade companies' that disappear without a trace after collecting hefty deposits from thousands of gullible investors.

A customer who knows what he is doing will keep his goal in mind—to get value for money by shopping in the market for a reputed reliable product/service that lasts and is trouble-free. He would pick the product/service if it is of good quality and reliable at the right price. Among the competing brands, he would choose the one that has a better market reputation for quality and reliability with features he wants.

Purchase decision→Quality/Reliability reputation

Customer decision-making is influenced by:

- Quality and Reliability
- Price
- Value for money
- Inducement

"There is hardly anything in the world that some man cannot make a little worse and sell a little cheaper and the people who consider price only are this man's lawful prey," so wrote John Ruskin years ago. The point John Ruskin made long ago is still relevant in our consumer milieu.

There are a few consumers who pride themselves for their smartness driving a hard bargain and getting something so cheap. Such 'bargains' could easily turn to be mere junks to be thrown away. But that doesn't deter such 'low-price conscious' individuals from looking for a bargain that could be the envy of others. 'Cheap and nasty' is an adage, which has never lost its meaning whatever the state of the market. Low price is the 'carrot' dangled by 'blade' companies and 'fly-by-night' operators to sell cheap and unreliable goods and services. Such enticements are good enough for those who believe only in 'bargains' and cheap products. It is said that one should not look into the mouth of a gift horse but where a poor quality stuff is being palmed off with a 'free' gift, wisdom certainly dictates that the quality of the 'horse' one is getting must be carefully examined. Such a 'bargain' could easily turn into a liability, with no takers.

A knowledgeable and responsible consumer will never compromise on quality of a product/service for the sake of enticements. He would not think of investment in something that's of dubious quality. Though many consumers would jump at the idea of shopping for 'discount, 'seconds', 'export surplus', 'export reject' *et al.*, a responsible consumer will think twice before going to such a place. Most of the stuff sold there is of poor quality and the question of refunds/replacements/exchange doesn't arise. Some goods could be 50–75 per cent cheaper than the market price but is such a 'bargain' worth it? Certainly not for those value their money and pride themselves on always looking for quality in whatever they purchase. So consumers beware and avoid seconds, export/surplus/ rejects and stuff like that!

"Earth provides enough to satisfy every man's need but not every man's greed!" stated Mahatma Gandhi. How very true even in this 21st century! Our planet's limited resources would be put to greater strain than ever before due to rising customers' expectations all over the world in the coming years. More goods and services would be required to satisfy millions of people who too want the share of the pie. At that rate the future is bleak for the coming generations who too have the right to quality of life.

"Progress is the myth that assures us that full-speed ahead is never wrong. Ecology is the discipline that teaches us that it is a disaster," as stated by an anonymous contributor who was aghast at the speed of 'development' that is plundering our resources. That means a knowledgeable and responsible consumer is the best guarantee that prevents over-exploitation of our resources to a point where the earth would become a barren hostile place to live. Such a situation is due to the unbridled expansion of consumerism to the exclusion of all other considerations like pollution, climate change and depletion of resources beyond a point of no return.

In India we have to think whether we should simply ape the advanced countries vis-à-vis consumerism. Do we need some fancy gadgets, which do not materially improve the quality of life? We are a frugal society and we should maintain such a lifestyle as far as possible. Why should we follow a wasteful 'throw-away' culture when we have been taught from a young age to be thrifty and use something till it's no longer serviceable economically? That means we do not have to copy every aspect of a consumerist society. We should be more responsible for our future generations who too desire a better life. That means we have to use the resources with care and consideration. Conservation of resources should find a place in our society.

Consumer [Rights + Responsibilities] = Environmentally friendly products and services

A few enlightened producers care for the environment and are not too concerned with the bottom line. "Keep the right goal in mind, don't look for money. Look for applause. If you create something of value, the sales will come," stated Robert Ronstadt, CEO, Lord Publishing Company. We need more such enlightened producers and business leaders to save our planet.

CHAPTER 3

MAKING THE RIGHT CHOICE

It takes a person who is wide-awake to make his dreams come true
—Proverb

The topic of making the right choice by a consumer is not only interesting but also challenging with the 'problem of plenty' as discussed in the earlier chapter. This chapter focuses on what a responsible and knowledgeable consumer (customer) can do to get the value for his investment, be it a product or service. Guesswork, inducements and "I didn't know" are not going help you to strike a good bargain when confronted by a multiple-choice market environment. Though we have made rapid strides towards a freer and open market economy, let us accept the fact that we have miles to go in reaching the consumerist standard of some of the advanced countries. It does not mean, however, we copy all that's happening in those countries where the 'Customer is King'. Surely, we cannot afford to waste resources on useless products/services when these are more urgently required elsewhere by millions of our countrymen struggling to eke out a living.

This is the right time to orient our priorities as far as production of consumer goods and services are concerned. We have no right to bring in products, of little value, which do not enhance the quality of life, just because it's an open market economy. The argument that responsible customers would reject such 'useless' products might be true. But why even think of investing valuable resources for such a product(s), in the first instance? There are ethical considerations as well as self-control in planning for consumer goods and services supposed to improve the standard of living of the people. It should also be remembered that some of the 'fancy' goods and services have a niche market and ordinary customers cannot even dream of possessing them as these are priced very high because of their 'esteem' value rather than utility considerations.

When a customer goes for shopping he/she is confronted by bewildering choice. A surfeit of information and ad blitz add to his/her confusion. More often than not the customer is confused as he/she is faced with new terminology he/she cannot comprehend. He might understand what a 'flat screen TV' is supposed to be. What about a 'plasma TV'? For a normal customer there is no apparent difference that's perceptible to him. He then wonders why he should pay much more for a new invention in TV that's not so obviously superior. Such dilemma confronts customers in these days of new inventions and 'breakthroughs'.

What used to be quicker and easier decision-making after seeing, hearing and touching a product or service, is turning to be more complicated with plenty of jargons to confuse. Such simple choice is no longer possible. For example, if a microwave manufacturer claims that his product is energy efficient with low radiation level, all that he can do is to use the product over a period of time and see whether the energy consumption is low as claimed. On the other hand, he has no way of testing whether the radiation is low as claimed. With more state of the technology products and services, it would be more and more difficult for a customer to make a meaningful choice for getting value for his investment.

The problem of informed choice extends to the service sector too where the customer has a wide choice of doctors, lawyers, hoteliers, holiday planners, event managers and investment experts, to name a few, whose services might be required. As we are aware, there are now doctors for every known disease as also super-specialists. Most of them appear to have similar qualifications and experience. So, how does one go about choosing a particular doctor for treatment for himself or some other member of his family? The family doctor is becoming an endangered species with the advances in medicine, surgery and technology driven treatment for diseases. In the earlier days, the family doctor was a trusted institution who would treat minor ailments himself/herself and advise, when deemed necessary, that the patient be referred to a specialist whom the doctor knew personally. Now ultrasound, MRI, angioplasty and the like are used extensively, whether these are essential or not is another matter. In the banking sector, it's now common to have ATMs, and ECS instead of the traditional cheque book and pass book. Paperless transactions are the order of the day.

Choice

What does a consumer do when confronted by several choices such as: Product A, B, C or D? He chooses the product that has better value for the money he invests. The more features that product has, the better. That customer would have already come prepared and better equipped to make his choice. He, under normal circumstances, won't be swayed by the tall claims of a particular brand as dished out by the dealer. The customer knows the dealer is doing his job to get a better commission. On the contrary, his interest would be served by choosing a product that has a good reputation, trouble-free, has better service facilities, and is competitive in price. Moreover, some of his close friends and relatives have bought that particular brand are happy with it. By no means he would be influenced by the price only for he knows the popular saying, 'Cheap and nasty.'

Choose wisely

It would be interesting to know how his counterpart in the advanced countries takes a decision regarding any brand. For him, multi-choice environment is taken for granted. He sees the advertisements in the electronic and print media. Moreover, he would have read the *Consumer Reports* magazine regularly to have an idea of the competing brands, he is about see and select one. He is armed with the information about ratings of products of various brands. The dealer, unlike in our country, is more customer-friendly for he knows he is dealing with customers who are knowledgeable and cannot be fooled by hype about a product/service. The dealer is neutral about recommending any brand lest the customer would be biased in favour of one brand or the other. Nevertheless, a customer would take into consideration the experience of his friends and relatives while making up his mind about a brand under consideration.

The overseas customers have the advantage of discount and genuine sale. These are not mere gimmicks at sales promotion, by artificially increasing the sale price and then reducing it when the product shows poor sales. Of course, the customer has the advantage of instalment scheme and easy financing, if his/her credit rating is good. Credit card is used extensively and it's rare for anyone to pay by cash, especially where the purchase price is high. Every sale, moreover, has a receipt unlike in our country where often the dealer wants to avoid sales tax and local tax by a direct transaction through cash dealings. The customer too gets a 'discount' for such a 'cash-and-carry' transaction. Such dealings are illegal and the time has come to stop such malpractices by one and all. It should be noted that a cash purchase might not indicate 'proof of purchase'. A receipt is a guarantee that the sales transaction has been done properly. Only such a receipt can be produced in a court of law while filing a complaint for redress. It is hoped that with the introduction of VAT (Value Added Tax) such illegal transactions would be minimized.

ADVERTISEMENT

Advertisement plays a part in the everyday life. Posters, hoardings, radio, TV advertisements, newspapers and magazines and now the Internet, bombard him. Starting with the morning newspaper, the magazine he picks up, unsolicited calls through the telephone/cell phone, mail/door-to-door soliciting, TV/Radio sponsored programmes, sports-promo by sponsors and the hoardings outside on the road-side, a person is subjected to a plethora of advertisements about various products and services, he may or may not be interested. The advertisements are often catchy, with the promise of a lottery, prize schemes and lucky winners provided the person buys the product/service. The celebrity endorsement has to come to stay. To what extent such endorsements appeal to potential buyers is a matter of debate. Advertisement budgets of big companies might run into crores of rupees. The idea is to make their product 'visible' all the time. Such an advertisement suggests that a customer who buys the advertised product/service would be a happy and delighted person.

The following paragraphs are meant as guidance, with ideas and suggestions, how an intelligent customer (consumer) manages his money while investing in products/services. For sure, we are now in a multi-choice business milieu, with the exception of services offered by government departments, semi-government organizations and local bodies, which include corporations, municipalities, gram panchayats and others where private participation is minimum or not at all. A word of caution is in order: The matter of consumer choice is vast and complicated and no justice can be done in one book. Some of the advertisements mentioned here could be topical but of no relevance later on. That's why these should be taken as broad guidelines so that the consumer is prepared in advance how a situation could be tackled.

There is no substitute to homework and knowledge about the product/service one is interested in buying. By all means, see and try the alternate brands. Do consult your friends and relatives before you buy. Read the ratings published by independent agencies, if available. Ultimately, it boils down to independent thinking and use of better judgment by a consumer confronted by conflicting claims of competing brands and also dealer's own interest as well as offer of freebies, gifts, lotteries, lucky draws, cash-back, low interest *et al.* as inducements to influence the purchase decision. All information, tips and guidelines about a brand should be welcomed to make a better decision. This is better than rushing into a store to shop on the 'spur' of the moment to regret later on. Also, it would be unwise to trust one's luck all the time while making a purchase decision. An informed consumer would see through tall talk and claims by a dealer and will not be swept by a tide of 'glib' talk by any sales-person.

Important points to note

1. Some of the suggestions given in this chapter are meant for guidance only. These are neither binding nor can be taken as authoritative.
2. Always check for the latest and authorized information before taking an important decision. Remember that 'ignorance of law or rule' is no excuse.
3. The author neither endorses these advertisements cited here nor disapproves them. It's up to the reader to decide the truth or otherwise himself/herself.

4. The above remarks apply to all the advertisements mentioned in this chapter and subsequent chapters, picked up at random and gleaned from newspapers/magazines/hoardings/product and service advertisements *et al.*
5. The author disclaims all responsibilities for anyone who might be affected adversely by either following or ignoring the ideas and suggestions given in this and subsequent chapters.
6. These ideas and suggestions are given in good faith and the author hopes that these would be used as additional tips and suggestions by an intelligent and informed consumer to improve his/her decision-making in a multi-choice market environment.

Let us examine a few advertisements and see how a consumer can cope with these. These are taken from various sources as appeared in the print/hoarding/electronic medium. Some of these are dated and so their relevance might be limited for the present as well as for the future.

1. *"Drive away a Honda City for just Rs. 5.13 lakhs. Pay the balance through an interest-free loan of Rs. 2 lakhs."*

Check for hidden costs. If you have the cash, or you can get a car loan at reasonable interest, go ahead.

2. *"BPL presents "Quadra Point Focus" (QPF) raise your vision to the power of 4, the new definition of vision, raises sharpness, contrast and depth and clarity to the power of. QPF means greater sharpness, higher contrasts and depth, rich natural colours, corner to corner clarity."*

This sounds great! Can you see the difference between an ordinary TV and this newer version? Do visit a BPL showroom and check out all the fabulous claims made. For the sake of comparison, check out a 'normal' TV too. The important point is how much the new design QPF will cost you. Are you prepared to pay so much for a difference, which after your personal check is not all that significant? But, if you are really convinced the QPF is the model for you, then go ahead. After all, it might just be the model you were waiting for enjoying a better TV picture quality and sound these years.

3. *"Flying KLM's World Class", "Yet it leaves your feathers unruffled." Ease, luxury and comfort at your service, special meals, in-flight entertainment maximum choice from a variety of movies or audio entertainment, wide range of reading material and newspapers. Selection of some of the world's best wines and champagnes. Our lounge offers easy accessibility to phones, fax machines, PCs and private workstations. Refresh yourself with complimentary snacks and beverages or simply get down to business right away.*

Sounds good. Most of the airlines which offer First Class/Business Class/Executive Class pamper their patrons as these seats costs much more than the economy class. Check out the fares of other competing airlines for the same class of service. If you are a frequent flyer stick to one or two airlines for maximum benefit. It is important that the airlines you choose should be punctual, on-time departure and arrival. Frills are important but not at the cost of reliability and quality of service.

4. *"Japan's No. 1 now in India with the power of Double Cascade: National 'Niagara' double cascade washing machine." 'Always with you' unique double cascade action for up to 50 per cent more cleaning power, 'Fuzzy Plus' with four sensors—wash load, temperature, motor action and tangle sensors for more efficient cleaning, smart compact size, it fits into the smallest corner, 8 different wash courses to handle any kind of washing, tough, 100 per cent made in Japan, body for longer life, plastic base to prevent rusting and corrosion.*

You might wonder what's 'Fuzzy Plus', 'Double cascade action' mean to you. Doesn't it sound too complicated? Who needs 8 different courses? The more sophisticated the machine, the more costly it's going to be. And what about service? Are there authorized service personnel to do a good job? What about the initial investment? How much does it cost compared to a 'normal' simple washing machine without all the features. This advertisement sounds too complicated for an ordinary householder. Avoid it and go for a simpler sturdier machine, which is easy to operate and with normal maintenance. Moreover, cost is another important factor while you invest in a machine that's too sophisticated.

5. *"Videocon mega monsoon exchange offer. Get up to Rs. 3500 off for your old washing machine (exchange price only, handling charges Rs. 1200)."*

This is a time-tested promo drive to increase sales. There are customers waiting to exchange their old machine to a new one. That incentive of 'exchange' is too powerful to resist. That the customer gets a small price for his old machine is a fact of life. The customer is happy to get rid of an old machine and buy a brand new one. Generally, a customer would like to go in for a later model from the same company—that's due to the 'loyalty' factor, which is hard to resist.

6. *"Plug-in to our most technologically advanced PCs without blowing up your wallet—Alpha Computech (India) Ltd. One-year on-site part replacement warranty. 100 per cent Y2K compliant."*

Check the models being offered and compare with standard brands available. See if there is any compulsory annual maintenance contract which tends to be costly, and often, not required. Is there an adequate support staff? Often, these computer companies start with just one or two people, assembling computers. Sometimes they do not attend to complaints from neophytes after the sale is over. We do need some support once in a way. Though one would like to buy a computer that's cheap, in the long run it pays to go in for a standard brand, not necessarily the costliest in the market, with good customer support.

7. *'We change lives' —APTECH computer education. India's first ISO 9001 certified computer training institution for education support services.*

Getting an ISO certification is a plus point. Check whether they are maintaining this certification regularly. Shop around for competitive computer training institutes that have sprung up of late. However, one should note that APTECH is not a registered university under the UGC Act. AICTE, AIU, UGC, State Governments and Government of India do not recognize it. Some of their advertisements do mention this fact. Unlike a few others, APTECH appears to have the expertise to train people on live projects and it has a placement service too. NITE is another training institution, which has a good reputation. Though UGC and others do not recognize these, some of the industries do employ such people. It's better to opt for training in an institution, which is recognized by UGC and others for a better future. Pay a personal visit to see the infrastructure, the number of tutors, number of computers per person and so on. If possible, get in touch with those who have trained in such institutions and hear their experience, good and bad. The fee structure is an important aspect of these institutes that should be checked if these are reasonable. You, as a customer, have to decide the type of computer training you would like to have and the fee you are willing to pay.

8. *"Java, HTML, WINDOWS NT.....diploma in INTERNET programming, learn the leading-edge technology the world is looking for, enroll today, First Computers."*

With the widespread use of PC/Internet, computer education and training is mushrooming. Points made above are valid here too. Check the quality of the programme by visiting personally and checking out on the infrastructure. See how the fee structure compares with others. It's important to note how the market views the diploma issued by this organization. Is there any placement service too?

9. *"Imagine getting this international degree right in Chennai, University of Lincolnshire and Humberside. Subjects taught: business, finance, IT, marketing. 18 months full time course. Not regulated under the AICTE Act or any other State Act."*

After spending so much money and time, it's important to find out, in advance, what to expect from such a degree regarding placement, higher studies and so on. A number of foreign universities are advertising, holding workshops, seminars, open houses and so on to entice Indian students either to go overseas for studies or study in India to get a foreign degree. However, one has to be wary about an unknown university to check its credibility. Also, it's important to note whether UGC recognizes such degrees. Great caution and much homework needs to be done before paying so much money for a degree which might not have value either in our country or even overseas. However, if a recognized and well-known university like Harvard has made arrangements to have an associate local college/university to award an equivalent/associate degree, that's fine.

10. *"Are you slow in typing? No typing tutor required but individually it will be taught in different methods just in 4 hours. Take a free trial class to believe it. Eligibility needed—just to read and write ABCD. No age bar. Stop thinking for yourself and come and clarify only at SUPERSONIC Computer Typing Institute. Nothing is impossible to man."*

Wonderful, how one wishes such tall and lofty claims turn out to be true! If you are curious but not serious, do pay a visit for a trial class to find more about that 'miracle' lesson which improves speed of computer typing.

11. *"Canon camera features: SURE SHOT WP-1; the all weather camera, sunshine, dust storm, hail storm, rainfall, 40°C, minus10°C. Big viewfinder, self timer, special anti-slip grip, auto film loading, fully auto transport, magnified counter display, auto flash with redeye reduction, high quality auto-focus, 32 mm, 3.5 lens, W / Macro and Focus lock, auto film speed set, 1 year warranty."*

Consult an expert *before* buying. There is no reason to doubt the features described by Canon the world's leading camera manufacturer. Go for a reputed brand. Satisfy yourself that you need all the features that are described. Suppose you are an amateur, may be a low-price camera could suit you initially rather than a sophisticated advance camera whose features you might not need or use. However, a professional would invest one-time in a costly camera, which has all the features to take excellent quality pictures. Now digital cameras are the in-thing. So, you may not get spares/repair facility for old style traditional cameras.

12. *"G K Vale's Mega exchange offer. The best time to get the coolest deals for your old camera. Any make. Any condition and get a fabulous exchange price for any camera of your choice at G K Vale. Hurry, offer open only until stocks last." In fine print: 'Conditions apply.'*

First of all find out what the conditions are. In general, the exchange price for your camera would be a small amount. You need not rush to exchange your camera just because there is such a 'tempting' offer. These are sale gimmicks, once in a way, to clear old stocks. Often you get a good price if you find a seller yourself by inserting advertisements. Apart from exchange, dealers offer discounts when they want to get rid of their stock. Watch out for such offers too. In principle do not buy because of such offers but because either you need to buy a camera or you want to go in for a better camera. Remember that digital cameras are now in vogue now.

13. *"Ruggers takes wrinkles out of flat fronts"* —Ruggers casual wear.

Find out the experience of your friends about such a claim. Check price of other competing brands.

14. *"No entry fee. Attractive prizes. All you have to do is fill in the numbers in the squares so that it adds up to 21 vertically or horizontally. Hurry and send in your entries to the address given."*

Beware, you are at great risk of losing your money! It could be a fraud. No one gets anything free. There is no free lunch, as they say. You would be asked to send an MO if you want to get a 'prize' and that's the gimmick. Avoid such schemes.

15. *"Kanchipuram silk sarees at wholesale prices up to 50 per cent off. Bring this paper cutting and get 5 per cent extra discount. Last 7 days."*

More such advertisements designed to attract customers appear from time to time. First of all, you must make sure the stuff is genuine and not some rejects or seconds being sold as new. It would be better to buy in reputed shops where you have a guarantee of quality and genuineness. Sometimes, they exchange too. Don't be misled by low prices.

16. *"KSIC Deepavali discounts. Add sparkle to this Deepavali with radiant silks from KSIC, 10-20 per cent discount, attractive discount on bulk purchases and package deals."*

If you are looking out to buy sarees, jewellery and the like, it's the festive season that's best where you get good deals. Try to shop only at factory outlets or reputed shops or departmental stores.

17. *Bhima Jewellers 'Anniversary Golden Challenge Offer' 10, 11 and 12, November, 2006. Best prices. Best quality. Best collection. Best service.*

If you are interested check out for yourself these claims.

18. *"Situation vacant. Overseas opportunity. Saud Bahwan Group. Muscat. Parts salesmen/Consultants. Graduates males only." Contact Tel. No.......*

You need to check out how reliable is this placement service. If possible, you should talk to anyone who has being sent overseas. Caution is needed and you must see fine print and terms of contract. Do not part with your money unless you are absolutely sure how genuine the placement agency is. Unfortunately, some of them have left their clients in a lurch in some strange country.

19. *National Consumer Fair. A unique shopping experience combined with more than 10 amusements for children. A perfect outing for the entire family. At Jalahalli Circle, Bangalore.*

It could be fun. Just do not buy anything on impulse.

20. *"Own your own home @ a first home buyers expo 2006. Koramangala Indoor Stadium 10, 11 and 12, November, 2006."*

Such expos are useful. Prospective buyers should visit such expos and make enquiries where there could be a better choice.

21. *"The right place for right deals. Used cars. Auto-loan by HDFC Bank." Call Tel. No...*

You can get a better idea of the price of used (pre-owned but mostly certified by auto companies or their authorized dealers). You can either trade in your used car or go for a later model pre-owned car of your choice. In general, most car companies such as Hyundai, Maruti, and Tata organize auto-melas periodically.

22. *"Fuel saving on MRF Formula Special Truck Tyres? That's exactly what these transporters are claiming."*

Check this out.

23. *"Live in a stretch of paradise...created specially for you. Independent houses on Tumkur Road. Rs. 12,50,000 onwards. Round the clock security. 9 ft. compound for the entire layout. 24 hours water and electricity. 24 hours cable TV. Tastefully landscaped garden for each plot and layout. Proposed BMRDA layout."*

Check out carefully such advertisements. You are investing a lot of money. All the papers must be in order with the approval of relevant authority.

24. *"Travel Bazaar. Return air tickets. Bangalore-Bangkok Rs. 5800. Bangalore-Male Rs. 5000." Call Tel. No...*

It might sound strange but it's true that the price quoted is without taxes, which could be as much as the price mentioned, if not more! So check out which is the airline that's quoting the price and the total money to be paid as well as any other hidden costs and conditions. .

25. *"MBA. ICFAI Flexible Education. Eligibility: Graduates (any discipline)." Contact Tel. No...Website:* www.icfai.org.

It appears to be interesting. Find out more details before you enroll in such types of programmes, which will help in your career.

26. *RADO, shaping the future.*

This is a simple and elegant advertisement for a watch. Have a look, compare prices and decide it for yourself

27. *"European Higher Education Fair, Experience Europe – Education unlimited. 25, 26 November 2006."*

Such fairs are good to go round and get an idea of the cost and the facilities available with foreign universities.

28. *"100% value holidays to the Far East. You'll love the experience. And the price too. Thomas Cook (India) Ltd."*

Check out this offer and compare with others. Also, meet or talk to those who have taken up similar tours with this company. Stick to reputed experienced tour operators.

29. *"Apollo Sindhuri Capital Investments Ltd. Buy and Sell Sensex. Contact nearest branch." Website:* www.apollosindhoori.com

Find out how long they are in the business and their reputation in the market.

30. *"Knock, Knock, Knock Opportunities keep knocking, post your resume online today and see more doors open for you. Naukri.com India's No. 1 Job site." Website:* www.naukri.com

Check this out and see the response.

31. *"Airtel Broadband @Rs. 250 p.m. Conditions apply."*

Now there are a number of broadband service providers. Check out how this company's broadband works.

32. *"Inventors. Innovators. Forward thinkers. Calling all top-flight IT professionals. Google"*

You should see what Google has to offer you, in case you fit into their description

33. *"Kennel & Pets: A Alpha Kennels offers quality Rottweiller, Doberman, Danes, Golden Retriever, Pugs, Boxer, Daschund, Mastiff." Contact Tel. No....*

If you are a pet lover, then you should approach only a certified kennel. Do visit this kennel and form your own opinion.

34. *"Study in London, UK For free admission and counselling meet Mr....."*

You should talk it over and find out more details, in case you want to study in the U.K.

35. *"Simplicity is a tube-light that saves you more. Philips lighting."*

You should be on the look out for such innovative products/services that saves you money.

INDUCEMENT

1. *"Ruggers, 'Flying Machine', casual wear. If anybody tells you that you don't get up to 40 per cent off on the Flying Machine and Ruggers Range, ask them to make a beeline to the nearest Flying Machine terminal and check it out.*

This is a limited period offer available only at exclusive Flying Machine terminals. Conditions apply."

Discount is welcome. Check how old is the stock. Do not buy it because there is discount but you need one. Such offers are mere inducements to clear stocks. Such information about discounts should be checked out while buying at any outlet. Shopkeepers may not be so helpful to tell you there is a discount on a particular brand. Remember: shops do not, in general, allow refund/exchange under their sales promotion drive.

2. *"One + one = three offer! Buy any 2 Byford T-shirts, pick up a third T-shirt absolutely free! But hurry! This offer ends on 25th July. Available at all Peter England outlets and other leading menswear stores. Byford T-shirts also available without this offer."*

Such inducements are common. The buyer gets a feeling he is getting something 'free' for nothing. Alas, most of such offers do not mean the shops are selling at a loss. Perhaps they would have recovered the cost of all three shirts by selling just two. It's up to you whether you would like to buy just one or would like to stock up three! Most of such offers have a deadline—just to make feel you have to take a quick decision otherwise you would lose out on such an attractive offer. Again, you buy T-shirts if you want, not because there is an offer, however attractive it could sound.

3. *"1 kilo Rs. 250 only. Knits India 100 per cent cotton export garments for the first time in your area. Biggest export wear sale due to export order cancellation. Grand offer for the summer season. Just grab this golden opportunity."*

Beware, you buy such items at your own risk! These are export order rejects perhaps, may be genuine or may not be. There is no guarantee of quality. Don't be fooled by the label 'export' which really means nothing. There is no exchange or refund after such a sale. It's a bad bargain minus quality!

4. *"Wear what people wear in England. Choice of millions worldwide, now in India. Inaugural sale 60 per cent off. Alan Paine, England."*

Check the material and price. Do you really want to wear what people in England wear at that price? Are there no Indian or foreign labels which are equally good? Are you tempted by that 60 per cent off? Perhaps it's a sales gimmick to introduce the brand in India. No harm in checking out for a bargain, as it's a reputed brand.

5. *"For ladies: One exclusive unstitched salwar suit with every salwar suit you buy. For men: One shirt free with every shirt you buy. For girls: One frock free with every frock you buy. For boys: One shirt free with every shirt you buy. Favourite shop."*

So the entire family gets a deal! Make sure the prices are right and the quality is good. Check up with someone who has experience with this label material.

6. *"Satyam On-line: India's most preferred Internet connection.* www.satyamonline.com. *Free software worth over Rs. 4000, choice of connections." The window to Internet.*

Presently, the customer has a choice with three or four leading Internet service-providers in the market. Choose the one that meets the need and see how the connectivity and quality of connection is. Check with those who have Internet connections about their experience. Another Internet provider, 'Mantra-on-line' has, apparently, gone out of business after making waves in the beginning. So we need stable service providers, as far as possible. There are a few Internet service-providers like: BSNL/Airtel/Siffy/Rediffmail and so on. Shop around for the best deal that suits your requirements.

7. *'Exclusive offer' for 'Flying Returns' members at Crowne Plaza and Holiday Inn. When you stay at Crowne Plaza and Holiday Inn hotels from 15th August to 31st October, you will earn 1000-add-on mileage points per night at special rates with complimentary American breakfast.*

This is a special offer for frequent flyer members who are rewarded for their loyalty with special stays at hotels while earning additional miles. Such inducements tend to build up a loyal clientele who want to earn mileage points by sticking to one or two of their favourite airlines. There is added attraction if one buys VIP products that carry add-on mileage. A special gift also waits such frequent flyers as a reward. No doubt such added attractions are important. However, the bottom line is you choose an airline that is reliable and punctual without hassles. All other considerations are secondary. In the USA newspapers publish regularly the performance of airlines, the most important being the percentage of flights that took off and landed on time. Anything above 90 per cent is considered good. Another factor is the number of passenger complaints per 1,00,000 miles, which is an indicator of how efficient the airline is.

8. *"Sahara take off' Take off with Sahara and win exciting free gifts and holidays including free Handycams and 29 inch colour TVs."*

Check up whether such an offer is applicable to all sectors or limited to a few selected ones. Validity of such offers is limited and moreover such offers cannot be combined with anything else. Certain other conditions too might apply. Read the fine print to make sure. There could be some other strings attached. Just check up all the terms and conditions to make sure. An important factor is whether you want to fly with this airline at all. Perhaps you are already enrolled in some other's frequent flyer mileage. You decide.

9. *"Fabulous airfares. Everyday first flight in the morning and evenings BLR-BOM one-way Rs. 3333 instead of Rs. 4045. BLR-BOM-BLR return Rs. 6666 instead of Rs. 8090." Contact Meridian Air Travel Pvt. Ltd.*

We have come a long way from such fares. Now much cheaper air-tickets are available with several low-cost airlines filling the sky, like Air Deccan, GoAir and SpiceJet. Even the well-known airlines have reduced their fares to stay competitive. Note that most of these low-cost airlines do not have travel agents but booking is done on-line through credit cards. The more in advance you buy a ticket the better for getting a low-fare seat. Air-travel in India has never been so good. However, there are a few horror stores of low-cost airlines that cause problems due to delays/cancellations. Some of these budget airlines could disappear after a while such is the competition.

10. *"Service your Sumo and win Rs. 10,000 (There is a winner everyday). Conditions apply. A Tata Sumo at our showroom is filled with balls. All you have to do is to guess the correct number of balls in this car. The closer guess will win a cash prize of Rs. 10,000."*

Try your luck while you are at the service station servicing your Tata Sumo. It's presumed that the service-agent is authorized by Tata. You have nothing to lose and it's fun guessing.

11. *"Just pay Rs. 999 for 24 months and ride your favourite Hero Shakti 3G. Finance at the sole discretion of HFSL."*

First of all you decide whether Hero motorbike is your favourite machine. Now-a-days there are car/mobike melas where either old vehicles are exchanged or newer ones bought with easy finance. Just make sure your car/mobike loan is competitive. Getting a loan has become easier with various options. Check for hidden costs. As always, check out that the price you pay is commensurate with the performance of the machine.

12. *"Videocon TV offer. Exchange price only, handling charges Rs. 1500 extra, offer valid on CTVs in working condition with remote. Offer available on models shown in the advertisement and is offered by Videocon dealers only."*

Remember you get a pittance for your old TV and such an exchange does not benefit you much. However, the advantage is getting something back at least and in the bargain a new TV set. Make sure you want to buy the brand as advertised. Shop around for other brands. Some of the dealers do exchange any brand TV set just to make you happy and effect a sale. The 'handling' charge appears to be unreasonable.

13. *"Free, a Solace-Whiteline mixer-grinder worth Rs. 2295 with every washing machine."*

This appears to be a tempting offer. Are you sure you want to buy the brand of washing machine that's advertised? If so, go ahead and get the freebies. However, if you do not like the product, forget the freebies and opt for a standard brand you are familiar with.

14. *"Sweekar oil MRP 55, sale price Rs. 47, Annapurna extra fibre atta 5 kg + 1 kg sugar: MRP Rs. 110.50, sale price Rs. 92—Foodworld."*

Always look for a bargain sale, which involves standard products from reputed outlets. There are departmental stores who sell products as per MRP only, unless these are discounted when they are not moving fast. On the other hand, retailers offer better discounts as they have a margin for profit on the MRP. Look for date of manufacture and do not buy outdated products even offered at 50 per cent discount. Like in the advanced countries, the trend in our country is to offer low prices on bulk purchases. For example, 1 kg of good quality rice is sold for, say, Rs. 21. The same rice if bought in a 25 kg bag would work out to be, say, Rs. 19 per kg. However, shop according to your needs, as long storage of food items have their own problems. Do not compromise on quality of food items as they could have adverse impact on your as well as your family's health. Say NO to buying of 'cheap and nasty' food items.

15. *"Avail great coaching at your doorstep. We provide coaching classes for II PUC, BBM, MBA, BE. Get free: Career guidance, tips to answer questions, scholarship, personality development, Josephites Academy of Brilliance."*

Check out the credibility of the institute before you think of joining the coaching class. If possible, meet students who have being coached by this institute. Check out on the fee and other costs involved.

16. *"We guarantee a Flat Bed in Business Class" — British Airways.*

If you are a frequent flyer of British Airways or you want their 'flat bed' by all means buy a ticket and check it out yourself.

17. *"Surya Enclave. Choose class living. Mega residential layout. BMRDA approved. Special inaugural offer." Contact Tel. No...*

You will have to study the offer in detail. Consult lawyers and experts. Visit the site. Then only make up your mind about investment in such layouts.

18. *"Call Centre training. Get a free silver coin on admission at JETTA. 100% placement." Contact Tel. No...*

Meet anyone who has been successfully placed. Visit and see the facilities and the staff. Don't be in a hurry to enroll because of the freebie.

19. *Buy the best. Treo 650. Mobile phone. Free: Additional battery, additional stylus, 256 MB memory card, and screen protector. Rs. 24,999" Contact Tel. No....*

See if this is the model you want to buy at this price. Ask those who have used this type for their experience.

20. *Up to 70% off on books. The Great Crossword sale. Crazy but true. In association with HDFC Bank. We understand your world. 11th November to 10th December, 2006.*

Take the family with you. You might some interesting books at discounts.

21. *"On the occasion of our 1st anniversary, we are giving away 1,00,000 free tickets. Across all sectors. Rush! Offer valid till 15th November, 2006. Offer valid for travel till 31st March, 2007. Schedule subject to change. DGCA and other regulatory approvals. Fly Smart. GoAir." Website:* www.GoAir.in"

Try if you are lucky to get a free ticket. There is 'no free lunch'! Perhaps there are hidden costs. Check out!

22. *"It happens only at Raj. Tours departing on 24, 25 and 26 December, 2006 are also SOLD OUT. Exotic Far East only with Raj. Book this tour and get complimentary return journey on Raj National Express to any sector in India from Mumbai."*

If you are interested in a conducted tour, check this out offer along with competing travel operators/agents. It all depends upon on their reliability and service during the tour.

23. *"The hottest offer on the Ford Ikon this November, 2006. Get free insurance for the first year with every Ford Ikon Flair. If you find a better offer in December we'll refund the difference."*

If you are interested in exchanging/buying a new car, check this offer. See if can get any other offer that's equally attractive. It depends upon your brand preference too.

24. *"It's winter. You should be out in the sun. Taj Holidays. Special 20% discount on the rates on stay till 30th November."*

If you want to holiday, check this out yourself. Find out the hidden costs.

25. *"Why to Kancheepuram and Chennai for buying pure silk sarees? Experience the happiest shopping. Visit S.M. Silks. Up to 50% off."*

Sure you should visit, in case, you are thinking of buying silk sarees. Check out the price and quality.

26. *"The largest sale of winter jackets and track suits at unbelievable prices. Sale from 15–25 November, 2006. The Wearhouse."*

Do you need winter clothes? By all means visit and see for yourself the range offered and their prices.

27. *"Don't miss this golden opportunity. Introducing 'Alice Cash back' offer. Step into Alice and be dazzled by the best offer in town. Alice Jewellery. Government of India approved jewellery valuer. 100% buy-back guarantee for gold."*

You might go and see the variety of designs and the cost aspect yourself and then decide about buying.

28. *"Free holiday package with every mobile. Phones starting from Rs. 1999 onwards." Just Call Tel. No. ....*

Read the fine print the terms and conditions of the 'holiday package.'

29. *"India's No. 1 Colour Television. Upgrade to an elegant lifestyle and get paid for it as well. LG Electronics."*

If you are thinking of upgrading your TV set you may consider this offer too.

30. *"Best cars are limited. So are the best offers...Last 7 days only! Gift cheque Rs. 15,151 for Maruti 800 and Rs. 11,111 for Alto."*

Check out whether the offer is for exchange or for a new car. Check if you get a loan to buy the car on the spot.

HEALTH RELATED

1. *"Herbal. No pesticidal chemicals. No. 1 at driving away mosquitoes."*

Beware of all mosquito repellents. Use with care, if you have to. It's hazardous to keep a mosquito (repellent) coil burning all-night, day in and day out that is a health risk. A mosquito net is preferable at home.

2. *"Teka' capsules for a sharper brain. Who needs to take 'Teka' capsules? Children with stammering problem, students to increase concentration and intellectual capacity, executives and housewives to sharpen their decision-making skills, the elderly to rejuvenate their memory power and reflexes. Dosage–adults one capsule in the morning and one capsule in the night after food. Children (5–12 years) one capsule a day mixed with honey."*

Such advertisements will continue to be released whether one likes them or approves them or not. It's for consumers to decide whether they would take such medicines that could cause more harm than good in the long after investing money. Caution is the word while dealing with such advertisements. At best, you can consult your doctor before deciding to try these types of 'miracle' medicines.

3. *"The Healing Touch Naturopathy Clinic will arrange treatment for hyperacidity, gastritis, peptic ulcer, and constipation." For details contact phone.......*

Beware! It's possible the cure could turn out to be worse than the disease!

4. *"D-Diabetes is a time tested medicine made from a mixture of ancient ayurvedic herbs. It helps control blood and urine sugar, helps regain physical strength and reduces depression, enhances your vigour and vitality. Use as per doctor's recommendation." Available at ....*

Do not give up the present medication and try out the new medicine as described. Consult your doctor, if you decide to change your medicine. Sometimes such claims are not supported by scientific evidence. If you want to try this medicine out, then the risk is yours!

5. *"Kidney stone removal without surgery," by R G Stone, USFDA approved state of the art, Simens, Lithostar. All urinary stones treated. No pain, no anesthesia. Diabetes, hypertension, heart patients need not fear. CGHS approved. "Pioneers yesterday, leaders today."*

Check with a qualified doctor and also with those who have undergone this treatment for improvement. Find out the cost of treatment before you sign up for the operation.

6. *"Herbal medicine for asthma. The Gaur Brahmin Sangh will distribute free herbal medicines for asthma patients." Contact Tel. No........*

Any medical or scientific evidence does not support or approve of this 'treatment'. However, thousands of asthma sufferers, defying logic, go for treatment. There is no evidence that the medicines given cure asthma. Also, it's not known how many people really get cured and how many don't. It's a matter of faith. You decide this yourself!

7. *"Fish medicine to be given on June 8, 9 in Hyderabad. About 2 lakhs asthma affected people are expected to be treated by 'fish medicine' given by the famed Bathini Goud Brothers free of cost every year. 'Family secret' claim the brothers."*

For vegetarians, medicine is put into bananas. There is no medical/ scientific evidence of the efficacy of this treatment, though lakhs of asthma sufferers go to Hyderabad for treatment. It's faith cure that's all! Same as in point 6 above.

8. *"Self purification technique. The Vipasana Meditation and Research Centre is conducting a ten-day residential course on ancient technique on self-purification, which includes relief techniques from tension, stress, anger, anxiety and fear."*

If you have an open mind to try something different, you can see how this course works for you. There is a wealth of knowledge that's hidden in our ancient texts, which benefit an individual.

9. *"Arthritis? Fifteen days from now, you will mail us thank you cards. Sunova Nopane relief from agony of arthritis. Developed by Dabur Research Foundation, natural/non-addictive remedy in just 15 days, for best results use for 3 months continuously. Available over the counter."*

Such claims should be taken with a pinch of salt. At best, you might get some relief temporarily. Try it to see how it benefits you, if at all.

10. *"Be slim! Be happy! GARCINIA oral spray (Aqualogics): a product from USA, 5 pumps 5 times a day in the mouth, followed by a glass of water 15 minutes* *before food, for a slimmer you. For male/female both for home delivery. Call on Tel. No..."*

Danger lies ahead if you follow this regime! Do not attempt such 'treatment' without consulting your doctor.

11. *"French Neutro Slim' Shastric Siddha Medicine. Capsules that treat obesity by reducing weight at regular intervals without any side-effects."*

Same warning as above!

12. *"Beautiful skin' Florozone lotion and cream with allantoin makes skin soft, smooth and beautiful. Write for free literature to Hygienic Research Institute, Mumbai (price not stated)"*

Every human being wants to look beautiful. As such there are many ways of hooking the gullible to buy some 'magic' medicine/treatment or the other. If you are beauty conscious, do consult a recognized and well-known beautician and not buy some strange over-the counter-stuff that might actually harm you.

13. *"New formula ORGANICS root nourishing shampoo. Reduce hair breakage by 50 per cent."*

Is this from a recognized manufacturer or some vague company trying to fool the gullible? Use only time-tested brand and stick to it, unless proved otherwise.

14. *Literature and magazines connected with health, for example, 'Longevity and Health' which claims "a complete family magazine fore help, hope and happiness."*

Upgrading your knowledge about health-related matters is a life-long venture that would benefit you and your family members. But no self-medication please! Do not try something new because that's the in-thing. Use your judgment and consult others before you want to try something new or novel.

A claim such as "proper ergonomic chairs will ensure that your spine retains its right form," need not be disputed. However a claim, "Nature cure for diabetes," should send alarm signals before you venture into such a 'treatment'. That's true for claims like 'Yoga cure for short-sight'. You might give such methods/treatment a try but not at the cost of whatever treatment you are taking as prescribed by a qualified doctor. You should remember, that for every success claimed, for home medicines, nature treatment, over the counter pills and the like, there could easily be ten times more failures which the manufacturer, dealer, retailer won't even mention to you because their business is to sell.

An intelligent and informed consumer would exercise care in going for anything 'new' and 'novel'. He/she would have done his/her homework and prepared well before attempting something different. In health-related matters there are multiple-choices. However, it is a minefield to be negotiated carefully in view of so many claims and counterclaims. Internet has websites that educate the general public. For example, *www.webmd.com* is a useful website where you get expert advice on various matters of interest to the consumer.

15. *"White patches: By using this newly invented medicine it is 100% guaranteed that the colour of your skin will be changed surely within 20 hours. Send details of your disease or contact Chief Vaidya Raj over phone. Tel. No...."*

Beware of such miracle cures!

16. *"Dr. Batra's treatment not only reduced my hair fall, it also improved my hair texture."*—By a patient

Dr. Batra's is claimed to be world's largest homeopathy chain. Check out with those who have undergone such treatment and their experience. It's important to note the duration and the cost involved in such treatment.

17. *"On the occasion of 'World Diabetes Day' The Sagar Centre for Diabetes offers following specific packages" Comprehensive Diabetes Care Package; Diabetes Screening Package; Diabetes Review Care Package; Gestational Diabetes Package." For further information contact Tel No. Website: www.thesagarcentrefordiabetes.com*

If you are interested call or pay a visit for details including costs involved.

18. *"Breakthrough in research. To reduce blood sugar the natural way. Diabetes granules."*

Beware of such claims of 'breakthrough'. Check up with your physician. Do not stop your regular medication.

19. *"VLCC helped me lose two things, 21 kgs and all my old clothes," testimony by a patient. "Book for weight loss and 50% off on figure correction." VLCC. Slimming, beauty and fitness.*

Man/woman's eternal quest is for that perfect hourglass figure, especially the fair sex. Those on the higher weight side try to shed kilos by all sorts of methods—fasting, dieting, exercises, medicines and the like. Try to find out what exactly VLCC does for weight reduction, how long is the treatment and also the cost involved. Check with those who have lost weight their experiences. Consult a dietician too, if required.

In your quest for an hourglass figure, don't fall into the false promises of dubious weight loss clinics. Ascertain the following:

- Always go a reputed weight loss.
- Check whether they have a qualified doctor on call.
- If possible, ask for the references of fellow clinic customers.
- Don't go by their verbal claims. Ask for a written promise.

- Don't hesitate to go to Consumer Court for any mental or physical agony.

Advertisement by: Department of Consumer Affairs (Government of India) website: fcamin.nic.in. Call for free National Consumer Helpline No. 1800-11-4000 or log on to: *www.core.nic.in*

20. *"Quality health care at affordable cost. Manipal Speciality Hospital. Senior Citizen Club. Free RBS and BP test at the time of registration." For registration call Tel. No...*

Such offers are tempting. You will have to check on the cost aspect before enrolling in such schemes.

21. *"Now with Dr. Honey cough syrup get fast relief without drowsiness."*

Check this with your doctor. There are too many over the counter cough syrup formulations variously priced.

22. *Beware of mosquito repellents—killing you softly!*

Take care!

FINANCE RELATED

Savings account

Free! ATM card (accessing 139 ATMs countrywide). Free! Tele-banking, Free! Drafts and Funds transfer, Free! E-sec Account (Depository Account Opening), Free! Personalized cheque book, quarterly interest, extended timings and more.... Just open a savings bank account with us, IDBI bank, gateway to modern banking. Including 107 ATMs of other banks in Mumbai through IBA's SWADHAN network and 4 American Express Bank ATMs. Conditions apply.

Most of the above facilities are now available with practically every nationalized and major private bank in the country. You choose the one nearest to you with ATM and extended working hours (now mostly it's 8 am to 8 pm Monday to Friday and half day on Saturday, Sunday and public holidays closed). Check your pass book or bank statement regularly. Those with on-line bank statement can access their secure account as and when they want.

Caution: Use your ATM/Credit/Debit card with care and caution. Report if someone has stolen the card details and is using it fraudulently. Report loss of card immediately and ask for stop payment immediately.

Services offered by ICICI

Banking services including 24-hours ATMs in selected metros, bonds, depository services, car/home loans and a host of customer services including NRI. Leading analysts adviser you on what shares to buy and when to sell. All you have to do now is log in: www.icicidirect.com.

"Protect your savings. Never leave your cheque book unattended. ICICI Bank."

More such banks would be available in future with many foreign banks starting their operations in India. Most of the big banks, in the public as well as private sector, are competing with each other to woo customers. They provide good service. One has again to go by loyalty and one's own experiences in dealing with a particular bank. With more ATMs offered by various banks, banking is becoming 24 × 7 and easier. However, take care while drawing cash and look around for strange characters who could mug you if you are not careful enough. We should note an important point: Computers don't make mistakes but people do. So it's advisable to check up the banking transactions regularly to avoid nasty surprises. The more Internet savvy you are the better for easier transactions in future where more and more services would be available on the Internet.

Travellers cheques (TCs): Some tips

- Always keep proof of purchase in a safe place and not along with the TCs. This is essential when you want to claim refund for lost/stolen TCs.
- Report loss/theft of TCs within 24 hours to the nearest police station and get a copy of the First Information Report (FIR) for your record and further action regarding claim. You will have to inform the toll–free number of the TC company for their information and claim. Most of the TC issuing companies like American Express, Bank of Baroda, State Bank of India, and Thomas Cook have their own dedicated 24 hours line for customer service.
- Do sign all the TCs immediately on receipt to prevent fraudulent use by someone else. Note down the TC numbers in a separate notebook for your reference. Do not countersign the TC till you want to cash it.
- Do return the TCs to the agent/issuing company in case you find these later on. The TC companies appreciate such honesty.

Credit/Debit card: Some information

"India's only debit card now comes with its most valuable feature, your simile! Introducing: The Citibank Suvidha Photo Debit Card. Warmly welcomed at 1500 shops, no minimum purchase amount, up to 25 per cent shopping discount offers, reward points on every purchase."

We have come a long way from such advertisements. Now getting a debit card is easy and every savings/current account holder gets it as a matter of routine. However, getting a credit card is not easy, especially for senior citizens who are routinely denied a credit card, though credit worthy, due to some strange reason. In India the use of debit/credit card is limited, mostly, to metros. Even here some of the shops do not accept 'Plastic money' but only hard cash. There is also the requirement of a minimum purchase, like Rs. 250 per transactions. Not all credit/debit cards are accepted by all establishments but only well known brands.

Some features of credit cards

- In general there is an annual fee, though this varies. Some banks charge Rs. 500 to 1000 for certain types of credit cards.
- They have buying power in certain shops and transactions only.
- Not yet widely accepted in India unlike the advanced countries like the USA/UK where these are routinely accepted for almost all transaction.
- Free credit period varies, generally up to 50 days.
- Smart cash, which offers 24 hours access to cash at a number of ATMs across the country. The trend is to tie up with banks so that customers from one bank could access cash from some other bank's ATM without any charge.
- Exclusive travel services.
- Insurance benefits, which may be up to Rs. 10 lakhs in case of death.

[**Note:** The benefit package, and conditions like annual service-fee could vary from bank to bank. ATM has become quite a standard option at present. In fact, banks urge customers use their ATMs rather than use a cheque and teller facility.]

'Add power to your pocket.' The new Deutsche Bank Credit Card. A passion to perform. Deutsche Bank. Website: www.deutschebank.co.in

BOB Cards

Free credit card offer to Bank of Baroda Customers: Account holders of: Fixed deposits; Super savings bank account; Premium current account; Housing loan account etc.

Advantages BOB cards

- Lifetime free card—gold and exclusive (woman and youth)
- All other cards free for one year.

- Total family card—up to 3 add on cards free.
- Flexi limits.
- Minimum payment (5–10%).
- Service charges—1.99% p.m (@23.88% p.a.).
- Up to 3 bonus points on gold card and 1.5 bonus points on exclusive card usage.
- 50% cash back on bonus point redemption (one bonus point = Re. 0.50).
- Reduced service charges on cash withdrawal.
- Excellent reward points and discount schemes.
- No hidden charges.
- Total relationship management and personalized services.
- Strict compliance of GOI, RBI, IBA guidelines.
- All cards ATM compatible and globally accepted.
- Special services available from Master Card and VISA—host of services worldwide.

[**Note:** A customer has to be wary about use of credit card. Credit fraud is a multi-crore racket due to all sorts of malpractices. Beware of charges, which you might be debited, if you are not vigilant. Credit/debit cards are no doubt convenient but caution is the watchword to prevent misuse and wrong billing.]

Convenience cheques from Citibank

This innovation enables Citibank cardholders to issue cheques against their credit cards and pay utility and other bills where payment through credit cards is not yet popular. Designed to enable customers to make payments and enjoy the same benefits as they would if they had used their credit cards, convenience cheques are otherwise similar to cheques that are issued from savings/current bank accounts. They are accepted everywhere a customers' cheques are normally accepted. Convenience cheques come with the payment at par facility in six cities of Bangalore, Chennai, Delhi, Kolkata, Mumbai and Pune, thus enabling inter-city payments.

Credit card: Charge it now and pay later.
Debit card: Buy now and pay up immediately.

SBI card

The currency of modern India. A cardholder with Visa power from India's biggest bank—State Bank of India and GE Capital, World's biggest Finance Company:

- Accepted at over 100,000 outlets in India and Nepal.
- Interest free credit up to 50 days on purchase.
- Extended credit facility at finance charge of first 2.5 per cent p.a.
- *Buy when you want, pay when you can.*
- Cash facility wherever you go cash withdrawal facility at over 75 SBI card cash points in 5 cities, 11 cash points at Bangalore city (Latest info- these figures are much higher and available at many big towns and cities all over the country).
- Free accident insurance cover of Rs. 2 lakhs (now it's much higher).
- 24 hours SBI card help-line available for any assistance.
- Regular free privileges, special offers and mega value offers shall be mailed to all cardholders from time to time.
- Joining fee of Rs. 250 waived as a special introductory offer.
- Annual fee of Rs. 500 only.
- Add-on facility cards for all cardholders for a special fee of Rs. 250 only.
- Simple procedure, no need to open an SB account with SBI.

[**Note:** Some of the above could have changed over a period of time. Check with SBI on the latest conditions.]

The Hong Kong and Shanghai Banking Corporation (HSBC) Limited credit card:

- Low annual fee, after the first year, you pay only Rs. 500 annually for a HSBC Classic card.
- *Buying power:* A HSBC card is accepted at 100,000 establishments.
- *Free credit:* Of up to 50 days and an extended facility which allows you to buy now, pay a minimum of 5 per cent and settle the balance later.
- *Smart cash:* Offers 24 hours access to cash at over 60 HSBC Group ATMs across the country (Latest—could be much higher now).
- Exclusive travel services to take care of every detail related to your business or holiday.
- Excellent insurance benefits including a free accident cover up to Rs. 6 lakhs, purchase protection of Rs. 30,000 and a credit shield cover of Rs. 20,000.

If you avail of this offer, you also stand to win one of over 1000 fantastic prizes.

[**Note:** Check for the latest information with HSBC.]

With improved performance of banks, private as well as public, it's a question of loyalty and convenience. For example, you tend to bank at the nearest place, which is walking distance and where the service is prompt and personal. Moreover, you don't need all the services by some banks. Credit/debit card are useful while dealing with large amounts of cash, especially if you are a frequent flyer on company business. In fact, for such travellers, there are special promo schemes by airlines as well as hotels, travel-related services and other services. Still 'plastic money' has to gain better acceptability in our country. Moreover, some conservative spenders still with an old mindset wouldn't like to be in 'debt' to someone else. They would rather settle bills then and there. We have to understand the convenience of plastic money but at the same time be responsible enough not to overspend, because you don't have to pay now. There is an important concern of fraudulent use of credit card that needs to be safeguarded. Thus keep your credit/debit as safe as any cash and prevent misuse.

A point worth noting is that the information supplied to a credit/debit card agency may not remain confidential.

This can be seen from the following paragraph:

[**Note:** 'Authorization' wanted as a form of declaration by HSBC.]

"We hereby authorize you to inform the details of my/our transactions including default of payment that may occur, to any other credit card issuer, other banks, financial institutions, credit card rating agencies and other similar organizations as the bank may deem fit and proper in India, without obtaining any further oral or written consent from me/us."

Declaration by applicant: "Authorization to verify any information and obtain any credit card report including that of my family members, with any source at the discretion of the bank. The issue of a credit card is subject to banks discretion and the bank reserves the right to decline the application without giving any reason. Credit card may be used only subject to terms and conditions of the bank, a copy of which will be sent to me/us along with the credit card later."

Such one-sided rules and regulations smack of arbitrariness. We have yet to reach the level of credit card usage of the advanced countries. However, if your personal information has to be kept confidential, then you may not go in for a credit/debit card. In the advanced countries plastic money (various types of credit/debit cards by several agencies) have practically replaced paper money. However, fraudulent/misuse of credit card is rampant running into several millions of dollars every year. One should take care of all the possible precautions, yet there is a chance some one some time is bound to hack into your e-mail and get the information of your credit/debit card. So beware of such misuse all the time! The more vigilant you are the better it's for your safety sake! Even in the USA, where use of plastic money is widespread, there are a few who swear by paper money. They feel rich with wads of greenbacks and use these carefully because they can really see where they are spending.

Here is a real story by one of the credit card user:

"I'll never forget receiving a $99 restaurant charge on a monthly statement. I had been in another city on the day of the charge was recorded and thought my husband had entertained someone and neglected to mention it. When I questioned him, he said he had only gone to the restaurant for a cup of coffee. I called the credit card company and asked for a copy of the receipt. Sure enough, the decimal had been put in the wrong place, and the real charge was 99 cents."

So it's in your own interest to check carefully every single credit/debit card transaction you do

Home loans: Some information

HDFCís adjustable rate home loans (ARHL)

You can avail of loans at interest rates that will be linked to HDFC's Retail Prime Lending Rate (RPLR). The interest rate will be adjusted every six months. You have also the option of a Fixed Rate Home Loan, maximum 15 years. HDFC's latest (December 2006) rate of interest on housing loans is 11 per cent (fixed rate) for a period of 0–20 years.

Getting a home loan, either to buy/build a new home or renovate an old one, has never been so easy as of now with so many institutions offering easy and quick loans at competitive rates. Most banks now-a-days offer loans against fixed deposits or proof of salary. Elaborate documentation has now been simplified. Still, it's better to shop around, consult financial/tax experts and then only go for a loan, fixed or floating rate. While in the USA and other advanced countries, it takes just one or two days to get a mortgage loan, in India it still takes weeks, though this is likely to come down with increasing competition.

HSBCís home loan (The Hong Kong and Shanghai Banking Corporation Limited)

"10 good reasons why buying a home will never be the same again." Fixed or floating interest rate, low interest, design your own loan repayment plan, loans from Rs. 1 lakh to Rs. 1 crore, no penalty for repaying up to 25 per cent of your loan every year, loans for different housing needs, refinance existing loan and save money, loan against residential property, enjoy personalized service, special offer for valued HSBC customer. HSBC, your world of financial services. Terms and conditions apply.

ICICI Bank 'Loan against property'

Property overdraft—For the first time get an overdraft against your property.

Here is some information that could be useful for prospective home-loaners.

Booklet issued by Alacrity Housing Limited in public interest

- Key questions to ask while buying a flat.
- Urban housing: Whose rights and whose responsibility.
- Water issue for housing.
- Business and ethics.

Always read the fine print (for terms and conditions apply) and compare any offer with other reputed housing loan agencies/banks/institutions. Now customers have a choice of from whom to get a housing loan. Use it wisely and cost-effectively. Look for prompt and personalized service, preferably with a smile! A smart person who is about to invest in a house would shop around for good deals before choosing one that suits him. He should be monitoring the loan interest situation so that he can opt for renegotiating the new loan by clearing the old borrowed sum. It is logical to opt for a new loan whose interest is lower. One should keep that flexibility aspect in mind while taking any loan.

The repo rate rise by 25 basic points in the RBI's busy season credit policy pronounced on the 31st October, 2006, and subsequent tightening of housing loan norms are likely to place housing sector in some sort of jeopardy state some experts.

Here are some questions, which you should ask before investing in a house:

- Will the builder allow modifications? Is there room for future changes?
- Check what area of actual usable space you will get; is it enough for your family? What about when guests/relatives come over?
- Is it a duplex system? Do you have old people in the family who may not be able to climb stairs?
- Is it compatible with your lifestyle? Can you have formal as well as informal entertainment space? Will it accommodate religious functions?

- How is privacy important for you?
- Does the floor plan allow for good ventilation and natural light? Is the kitchen dark?
- If your children are small, are the balcony railings safe?
- Are electrical fittings inclusive of safety features?
- Are security and amenities adequate?
- Is the builder reputed? Is the brand an established one? What has been the track record?

Information: It pays to read about modern and ancient housing designs. There are newspapers and magazines which deal with real estate/ residence regularly which give a fund of knowledge and information. For example, wooden floors are strong and stylish.

Car loans

"Instant second-hand car finance, even for models dating back ten years. Finance available at the sole discretion of AVCO Financial Services Pvt. Ltd. Terms and conditions apply."

Situation for car loans has changed dramatically of late with many financial institutions coming forward to offer loans at competitive rates. Look around for easy payment and lower interest with a good customer service that's personalized. Documentation too has been reduced to make it user-friendly.

Car loan (by a panel of experts of ICICI bank)

1. *Advantage of using your own funds to buy a car:* No debt obligation, no interest outflows, pay actual cost, no paper work, no need to make a large cash outflow all at once.

Disadvantages: Blocks a fair amount of your funds, so you lose the opportunity to deploy it elsewhere.

2. *Advantage of using a car loan:* No need to make a large cash outflow all at once, repay in instalment, tax benefit (if you are a businessman).

Disadvantages: You pay much more than what you would have paid for an outright purchase.

So which is more beneficial, using your own funds or taking a car loan?

If you have an avenue of investment giving you a rate of interest exceeding the interest rate on the car loan, it would be beneficial to take a car loan and park in that investment avenue the amount saved by avoiding a one-time flat outflow. If you do not, and if you have the funds to make an outright purchase, it would be beneficial to use your own funds to buy the car. If you have a budgetary constraint on making an outright purchase, the only option is a car loan. There are *melas* where used cars are certified by car dealers and traded for new ones or go in for a later model. Car finance is generally arranged through a financial institution where the documentation can be completed. Most of the time, the documents required would be your salary certificate/bank statement/IT returns/proof of residence/personal ID and so on.

Investment risk

Credit rating is an indication of the risk factors involved in any investment.

The credit rating firms are:

- Credit Rating Information Services of India Limited (CRISIL)
- Investment Information and Credit Rating Agency of India (ICRA)
- Credit Analysis & Research (CARE)
- Duff & Phelps Credit Rating India Private Limited (DCR India)

It should be noted that rating once awarded is valid for a certain period only and it gets updated regularly. That's why the investor has to keep an eye on the credit rating before investment.

A word of caution: Credit rating agencies are not responsible for the safety of your investments. The risk is entirely yours and the credit ratings are for guidance only.

Rating AAA means the highest safety rating. Others are given below:

Rating		*Safety*
AAA	—	highest safety
AA	—	high safety
A	—	adequate safety
BBB	—	moderate safety
BB	—	sub-moderate safety
B	—	inadequate safety
C	—	substantial risk
D	—	default

Fixed income: Some tips

To get a fixed income over a period of time, the investor has a choice of investing in: fixed deposits in banks, corporate and financial institutions, corporate debentures, mutual fund schemes, public provident fund, postal-savings schemes. The highest safety is with nationalized and big private banks as well as with postal and LIC pension schemes. The interest on fixed deposits varies in a narrow band. Higher rate of interest promised by some institutions carry greater risk. The credit risks are: borrower not paying the contracted interest or not refunding the principal on time when due. You can get an idea of the risk factor while studying the ratings of institutions you wish to invest. It's better to consult an investment consultant to clarify any doubt. An investor who is in need of a regular income every month/quarter/six months opts for a fixed deposit, for a specified period of 1, 2, 3 or 5 years, whereas he might opt for as cumulative fixed deposit, which fetches a higher rate of interest at the end of the lock-in period, in case he is not wanting regular income.

Highlight of sound returns: Open-ended income fund. 100 per cent debt portfolio, higher post-tax returns, and no lock-in period, dividends exempt from income tax.

Fixed deposit (FD)

It is an investment of a certain sum of money, in a bank, Non-Banking Finance Company (NBFC), manufacturing company, for a specified period. It can vary from 15 days to 5 and rarely to 10 years. Interest rate depends upon the period of fixed deposit and varies. Senior citizens get an extra 0.5–1.0 per cent over the general interest rate. In general, the longer period the better the interest rate and is as per the Reserve Bank of India (RBI) guidelines. Interest payment can be flexible—monthly, quarterly, six-monthly or annually.

Fixed deposit allows you to withdraw the sum prematurely but you will lose interest and there could be a penalty too. You can take a loan on your FD but paying higher rate of interest than you would receive. If you forget to renew the FD then the amount will not fetch any further interest but your sum will be intact. However, some banks continue to pay interest with the expectation that you would renew the FD further. But don't assume this but renew the FD before it's due.

Investment in a FD can be 'liquid' in the 'Auto-Sweep' type of schemes offered to depositors by some banks. Suppose you have a savings bank account in a bank. The bank offers facility of moving funds, automatically, in excess of a specified limit to another to create a FD fetching higher interest. The advantage is that the 'automatic sweep' allows your 'idle' savings back amount to fetch better rate of interest. However, when you need funds, this scheme allows you to draw from the FD without penalty but losing the higher interest. This is known as 'Reverse Sweep' is a mechanism offered by some banks to honour your cheque when needed.

It's prudent to have a joint-holder account, whether it's savings bank, current account or fixed deposit. A joint holding allows one or more designated persons to operate the account conveniently. You can also have a nominee who can stake a claim only when the first and joint holders are dead.

We have come a long way from double-digit inflation and double-digit interest rates due to better management of economy and partly due to globalization. We are almost at par with the developed world as far as inflation and interest rates are concerned. The inflation is about 5 per cent and the interest rates vary from 6 to 9 per cent. However, those with fixed incomes, mostly from FDs and postal savings schemes, are in trouble due to reduced interest rates. That's why a few schemes like senior citizen's fixed deposits and pension schemes offer a better rate of interest of about 9 per cent which is safe because it's guaranteed by the government.

Cumulative deposit (CD)

Interest received, along with the principal, at the end of a specified period. The accrued interest gets added on to the sum invested. A cumulative deposit has a better Return On Investment (ROI).

Risk and Return in a fixed deposit (FD) (by a panel of experts of the ICICI bank)

Risk is directly proportion to the return. Greater the risk higher is the return. Strike the right balance between risk and return. Those who offer higher returns are found to be less reputed and so higher is the risk. It's possible you might not get regular returns as promised and there could be delay or even default on returning your sum invested. So watch out for such institutions, which promise a lot but fail sometimes to deliver. The credit rating of a company reflects its safety level and risks, lower the rating greater is the danger of default.

Tax deduction at source (TDS)

This is deducted at source when the interest in a calendar year exceeds a designated amount. Those who don't want the TDS to be deducted could fill out the relevant IT forms like 15H/15G.

Do study various exemptions under various sections of the Income Tax Act.

Investment in 'Penny Stock'

A Penny Stock is one which is set to 'shoot' up. The profits to be made on such stocks are very high. But one can rake in profits in a couple of such stocks but on a majority of such stocks, one is likely to lose money. A Penny Stock is a risky investment option. You may not make a killing but it may kill you!

A few lucky investors become millionaires overnight by investing and selling stocks at the right time. Spurred on by such success stores, other investors too want to try their luck in such stocks. Some of them invest their life's savings to realize soon that all their shares are worthless and are likely to lose heavily. Some of them become bankrupt too. So beware of such quick ways of making money. Please understand that not all can be lucky to rake in millions.

Stockbrokers and investment agencies advise their clients from time to time where to invest and how much to buy and when to sell. With the on-line share/stock trading matters have become even simpler. You watch for the share prices and decide when to buy and when to sell by the click of a mouse. A few avid investors look forward to buying each and every new company's issues at par so that they can make a fast buck later on. Investing in stocks and shares and depending upon it to make a living might not be as risky as gambling but the investors are warned that there is great danger of losing one's money if one is too reckless.

Caution is the watchword while trying to invest in stocks and shares. Let us face the reality—only a few make money, while majority lose. So the risk is yours when you want to play on the stock market.

Stock market could be a roller coaster ride. The Bombay Stock Exchange (BSE) index, SENSEX (upwards of 14,000) and the National Stock Exchange index (NSE NIFTY) (upwards of 4000) have touched unprecedented levels of late. However, on days it sheds hundreds of points with the result that those investors who thought of cashing in on the boom would be left high and dry. They lose thousands if not lakhs of rupees overnight. That's the risk in playing on the stock market. Some times stocks turn to worthless paper and those investors suffer a huge loss. No one but the investor is to be blamed for such a sorry state of affairs. The SENSEX is often speculative and does not reflect the actual position of the worth of stocks.

The Security and Exchange Board of India (SEBI) has imposed restrictions on wild fluctuations of stocks. In such cases there is an automatic circuit breaker that halts all trade for that day. But SEBI cannot guarantee that every investor in stocks makes money. An amateur investor might gain once in a way. However, he/she would be well advised to consult reputed stockbrokers who can guide investors to wise decisions. However, as mentioned earlier, with the on-line trading of stocks and shares, even average investor, over a period of time, can gain a bit of expertise and use his / her judgment better to maximize gains and minimize losses. Wise investors keep a small sum, say, Rs. 10,000, for investment in stocks as more of an intellectual challenge. At the other end, some investors, who have the money, invest lakhs hoping to increase their net-worth. For safety and a steady income there is nothing like a fixed deposits, postal-savings and pension funds guaranteed by government. SEBI takes up grievances related to issue and transfer of securities and non-payment of dividend with listed companies. In addition, SEBI also takes up grievances against the various intermediaries registered with it and related issues.

Contact SEBI: SEBI Bhavan, Plot No. C-4A, G Block, Bandra, Kurla, Complex, Bandra (East), Mumbai-400 051, Tel. No. 264490000.

Investment in bonds

Bonds are 'liquid' cash (a) early encashment option (b) put option—you can deem your bond at the time of the put option (c) call option—the company can buy-back bonds when it wants at the time of the call option. The investor may note that all bonds are not listed on the stock exchange. Bonds are transferable.

Bonds and debentures: Easily available because they are traded in the debt market. Interest rate offered on bonds, debentures are more or less same as FDs. Bonds and debentures are more 'liquid' than FDs.

Mutual funds (MFs)

MFs are set to replace direct investment in the advance countries. These attract savings of individuals thereby replacing bank deposits with commercial banks. However, in India the MF industry has not taken off in the real sense of the word though there is now MF as an additional option for investors. Of late, the keenness of investors to invest in MFs offering regular income with zero credit is being capitalized by many funds offering gilt schemes. Also there is a trend to divert savings bank and FD accounts of scheduled banks to the open-ended income schemes of MFs and gilt schemes. The reason is that the yield on government securities for comparable tenure is more attractive than the interest rates offered on FDs with the banks. The gilt schemes also offer any time liquidity. "Making Mutual Funds work for you," is a useful booklet issued by the Association of Mutual Funds in India. The prospective investor in MF will benefit by reading such information booklet carefully.

"Uncertain markets need not mean uncertain returns. Presenting PruICICI Equity and Derivatives Fund. Designed to work in all market conditions." You should consult a financial/investment expert on such schemes.

Attention NBFC depositors (Issued in the public interest by RBI)

Non Banking Finance Company (NBFC) includes leasing and hire purchase companies, loan and investment companies and excludes residuary non-banking companies. Invest only with NBFC registered with the Reserve Bank of India (RBI) and having RBI approval to accept public deposits.

Remember before making your investment decision:

- NBFCs cannot offer more than 16 per cent (this is changing) interest on public deposits.
- No official agency guarantees or undertakes the repayment of deposit or interest. This is the sole responsibility of the NBFC.
- NBFC deposits are neither insured nor backed by security.
- NBFCs cannot offer more than 2 per cent (this is also changing) brokerage.
- NBFCs cannot offer gifts/incentives.
- NBFCs cannot accept deposits for less than 12 months.
- All depositors must be issued proper receipts for deposits.
- Unincorporated bodies like individuals, partnership firms, Hindu Undivided Family (HUF), association of persons, trusts, clubs *et al.* engaged in financial business cannot accept public deposits.

Electronic clearing scheme (ECS)

(Issued in the public interest by the Indian Bank's Association on behalf of all members)

"So many benefits—So convenient"

"ECS, Save Money—Save Time"

How ECS benefits bank customers and investors in share/ debentures/deposits?

Direct credits: Dividend income from investment in shares/ debentures, interest income from FDs, pension funds, bonds, commission and other regular incomes, salary and pension, income-tax refund orders, and other inward remittances to your bank account.

Direct debits: Telephone, and water and electricity and other utility bills, loan instalment and insurance premium, school, college and club membership fees, credit card dues, water and property taxes and other regular payments to your bank account. This can be done only after proper authorization and you, as well as the agency involved could withdraw from the scheme. (**Caution:** Check each transaction carefully for errors of omission and commission).

Your advantage: Payment on due date, no more 'loss in transit' of bills or cheques, no fraudulent encashment, effortless receipt, no more correspondence with the companies, no hassles of standing in long lines for payment of bills, no more disconnection of telephone/electricity/water, account statement/pass book will show the source of credit and debit. All you need to do is to prepare the payment data and submit it to the 'sponsor' bank. And after that everything happens electronically

[**Note:** Make sure that happens].

ECS is the future way of doing paperless credit/debit which is the trend in India too.

But a customer has to be vigilant to see that the transactions take place on time and everything is in order as per his/her instructions. That's why a regular check of account statement is a must. Don't be surprised if someone else's bill is being charged to you or you get some credit, which is actually not yours.

DEMAT trading

Trading in dematerialized shares. It means replacing physical share (paper) certificates with a book entry in a depository account—similar to a bank account — with a depository participant. All such transactions, dividends, and bonuses are credited/debited electronically to such accounts. Most of the companies are switching over to DEMAT trading for sheer convenience. Often you may not be able to sell shares without converting your shares to the DEMAT format. So go ahead be a DEMAT account holder for easier transactions in tune with the times.

Performance indicator (PI): Life insurance corporation (LIC) of India

Of late more and more organizations publish their PIs, which is a statement of intention to serve the customers within a defined timeframe. The following are the examples of PI of LIC.

- Issue of renewal premium receipt at the counter for policies where the premium position is up-to-date and the policy belongs to the same branch: within 30 minutes.
- Registration of nomination/assignment on receipt of all requirements: within 5 days.
- Issue of maturity/survival benefit claim cheques after receipt of all requirements: where all requirements are received sufficiently in advance of the date of maturity: post-dated cheques in advance. Where all requirements are received after the date of maturity: 4 days.
- Issue of death claim cheques after receipt of all requirements: 4 days.

Life insurance corporation (LIC) of India : Some tips

(Issued by LIC for the benefit of the policy holders)

- Quote your policy number in all correspondence
- Pay your premium regularly and within specified time limit
- Get age admission
- Intimate change of address
- Transfer of policy to branch of your choice
- Ensure safety of your policy
- Ensure adequate cover
- Prompt revival of lapsed policy
- Get claims maturity
- Get grievance redress

More and more service organizations are devising PIs to continuously monitor these for control and improvement in order to improve their service quality. Service organizations have to be customer-focused for better quality of service. More public sector undertakings, due to competition, are coming forward to demonstrate their concern for the customers. Here is an example from the Income Tax Department, Government of India:

Citizenís charter

A declaration of our commitment to excellence in our service to tax payers:

- To be fair
- To be helpful
- To be efficient

We expect you:

- To be prompt, honest and accurate
- To pay taxes in time
- To quote PAN/GIR in returns and correspondence

A quick reference guide for investors

(Issued in the public interest by the Securities and Exchange Board of India (SEBI), Mumbai.)

Such guide booklets are useful to an investor and he should study before investing in stocks and shares.

RBI devises rating model for customer services in banks

The RBI has asked Indian Bank Association (IBA) to customize and adopt a model developed by it to rate for rating customer service in banks.

How to cope with a stock market that behaves like a roller skater? [by Prem Khatri, Vice-President (marketing) of Kothari Pioneer Mutual Fund]

- Don't react emotionally to market movements.
- Take the long-term view.
- Hold a mix of investments (invest in different instruments such as shares, debentures, mutual funds, and bank deposits as also postal-savings schemes). A diversified portfolio of investment can help you to offset the losses of one-category against the gains of another as very often, the same events affect two categories very differently.
- Invest regularly
- Set realistic goals
- Seek help

[**Note:** Invest wisely and cautiously. It is important to note that while there are very few who hit the jackpot, there are plenty who lose their shirt while playing on the stock market by sheer instinct].

How to preserve your bank pass book?

- Utilize nomination facility.
- Get pass book updated regularly, preferably every month.
- Do not put your signature anywhere in pass book.

- Do not fold the pass book.
- If a pass book is lost or damaged, a duplicate pass book will be issued on payment.
- Suggestions/complaints can be written in the book maintained by the branch.
- See the bank manager in case of difficulties or even higher up, if need be.
- Do check the entries in the pass book whether these are correct and bring any discrepancy immediately to the attention of the bank staff for clarification/correction.
- Keep the pass book safely at home

[**Note:** A few banks have dispensed with pass books. The accounts are accessible by Internet. Monthly-computerized statements are sent to the customer. Pass books are now-a-days printed from a printer in the bank unlike handwritten in the past].

E-commerce

You will hear more and more about E-commerce in future. E (Electronic) Commerce is not just a bunch of websites. It is a new world economic order. In the modern world, E-commerce has already reached the critical mass with never before cost saving and efficiency levels. E-commerce is sweeping across India too. 'Paperless' transactions, like Electronic Clearing Scheme (ECS) will become commonplace as part of E-commerce revolution. A few training institutes offer training facilities in India for E-commerce. There is no doubt E-commerce will become a multi-crore business soon. Customers should keep themselves informed about the developments in this vital sector, which will affect them in one way or the other. E-commerce is irreversible and we can see a rapid spread of this modern way of doing business across the country within the near future.

On-line shopping

This is catching up in a big way, part of the E-commerce, which is getting more widespread in India. Major on-line shopping sites such as Fabmall, Rediff, Indiatimes and Siffy have reported a business of Rs. 1180 crores, during 2005-2006 on their sites. This will increase much more in the years to come given the sheer convenience of such on-line shopping. Retail business is poised for a phenomenal growth, with shops of international repute entering the Indian market in the near future.

Here are some tips for safe on-line shopping:

- Don't pay cash. Your credit/debit card is in a 'secure' mode.

- Check whether the seller is reliable and reputed.
- Don't fall a prey to low prices. There is a catch somewhere or the product/service is really not worth even its low price.
- Do not disclose your credit/debit card information or any other information about your finance, investment, insurance, stocks shares and the like. Do not respond to queries on the Internet or through telephone.
- Check that the product/service you intend to buy on-line is what you want. Sometimes, it's better to check such items by physical means by visiting shops and malls where such products/services are on display.
- Take a print out of the order when finalized for your record and future reference.
- Protect your computer with updated virus protection.
- Do not open e-mail attachments from unknown companies or agencies.

Insurance

Compared to earlier where the behemoth Life Insurance Corporation of India and other nationalized insurance companies like The New India Assurance Company Ltd., Oriental Insurance Company Ltd., and United India Insurance Company Ltd., operated, we have a number of new players, some with foreign collaboration in the field dealing with general insurance matters. Some of these are: Aviva, Bajaj-Allianz, ICICI-Prudential, Ing-Vysa and Tata-Metlife. These deal with a host of insurance matters such as: motor insurance, health insurance, house-holder insurance, shop keeper's insurance, burglary insurance, fire insurance, hospital cash, critical illness cover, overseas travel insurance, electrical equipment insurance and so on.

Banks are always coming out with innovative schemes some of which you could utilize for your benefit. For instance, "Good news for UCO current and savings account holders. Just Rs. 6.99 per year and you are insured for Rs. 1,00,000. You can expect more from UCO Bank. Honours your trust."

OTHERS

1. *"Divine healing from Zen for physical, mental and emotional ailments." Contact healer ——, Tel. No.......*

You will see more and more of such advertisements when the modern lifestyle becomes hectic and brings with it all sorts of problems like anxiety, nervousness, depression, health-related issues. It all depends upon how much faith you have in alternate means of curing and stress relief. Some people take to Yoga and others to meditation under learned masters. Some seek solace in prayer, *bhajans* and religious discourses. No doubt some of the ancient techniques bring relief in case of chronic problems like asthma, high blood pressure, nervousness, and diabetes.

2. *"The school of yoga will be conducting a two-day workshop on hypnosis and Tai-Chi from—— to——." Those interested may contact Tel. No....*

Yoga practised under a trained teacher is certainly beneficial in many ways. But it's no panacea to all health and other problems. Some claims that yoga can cure diseases will have to be taken with a pinch of salt. Surely, yoga is beneficial in its own positive way.

3. *"The Kaginele Kanaka Gurupeeta will be conducting yoga and pranayama classes." Those interested may contact Tel. No.....*

Same comments as above.

4. *'Vaastu Shastra'*

The latest fad is to quote *Vaastu Shastra*, which is claimed to bring good luck, mental peace and happiness. The idea is that the human being be constantly connected to his environment in a beneficial manner in the way of the ancients. *"Vaastu is the outer expression of a deeply meditative mind."*

A few votaries of *Vaastu* are spending thousands to lakhs of rupees to alter their existing homes/buildings to fall in line with the Vaastu Shastra's directive on the way a home/building has to be built. A few homebuyers insist on the correct Vaastu Shastra built home/buildings before they invest.

How much science and how much 'hocus pocus' is involved in Vaastu Shastra, at least as practised by some persons, is difficult to state. It's all in one's mind and no logic can work for such persons. Any misfortune will be directly put on the home/building they are residing. At least, you should guard yourself against self-styled Vaastu 'experts' who suggest demolition of the house or at least a portion to avoid the 'ill-effects' due to the wrong Vaastu. However, there are other Vaastu experts will tell you, for a fee of course, "You don't have to demolish your existing structure but make a minor modification."

Chinese Vaastu: A corollary of India's Vaastu Shastra is Chinese Feng Shui, which is claimed to be a science, which is part art and part skill. It locates the imbalances in the way we live. In simple words, Feng Shui is a method of arranging our environment in such a way that it is as beneficial to us as possible. Same comments as in the above paragraph.

5. *"Teak, mango, fruit trees plantation scheme, free supply of rice and vegetables for ever."*

Such schemes were being floated sometime back and a few gullible investors put their money into these schemes. They were rewarded with interest and a place where they could see their plantation was coming up. Others got free rice and vegetables for a few months. Then one by one these schemes just folded up without a trace. Most people who invested lost their capital. A few got a pittance of compensation.

Caution: Do not be swayed by such too-good-to-believe schemes, which promise a lot but fail miserably on delivery.

6. *"Promises by agents who promise a job in the Gulf or elsewhere and they fleece you demanding Rs. 1 lakh."*

The lure of going to the West is so strong, for enjoying a good life, that people are desperate and willing to do anything including aiding illegal shipment of human beings under horrible conditions for hefty sum. Do not fall into such a trap whose consequences could be very serious — death or imprisonment. If you are keen to migrate, follow the right royal route and try your luck.

7. *"Unbelievable rate of interest 23 per cent with gifts, lottery, prizes and early bird incentives."*

Simple rule: Do not believe such shady deals and lose your money.

8. *"An Australian MBA at less than one-fourth the Australian cost," claims an institution in Bangalore.*

Check out hidden costs. See if this institute is recognized. Check out whether anyone has got the degree and his/her experience of dealing with this agency that promises a foreign degree at one-fourth cost. A case of too-good-to-believe?

9. *"The mega-mileage holiday from Club Mahindra: A free 3 day/2 night holiday (if you sign up for Club Mahindra's 33-year holiday plan)".*

Do you want to join a Vacation Club? Is the incentive so attractive that you have to decide on this vacation club immediately? Think before you take out your cheque book. Check out competitive offers. Decide whether you want to invest a big lump sum to be vacationing for 33-years with the same company. There are always conditions printed in small letters, "Offer includes accommodation only. Holiday can be availed only between July 1 and September 30."

10. *'Pure Water Maker', Rs. 2290 only. Clear Water Maker, Rs. 590 only. Requires neither electricity nor plumbing. Claims: completely eliminates bad odour, bad taste and any bacterial content in water. Absorbs Chlorine and other solvents. ATLAS FILTRI SANPAR Pvt. Ltd.*

Beware of such advertisements, which promise many things so cheaply!

11. *"Home self-testing. Home pregnancy test-kit. Home diabetes testing kit, BP monitoring test-kit, Urinary track infection test-kit, Tele-ECG test via telephone (Tele-cardiology)."*

Warning: Consult your doctor before you buy the self-test kits. In case of problems with the test results, consult the doctor immediately. Do not start home treatment on your own without checking out with a doctor. That could be dangerous. Always establish a correlation between the home test-kit and a recognized laboratory. Check this regularly so that you are assured you are on the right track.

12. *"Astrology: Ace astrologer from India........is in Bangalore again at hotel......for 4 days. To know about your future, promotion, business, foreign trips, education, health, love, marriage and children according to the systems of astrology, numerology and palmistry."*

The claim, "Accurate prediction with astonishing intuition and flawless scientific analysis," has to be taken with a pinch of salt. It all depends upon you whether you want to know what is going to happen in future through astrology or you want to adopt a philosophical view of life such as *'que sera sera'* 'whatever will happen will happen'.

13. *"Golden chance, second time in your city famous astrologer and palmist — (Tantrik) for your profit/loss in business, marriage, service, achievement in politics, family troubles—contact Tel. No..... for appointment."*

That great desire to know one's future is irresistible, defying all logic and scientific evidence. In ancient times, the Greeks consulted the famous oracle at Delphi. Whether it's a politician, doctor, engineer, students, businessman belief in astrology is strong. In fact, even in the advanced countries there are people who believe in astrology and the predictions. It all depends upon one's mental make up. Some refuse to go to an astrologer whatever might be the difficulties, hardships and calamities they might be enduring. They do not believe that it's possible to avert one's destiny by any means — prayer, *homas, yagnas,* visit to pilgrim centres and the like. All these are undertaken for one's mental peace that's all.

Ultimately, it's the customer who makes his choice, product or service:

Consumer exercises his option→Decision→Buy/Do not buy

The suggestions made in this chapter, hopefully, could improve the decision-making of customers confronted with multi-choice market environment. He/she has a tough choice given the sophistication of the goods and services as well as confusing/conflicting claims by producers and service providers. Technology is more and more complicated and it's no longer possible to make an off-the-cuff simple decision about a product/ service. One should be informed in advance to improve one's decision.

Customers should be alert and not get carried away by tall claims/ talks, freebies, inducements, on-the-spot finance and the like. We should understand that there is a conflict between what a customer wants and what a seller wants. For example, a customer would like to have the best value for his investment. On the other hand, the seller wants to maximize his profits by all means possible — sometimes fair and sometimes not so fair. A customer has to guard himself against being carried by claims such as 'ancient' herbs, ayurveda, yoga, tantrik, natural, and herbal to mention a few. One has to be extra careful while accepting any medicine/ treatment that's not in the mainstream. An investment has risks, the more you know about such risks the better so that you can manage your finances better. Education is another field where students and others could be led up the garden path, if they are not careful and check the credentials of those who make tall claims.

Consumer is the King, only if he/she acts wisely and knowledgeably

General

- Read available literature on the subject in which you are interested. Internet, with various websites could give you the latest information free of cost.
- Buy reputed brands, preferably with quality certification/BIS or any international.
- Do not compromise on quality and safety because of low prices.
- Life-cycle cost is important while buying a consumer durable or even a car.
- Look carefully at warranty/guarantee/return goods policy, in fine print. Ask questions if you have any clarification required *before* you decide to buy.
- Check adequacy of service outlets near your place of residence. Do not sign any annual maintenance contract, without checking the reliability of the service personnel and their competence. Otherwise this would be just a waste of time and money without getting anything worthwhile in return.
- Always see the 'conditions apply' terms carefully to avoid surprises later on.

- Study features/price of competitive products/services. See if an independent report on rating of the product/service under your scanner is available which would make your buying decision easier. That's the best bet to get an unbiased opinion about the goods/services.
- Consult your relatives and friends who might have same or similar products/services in use.
- Do not rush to buy something you are not aware of it. Make a calculated decision.
- Do not take 'no' for an answer from a dealer/service person, in case you have a problem with the product/service you have bought and that too in the guarantee/warranty period.
- Do not allow unauthorized person to handle repairs. It could prove 'pennywise and pound foolish'.
- If you want to try a new medicine/treatment be cautious and better to consult your doctor. Sometimes, the cure could be worse than the disease.
- Be wary of offers, which appear too-good-to-be-true. There will normally a catch somewhere or the company could be just a blade company to catch the unwary and disappear after taking money/deposit from people.
- If any advertisement in the print/electronic media offends you, you have a channel to bring it to the notice of the authority which is supposed to take note and initiate action. You might inform, with all the details when the ad appeared, the channel and the timing and so on to "The Advertising Standards Council of India", Mumbai (Regd. Office and Secretariat: 205, Bombay Market, Tardeo Road, Mumbai 400 034. Tel. No 4936863/4937066) they have published a booklet "The code for self-regulation in advertising," for the information of the industry and the public. Read it for more details.
- If you buy seconds/export surplus/export rejects/items at 'throw-away-prices', you don't expect quality or exchange or refund on such a sale. The risk is entirely yours.
- Encourage eco-friendly 'Green' products/packages.
- Patronize those who care for the environment and the community, with their social commitment, and who render community service and bring out only ethical eco-friendly products and services.

In summary

Consumer→New/Tall claims→Caution→Consult→Decide
Good business→Ethical products/services→Friendly dealings/services→Consumer-friendly→Patronize
Fly-by-night operators→Hoodwink the gullible consumers→Short-term profit→Avoid such business

In a multi-choice market environment, with more to come because of globalization, the consumers of today and tomorrow would be in a difficult spot to make a meaningful choice that suits them. That's why the more knowledgeable a consumer is the better for good decisions that are better value for money. Internet, as a source of free and credible information, should be utilized to the maximum. Latest trends in products/services would be available by surfing the Internet. Then there are consumer magazines that give out ratings and expose frauds. Newspapers and magazines are other sources of information that should be consulted regularly. Technical publications like 'Understanding My Computer', written in layman's language, should be read to update one's knowledge. It's better to consult experts in the field, be it lawyer, doctor, education expert, and financial consultant, to get the maximum advantage *before* one wants to invest one's hard earned money. It's better to avoid impulsive buying when dealing with huge investments. A careful look into all the aspects of the product/service could prove useful in avoiding surprises later on. Those who have already used a product/service are the best judges about such a product though a degree of personal bias cannot be avoided in such information.

The book especially this chapter is, hopefully, a step towards empowering consumers in exercising their choices wisely while helping them to maximum return on their investments.

CHAPTER 4

RETURNS, WARRANTY AND PRODUCT LIABILITY

Anything bad that can happen will happen
—Murphy's Law

A consumer (customer) is defined as one who has bought a product/service by paying money. Unless there is an exchange of goods/services for money, it doesn't become a sale. A patient who gets a free treatment in a government hospital or facility cannot consider himself/herself as a consumer. Suppose there is a mass medical camp where volunteer doctors treat patients free of charge, then the people involved cannot be considered as consumers. That applies to a client who gets free legal advice from a lawyer or a person who has a free consultation with a financial expert. The risks in such cases are entirely that person's and no one else can be held responsible for any problem arising out of such advice.

We have a strange dichotomy in our social milieu. We act differently when we are consumers and when we are sellers. The fact is sometimes a consumer becomes a seller such is the inter-dependability. No one can hope to be totally independent of another person(s). The approach of a seller is to sell and maximize his/her profits. Whether such profits are made ethically or otherwise doesn't worry someone eager to capitalize on the sales. On the other hand, as (a person) a consumer he/she has high expectations. A prospective consumer wants to maximize the value of a product/service the sale of which is about to take place. He is disappointed when the sale doesn't benefit him much in his favour but is loaded in favour of the sales-person.

The moment a sale is concluded, the product/service becomes the property of the consumer, unless there are hidden clauses but the ownership does not fully go to the consumer but that person is just enjoying the same for a period of time. For example, anyone who goes into a home, after taking a mortgage, the true owner will be someone else but the householder can stay and enjoy the benefits of that home, within certain terms and conditions as laid down at the time of the mortgage agreement. That's equally true of a hire-purchase agreement where certain services/goods are used by a consumer after paying the required money. In that case too the consumer cannot be considered as a true owner of that product/service.

However, if the terms and conditions of mortgage/lease agreement are in order, that person who has bought the product/service is the true consumer albeit during the time period mentioned in the agreement. Of course, such a consumer has to enjoy his product/service within limits/restrictions as stipulated. On the contrary a person who has paid for the product/service in total becomes the 'absolute' owner. For instance, certain lands/flats are bought as on 'lease' for, say, 99 years. On the other hand, there are properties which are 'freehold' which means the owner enjoys the property/ownership in perpetuity. But as per the definition, both the persons are consumers.

Let us take an example of a car, which a consumer has bought it for, say, Rs. 5 lakhs. The moment the car leaves the garage of the sales-outlet, the depreciation of the car begins which could be easily up to 25 %. If everything is fine with the car, the owner is happy to drive around for the benefit of his family and friends. However, if he notices that the brake is not smooth but works with jerks or comes to a stop screeching, the first reaction is of disappointment and secondly of anger. "How can the dealer palm off a sub-standard car as new after paying such a big amount?" would be his immediate reaction. He would take back the car to the sales-outlet and confront the dealer soon afterwards. The dealer could be polite and see that the car is repaired immediately with an apology. Or the dealer could be gruff and tell the owner, "Sir, we have many cars to be repaired. What can I do if the car manufacturer has made a mistake? I shall certainly take it up with the manufacturer. Have patience," he would advise the customer. The customer has no option but to wait patiently and waste a few hours till the car is repaired. It's rare to see a dealer/service person/retailer accept any problem as genuine and try to redress the grievance of the customer quickly.

OVERSEAS MARKETS

There is a sea change in the attitude of the customer service in the advanced countries where customer is treated as a king. No question is asked why a customer is returning an item for exchange/refund/replacement.

A customer service section deals with such complaints routinely. Generally, a receipt is needed to prove proof of purchase but is waived in exceptional cases. Moreover, items from one shop could be exchanged in another outlet, in the same town, or even another one, in exceptional cases. A computer-based data is created which keeps a tab on those who return goods frequently. However, shop assistants trust customers and do not ask questions. Even when there is a matter of choice, a customer prefers to shop at a particular outlet since he/she gets a personalized service with a smile. Some of them are on first name acquaintance, especially in small towns. Sales girls who are pleasant and prompt have already won half the battle for that stores as the customers' loyalty is built upon such a personal relationship. Every sales outlet, worth its name, has to be customer-friendly if it has to retain loyalty of customers and bring in newer customers. Shopping should be a pleasant experience and not a burdensome chore with unfriendly sales-persons.

Here are some tips a consumer should keep in mind while purchasing a product/service. When a purchase is about to be made, the customer has the responsibility of checking whether the product/service is free from defects he/she could easily see. It would be much easier to look for another item rather than go home, get disappointed and waste time and energy in returning it. No doubt a customer expects items in the shop for sale are free from defects. But in the Indian context, we still have to make checks, within our capability to make sure that the item is good at least to look at. For instance, a saree about to be purchased should be examined in all its full length at least cursorily to make sure there are no weaving faults, holes or damages.

Here are some more tips that could save time for the customer if he/she is a little more careful in the first instance at a shopping outlet:

- If you buy a piece of cloth and find it is damaged when you take it home and check it, it is likely that you'll have a problem getting a replacement or refund, if that is possible at all. The shopkeeper might say, "Sir/madam, why didn't you check such an obvious damage when you bought the material? Sorry, no replacement or refund." That's why you should examine whatever you could when you buy something; that's your safety.
- On the other hand, if you wash the piece of cloth you bought it with a normal detergent and the colour 'runs' then you have a problem on your hands, at least in our context. You think you have a genuine complaint that should be redressed by the shopkeeper. It's logical that the customer at the shop outlet couldn't

have checked this property of colourfastness by looking or by feeling. It's possible the shopkeeper might state, "Madam, I didn't tell you the material is 'colour fast' after washing. Sorry, no refunds or exchange. May be you have used a bad detergent and that's why the colour has 'run'." This is like adding insult to injury but we have to accept the worst in our business environment. It is always better to shop at a reputed shop where you buy only reputed brand material. You should ask the shopkeeper whether the colour is guaranteed and if so can the customer get a refund/exchange if the colour 'runs' after washing.

- A few film-developing centres print a specific warning. "Colour matching: Colour or density matching cannot be guaranteed in reprints and enlargements due to unavoidable fluctuations in daily conditions and in the sensitivity of individual colour emulsions used in the laboratory." Such limitations should be understood by consumers so that they are not disappointed after seeing the final quality of reprint/enlargement.
- In a restaurant you order your favourite wine and the waiter shows you the bottle with the label clearly visible to you. You can see the label and then decide. He opens the bottle and gives you a sample in a glass. You sniff the contents like a connoisseur and like the feeling on your tongue. You can refuse the bottle at this point of time because it's not the wine you wanted. But if you tell the waiter it's OK and then he pours the wine in the glass the deal is as good as done. You cannot now drink a portion of the wine and call the waiter and tell him you didn't like the wine. So, now you expect a wine of another make to be brought to you. However, the waiter is within his rights to refuse to replace the bottle as you could have done it earlier and not after sipping the wine. You cannot change your mind or complain about the quality of wine after drinking a couple of glasses.

The above examples illustrate how a consumer can make an informed choice after checking out the product/service and *before* paying for it. The consumer should observe certain basic rules so that he/she can make the right choice. It's useful to note that a consumer cannot merely complain without solid facts to back him up. In fact, a consumer court is sure to ask various questions, which a consumer should be able to answer. It would be better if the prospective consumer has facts that would enable him to make meaningful choice. The more homework he does about the product/service he wants to buy the better to avoid surprises. Moreover, he should know what questions/clarifications he should ask the dealer/shopkeeper/ sales person and what to check before buying a product/service. An informed and knowledgeable consumer has already won half the battle of wits with the sales outlet personnel.

Consumer's choice→Make sure your choice is right→Check out whether you got what you wanted→You have time to decide before paying the money

RETURNS

Every consumer wants to enjoy the product/service that he/she has invested, the sooner the better. No responsible consumer will ever think of returning it when it is working satisfactorily. Imagine that person's feelings when he finds the product/service failing after a few hours. He would curse the dealer and the manufacturer for such shoddy work. But a dealer/retailer has a different perspective. He only feels that the consumer is making a fuss about nothing. The first thought he has is, "God, here comes another ignorant consumer. I am sure, he has spoiled the product/service. Now I have to waste my time and get it repaired." This is a typical attitude of all dealers/retailer whenever a consumer comes back to his shop stating the product/service has failed. Strangely, when the very same dealer/retailer becomes a 'consumer' he expects something different. He would then grumble if the dealer/retailer from whom he had bought the product/service is not responsive to his complaints. That's why a dealer/retailer has to keep in mind that sometime or the other he would be in the same position as that of a consumer and he has to have a sympathetic attitude to any consumer who comes to him with a complaint.

We have been brainwashed that the dealer/retailer/shopkeeper is supreme and a consumer has little or no rights. Otherwise how could we have tolerated prominent notices in shops and on printed receipts, 'Goods once sold cannot be exchanged or refunded, or replaced,' 'Fancy items, no guarantee,' 'Errors & Omissions Excepted (E & OE)' 'Cash only, No credit' and so on? This is sort of warning to the consumer, "beware, or else!" he cannot expect much when the product/service goes bad. We have been told that the onus is on the consumer to see that everything is fine when a product/service leaves the shop. He is also expected to look after the product/service with due care.

One can understand if an item is bought in a discount 'sale' which may not be exchanged or replaced. But it's strange that even in reputed shops, there is little enthusiasm to redress consumer's genuine complaints even within the guarantee/warranty period. It's an interesting, but a painful experience, for any consumer to be confronted by a wall where the dealer/retailer/sales-persons all conspire to see that the consumer gets the least welcome. Often a consumer feels embarrassed when he goes to a shop complaining about a defective product because he has to undergo an inquisition by the shop personnel. It's like adding insult to injury. They go into a huddle to decide how to deal with such consumers who dare to complain. There is a high level discussion how best to get rid of the consumer as fast as possible so that they could resume their normal business. In fact, they are aware that as long as a complaining consumer is present in their premises it's a bad and adverse publicity that could affect their business.

"Sorry, Sir, we cannot do anything. The product was perfectly OK when it left our shop and you too were aware of it," would be the first blow from the shopkeeper and others. "But, what can I do, if your product goes bad?" would be the pleading of an aggrieved consumer. "Then you must have done something wrong or followed a wrong procedure," would be the second line of defense by the shopkeeper. "What do you mean by that insinuation? Can you please explain how I could make the product bad? You can see the seal is intact and obviously I have done nothing that could make the product bad," would be the strong defense of the consumer who gets more and more annoyed and frustrated by the totally negative attitude of the shopkeeper and others.

There could be happy ending to the above story if the shopkeeper gets a feeling the consumer is tough and might, after all, be right. He would then call his assistant to check out the product and see if anything could be done. The assistant would make a show of checking and come back to his boss to whisper to him that he couldn't do much and it has to be sent to a service centre. The consumer can do nothing but grumble and go home unhappy. He is sorry to have bought a product, from that shop and of that particular brand to have such a poor quality service in such a short time. A tough consumer might get angry and ask the shopkeeper to replace the unit immediately or give refund on the spot. That's asking for too much under our conditions of business ethics. Getting a refund is next to impossible. At the most one can expect a replacement or exchange for something else of almost equal value. If the replacement price is higher, then the consumer has no choice but to pay the difference in price to acquire the replaced unit.

The post era of liberalization and globalization is hailed as the golden age for consumerism. That would mean the customer has a wide choice at competitive price. All that's fine. Has anyone really studied the impact on the culture of service after a sale? Unfortunately, it's business as usual for most sales outlets, big or small. They are keen to sell but reluctant to redress consumer complaints which they feel is a nuisance and hinder their sale. That's why some of the big shops conveniently divert the customer with a service complaint to their service centres to get the unit repaired. The question of replacement/refund is the least priority in any sales programme. First of all you have to talk it over with the shop assistant. Then he will direct you to his boss and may be even the manager. Everyone behaves as if you have done something wrong and so you have to run from pillar to post to get your complaint redressed. If some customer gets fed up with such a bureaucratic set up, that should be no surprise to anyone. There is no visible change in the attitude of those who service customer complaints. It's business as usual — keen to sell but not at all interested in attending to customers' grievances.

The culture of service and promptness in attending to a customer's complaint should start by reposing trust and confidence in the customer. When he says a product/service doesn't work, the sales outlet should believe it, not with ifs and buts. Liberalization and globalization can only have a real meaning to Indian consumers only when the service element in the chain of product selling is strengthened and becomes at par with those advanced countries where customer is treated as king.

Right now Indians can only dream of the lucky consumers of the advanced countries where they could just visit the shop from where they have brought the item and get it exchanged/replaced/refunded as a matter of routine in a matter of minutes at the separate customer service centre within the departmental store or any store. There are no questions asked and the sales-person smiles as the exchange or refund is done quickly. He/she feels that it's part of a sales job and there is nothing wrong if some unhappy customer wants to get something exchanged which he/she doesn't like. In fact, the sales-person by his/her prompt service is requesting the customer 'please do come again.' Contrast such an approach with that of our Indian service personnel who think it's a burden to redress customer complaints promptly. The more the delay the better they think, just to show how important they are and what a wonderful service they are rendering to an unhappy customer. Such personnel fail to appreciate that a prompt and personalized service could be a plus point in promoting that store or brand. It's hoped that at least good businesses would realize that servicing of customer complaints should be given priority in these days of stiff competition.

The service factor could make or mar the image of a company or a brand.

We expect private sector to be more responsive to customer's needs because a business is based on customers' goodwill. That's not generally the case when it comes to redress of complaints. Delays and conditions are galore when it comes to attending to complaints. Some of them charge for parts, some for labour and a few for both. Nothing is free when it comes to settling complaints. No sales-person accepts the genuineness of a consumer complaint on its face value the first time. He/she always thinks the customer is at fault and that's why the product/service has gone out of order. Such is the apathy towards customer's problems. The public sector undertakings have been apathetic to redress of complaints. Since there was no competition, there was no incentive for them to improve their complaint redress mechanism.

Here is an example how as public sector bank used to warn its customers 'customers beware' when it came to handling cash: "Issuable notes: The slip on the bundle of notes states, "Denomination of notes 10, containing 100 pieces, signed/examiner, date."

[**Note:** "Please satisfy yourself before leaving the counter that the cash received by you, is in order in every respect. No claim will be considered under any circumstance thereafter." Such a statement of no liability by a reputed nationalized bank notwithstanding the fact the bundle of notes has been counted at least once and rechecked once again and the notes have been stapled together with a printed slip is amazing. Does it mean we cannot trust anyone and also the bank won't trust a customer when he/she comes back and complains there is excess or shortage in the bundle just then taken? However, the RBI has banned stapling of notes of late as it affects the life of a note. This is one more reason why the bank won't accept a customer's complaint regarding short or excess notes in a bundle issued at the counter.]

One must say there are some banks where they believe a customer's complaint regarding any shortage or excess notes and they have addressed it satisfactorily, though it's the exception rather than rule. Let us also accept the fact that a few customers, may their tribe increase! report excess notes issued to them and return the same to the bank without any hesitation or in expectation of any reward or appreciation. Their conscience doesn't permit them to keep with them anything that is not theirs legitimately.

This is not a general indictment of poor customer service by government and semi-government departments and agencies. Most of them acknowledge a letter or a complaint promptly. However, it would take time to get a final reply on any complaint due to bureaucratic delays that are inevitable in any big department or organization. Rarely, they acknowledge they made a mistake and regret it. This is in sharp contrast with the manner which organizations/stores/agencies respond to customers' complaints in the advanced countries, as can be seen from the following:

A big departmental store chain 'Target' has the following goods return policy:

"If you are not fully satisfied with your Target purchase, please return it with the original sales receipt within 90 days. If you have a receipt, we will exchange it for a similar item, return your cash, remove your credit charge or mail your cheque refund in 10 days. If you don't have a receipt, and we still carry the item, we will mail you a refund within 10 days. For all returns, with or without receipt, you may be asked to provide acceptable identification."

Here is an Indian example, which is the exception than rule:

"No questions asked return policy. At Foodworld, Chennai-based departmental stores, the unwritten law is to provide customers products of the highest quality at prices that are the most competitive in the market. But in the unlikely event of you being not satisfied with any product for whatever reason, you can exchange the same for another or get something else for the same price. Absolutely, no questions asked. We don't just simply claim but definitely offer you more value for your money."

Note the above and compare the return goods policy. Foodworld is silent on refund, it only offers replacement and or exchange unlike the Target policy of refund, which is an option. Moreover, it is still possible that an assistant at Foodworld could act high and mighty and deny an aggrieved customer the exchange promised, citing some flimsy pretext. Unfortunately, basic trust in each other—that's customer-trader is missing in our business environment barring exceptions.

Amazing refund

It's hard to believe some features of the refund order prevailing in advanced countries. Here is a true story:

Rohan, a student studying in the USA bought a dress shirt in a well-known departmental chain store in a city where he was studying for $8.50, the sale price after discounted sale that gave 50% of the marked price. He was naturally happy to have stuck a bargain at such a price. However, when he went home his happiness turned to utter disappointment as he noticed the shirt was one size too small! That meant he couldn't possibly wear it. That whole week he was busy and exchanging the shirt was his last priority. After ten days he went to the store with the shirt. To his utter disappointment he found that particular dress shirt design was not on the shelf. So his idea of getting the shirt exchanged to the next higher size couldn't be done.

He wondered whether he should make enquiries at the customer service center. Summing up courage, he approached the customer service center hesitantly. He wasn't sure whether they would consider refund since he couldn't get a shirt of his choice as replacement. He showed the assistant the shirt and the receipt, which he had preserved carefully. "Oh, no problem, Sir, we shall give you the refund," She replied. In a matter of minutes she busied herself on the computer. "Here is your money. Have a good-day," she smiled pleasantly as she handed over the cash to Rohan much to his relief and delight. As he went out of the store, he casually checked the amount given to him. To his utter amazement he had received $ 17.00, double the amount he had paid at the time of purchase. He returned immediately to the person who had given him cash. "Excuse me madam, you have given me $17.00 whereas I had paid only $8.50. So please take back the difference," he said as he handed over the extra cash. "That's fine, Sir. You see, we had a sale when you bought the shirt and so we collected $8.50. Now the sale is over and so I have to give you the full value of the shirt, which is $17.00. Have a good-day," she smiled as she went back to her work. That was amazing but true!

It is always useful to preserve the cash memo/receipt/warranty/ guarantee card while buying anything however small or big. Because this is the only proof that's acceptable in a court of law to prove that you are a customer who had paid the money to buy the stated product/service. The tendency to avoid a receipt encouraged by the shopkeeper should be desisted in the interests of good ethical business. The shopkeeper has his own vested interest in avoiding tax to be paid to the government, like local taxes. That's why he prefers a cash memo-less transaction. However, that's not in the interest of the customer as well as the government. That's why all responsible customers should insist on cash memo or receipt. Higher amounts should be paid by cheque/draft/credit/debit card, where they are accepted. While some shops exchange/refund when a product/ service is proved faulty, they insist upon proof of purchase. Rarely, they give the refund when there is no proof of purchase. In advanced countries, such a condition exists but sometimes it's waived in favour of the customer if the packing/label on the item is still there that could prove it's a product of their sale. Sometimes, it's possible to exchange/get a refund of a product/service in any store of their chain in the same city or even another city provided the receipt for purchase is there. That's one more plus point of sales in the advanced countries where customers are treated with respect and consideration. No one thinks of evading tax; that's ethics in business for you!

Rain check

Rain check is not supposed to be one of checking rain! It's a novel facility in the advanced countries where a consumer gets whatever he/she wants even though that item is out of stock when the consumer shops. What do you do when you shop and find that an item with a reduced price tag interests you but is out of stock? Simple! You just place your order for that item, at the reduced price, and the stores will call you or send a card by post informing you that your item has arrived and you could collect it anytime. Such is the concern and care for the consumer that the shop doesn't want to disappoint even a single customer but would go out of its way to please a customer.

Here is another store's commitment to the keep customers happy:

Sears, a chain stores in the USA has the following price guarantee:

"We'll meet or beat the competition's current advertised price on the identical item. Just bring their current advertisement to any of our stores. Excludes clearance, factory closeout and catalogue items."

The sellers are always looking for ways and means to improve their services to retain and woo consumers who have a genuine choice of goods/services in an advanced country like the USA. This is one way of cementing the loyalty between the particular brand sales outlets and consumers. Some of them have their own credit/debit cards which allow for shopping at their outlets and get something extra too, like bonus points earned on what customers spend. In this context, customer support services, like exchange/replacement/refund/service play a vital part in retaining customers. In our market environment, the aspect of customer support has to receive attention to render better service to customers. Right now they do not see much of a change in the attitude of the sellers, big or small. The culture of service has yet to seep into our business milieu. No dramatic change is expected soon, but who knows with stores of international re[illegible] which could have their outlets in India, spur the much-need[illegible] the attitude of dealers/sellers to become more consu[illegible] to imbibe the spirit of service by all those w[illegible] In fact this could be a strong plus po[illegible] it an important part of their [illegible]

To sum up the differences between our country and overseas as far as customer support is concerned:

	Repair	*Refund*	*Exchange*
India	Sometimes	Rare	Often
Oveseas	Mostly	Always	Always

WARRANTY/GUARANTEE

Warranty and Guarantee are used interchangeably throughout the discussion which means the manufacturer/producer/seller gives assurance to the buyer that the product/service sold will be attended to, if need be, free of charge for a specified period/number of kms run/hours used and so on. Without such a guarantee a buyer would hesitate to buy any product/service as the consumer doesn't know what to do if the same doesn't work as required. "What if something happens to the product/service I am using?" is always a worry with a consumer unless backed by a guarantee assurance that he need not have that worry or fear during the guarantee period at least. A warranty is meant to cover the risks at the consumer's end if a product/service fails to work as desired. Most consumer durables, air-conditioner, car, electric-iron, food-processor, mixer-grinder, refrigerator, TV, two-wheeler, washing machine, and so on are covered under the guarantee period of a specified number of years or miles in case of vehicles. But some times a warranty is no guarantee as we shall discuss some of the problems consumer face while getting free repair done to their product/service though within the guarantee period.

A warranty card, with the serial number of the product/service, address of consumer, address of the dealer, authorized signature of the dealer with the office stamp comes along with the instruction booklet. Often, it's necessary to send details of the product/service to the main dealer/producer for their record. A retailer might not have the service facility and so he will ask the consumer to contact a service centre in the town/area, with the address and telephone number provided for such access. Without such a warranty card, the consumer might not get any free service by a service centre. If a cash purchase is done, it is likely that ... dealer might not issue the warranty card unless agreed upon earlier. ... of of purchase and warranty card a consumer's complaint for ... be admitted in a consumer court.

... booklet along with a consumable durable is ... mer starts operating the equipment/ ... so confident that they bring the product and start connecting it to the mains without any further thinking. There could be instructions for use that says: "Connect the equipment to a three-point socket only. Use 'earthing' to prevent any electrical shocks when touched." Those who neglect to read the instruction booklet are in danger of hurting themselves or damaging the product at the time of connecting to the mains supply. Instructions for use of a computer, refrigerator, and TV might say, "Use a voltage stabilizer before connecting to mains to prevent damage to your product."

By not reading the 'Instructions for use' manual the customer might damage the product/service which is good enough reason for a dealer/ service centre to refuse free service/replacement. In fact some warranty terms and conditions clearly state: "The warranty is not valid in case the product is not used according to the manual, defects are caused by improper use, or neglect, or mishandling, or accident, or not handled by qualified service technicians." We should keep in mind that a dealer/ service centre is keen to point out the mistake of a customer that gives them a valid reason for not providing free service. So it's in the interest of every customer that he/she must read the 'Instructions for use', *before* he/she begins to operate any equipment/service.

In ancient times craftsmen took pride in what they did. They aimed at 'perfection' and often achieved it. They would be unhappy if a customer would come back to them and told them, "Sorry, I don't like your product." The craftsman would be unhappy and feel guilty that his/her customer was not satisfied. He would offer to exchange it for another one without any further discussion. Surely, that craftsman would ponder what went wrong and how he could improve so that no customer needs to complain again. It was their pride at stake and they would do anything to keep their reputation in tact. They also knew that a customer's confidence was easily shaken but difficult to regain it soon. In fact, in ancient times, long-term satisfaction was assumed without any conditions.

Here are two warranty terms:*

Warranty A: "This warranty is not valid in case the product is not used according to the manual, defects are caused by improper or careless use, or neglect, or mishandling, or accident.

Warranty B: "As concerns the gold ring set with an emerald, we guarantee that for 20 years the emerald will not fall out of the gold ring. If the emerald should fall out of the gold ring before the end of 20 years, we shall pay unto Belnadin-shumu an indemnity of ten mana of silver.

*'Managing Quality', A Practical Guide to Customer Satisfaction, by D.B.N. Murthy, Response Books, 1999.

Warranty A refers to recent times and warranty B to a period of between 465 B.C. and 425 B.C. during the reign of Artaxerxes I, King of Persia.

Moral: A warranty must be customer-friendly.

Compared to the earlier times, where items were produced mostly one at a time and that too by hand using simple tools, the modern production techniques involve many products and processes at a time and in a day thousands of such identical items could have been produced by machines, technology and processing methods that aid mass production. However, when we refer to 'identical' items, there is a catch. A few of them might slightly deviate from the average norms of production and which could cause problems at the customers' end. "Oh, we produce 10,000 pieces in a day. What can we do if 1 per cent goes out of control? That's inevitable, you know," would be the comment of the production unit's personnel, right from the top to the bottom. That's a small consolation to the 100 customers (1%) who are saddled with defective products. They want every piece to be working right from day one to as long as possible. They just don't buy the idea a certain percentage defectives are 'inevitable'. The customer's argument is simple — "I have paid a price for the product/service and I expect it to give me satisfaction and happiness continuously from the moment I buy it." Who could possibly counter such an argument in these days of supposedly customer-friendly business?

Happy customers

A good business strategy is to keep customers happy and satisfied and retain the loyal ones while wooing others. That cannot happen if the market has a poor opinion of that business, especially quality, reliability and safety. What's not appreciated is the fact that a warranty/guarantee terms is a good sales feature. Some producer might claim, "Our products do not need any service/repair/maintenance as long as they last," is an excellent statement and a positive sales point. An example is the maintenance- free car batteries produced by some manufacturers. There is no need to add distilled water regularly or use acid to regenerate it. A customer would be more than happy to own such a product that lasts long without any trouble and that too without maintenance. Such a brand would have an edge over another, which does not have that maintenance-free feature.

At the other end of the spectrum are products/services that do need technical support, periodical maintenance and a certain degree of care continuously till the product/service is in operation. That's why there are customer service centres precisely for that purpose, some have a

24 hours toll-free call lines or interactive sites on the Internet that provide technical support (Help) to customers spread all over the world. Some products/services have 'Trouble-shooting' tips as part of their technical booklet supplied along with the goods/services. This is helpful in locating faults and find out the possible causes for the problems faced by customers from time to time. For instance, 'Help' feature in a computer is meant to assist a customer to solve simple problems faced by him from time to time. However, when everything fails to bring relief to the customer he has no option but to call the help of technical support group located in the customer service group or in a different location.

Suppose a customer is watching an interesting cricket match at home. Suddenly, his TV goes blink and the TV set becomes 'dead'. Imagine his frustration. He would immediately call the service centre to help him. In general, no immediate help could be expected given the fact that the service personnel are overloaded with service calls. It's too much to expect the service man to rush to the customer's house to set the TV set right. However, a sympathetic customer service man would politely explain how it's not possible to come to his home immediately. He would suggest that he should bring the faulty TV so that he could see what he can do about it. That works sometimes if the customer is desperate. He would take his vehicle or hire one and take the TV set along with him and land at the customer service centre. He then expects to get his problem solved. A customer-friendly service person would look into the problem and if possible to fix it. If not, he would offer a spare/service TV set which the customer could take it and use it as long as his TV set is not repaired. This is a standard practice with some dealers to keep the customers happy. For instance, a car battery dealer might offer a service battery while the customer's battery is getting charged.

The following paragraphs contain information on various types of warranty/guarantee that's offered to customers (consumers). By no means, these can be considered to be complete or comprehensive. These are for the purpose of illustration only. Also, it should be noted that these terms could differ from time to time and from one dealer/manufacturer/sale-outlet to another. It's always necessary to check these terms carefully and read the fine print. Most of the terms are printed in the technical literature/pamphlet/instruction to use booklet and so on. In general, one shouldn't accept any durable goods or service without a written warranty/guarantee.

Two-wheeler warranty

- Valid for 12 months and 10,000 kms whichever occurs earlier.
- Liability of the company is limited to exchange or repair. Every form of consequential loss or damage is expressly excluded.
- Rubber components, bulbs, and propriety items are covered by such manufacturers' warranty for such parts.

[**Note:** It would be difficult for an ordinary consumer to find out what are such warranty conditions. How does one contact these manufacturers? Why cannot the company selling the finished item take responsibility for the warranty of the parts they are getting from their vendors?]

Television set warranty

- Warranty for one year, sometimes up to three or even seven years.
- Cost of transporting the set to the company's service center shall be borne by the purchaser.
- Warranty does not extend to any TV set, which has been subjected to misuse, neglect, or accident. Further, the warranty does not extend to any TV set, which may have been tampered with, altered, or serviced by any agency not authorized by the company.
- This warranty confines to the first purchaser of the set.

Two-in-one radio recorder warrantv

- Warranty against any defect due to defective materials for a period of one year, excepting the semiconductors, is for a six months only.

Portable fan warranty

- Warranted for a period of 2 years from the date of purchase against any manufacturing defect, provided the defective product or component is delivered/returned to us or to our nearest branch, distributor, wholesaler, freight paid.
- The warranty is not valid if: The fault or damage is caused due to customer's ignorance, mishandling, negligence, incorrect connection, misapplication, voltage fluctuation, accident or general wear and tear; the fan is not purchased from an authorized company dealer; the fan is opened by or handled by any unauthorized person; the serial number of the fan is missing, deleted, defaced or altered; the fan or the component is not properly packed while returning to avoid damage in transit.

- Our liability, however, will be to the maximum of the cost of rectifying the defects or the price paid for the product whichever is less and we shall not be held liable for any other indirect or consequential damage.

[**Note:** Just look at the way the warranty/guarantee is framed so heavily loaded against the customer. This gives a chance to the dealer/service centre to deny free service citing one reason or the other. The onus is on the customer that he has used the product properly yet it failed to work. Of course, the customer is expected to take all possible precautions to see the product/service he has bought is used properly and with care taking all possible precautions that are necessary.]

Refrigerator warranty

- Warranty one, three years or more from date of purchase.
- Warranty shall not apply to: any defect, which in the company's opinion, arises by reason of misuse or neglect or accident or damage caused during shifting or transportation; any defect not notified within 7 days to the company or to the company's authorized dealer/service contractor; any refrigerator, which in the company's opinion, has been improperly installed, repaired, or altered or any part not manufactured or sold or not recommended by the company has been fitted; light bulbs and crispator glass in models so fitted.

Mixer-Grinder warranty

- Warranty for 12 months from the date of purchase.
- Warranty not valid if the fault is caused due to customer's mishandling, negligence, misapplication, accident or general wear and tear; the appliance is opened or tampered with by anybody except our authorized service centre or mechanic; serial number if removed, defaced or altered, the appliance or parts are not properly packed while returning to avoid transit damage.

[**Note:** It's intriguing to note that 'normal wear and tear' is excluded from the warranty clause.]

- Our liability shall, however, be to the maximum of the cost of rectifying defects or the price paid for the appliance (whichever is less) and in any case our liability for consequential loss is neither accepted not implied.

SONY floppy disc warranty

- Full lifetime warranty.
- This product, if found defective in materials or workmanship and returned postage paid with proof of purchase to the appropriate address, will be replaced free of charge.
- Replacement is the sole obligation under this warranty. This warranty expressly excludes incidental and consequential damage caused by use of, or inability to use.

[**Note:** In some countries such a clause can be challenged in a court of law.]

Mathey-Tisot watch

- We guarantee your timepiece to be in perfect working order. It has been inspected to ensure mechanical perfection, and with reasonable care, will keep very accurate time.
- This is a lifetime guarantee and good for as long as you own the watch. This guarantee extends solely to the original purchaser and is non-transferable. The liability is at the sole discretion of the company, which may be anyone of the following:
  (1) Return of the purchase price.
  (2) Repair of the watch movement.
  (3) Replacement with a watch of comparable value. The company disclaims any liability for consequential or incidental damages for breach of and written or implied warranty of this watch. This warranty gives you specific legal rights, which vary from state to state. This warranty is good only in the USA.

Band box cleaners and dyers

- We are not responsible for colour running of sarees/dresses.
- No responsibility can be taken for shrinking or damage or defects becoming apparent during treatment, which are due to defective manufacture, to adulteration and deterioration or wear and exposure.
- Quality of texture, colour, trimming etc., is entirely at owner's risk. The company does not hold itself responsible for delay, loss or damage to any article arising from unforeseen circumstances or causes beyond control.
- The firm does not hold itself responsible for articles not called for within 3 months from receipt of the same.
- Fifteen times of our washing cost at the ordinary rate will be given for articles lost, except small articles and cotton articles after one month.

[**Note:** So you are aware of the conditions that the manufacturers/dealers/service centres try to protect themselves. But don't worry. It's possible that some of these conditions/rules against customers' interests will not stand in a court of law.]

Exide car battery warranty

- The tear off portion of the warranty card needs to be filled in completely and handed over to the dealer from whom the battery is being purchased. The dealer will arrange to send this to the nearest company branch for registration of warranty.
- The warranty card must accompany all claims arising within the warranty period.
- It is advised that service checks at least once in six months are adhered to.
- The service record must be filled in by an authorized dealer of the company as proof of specified maintenance. Without this record your claim, if any, is liable to be held invalid.
- Our batteries are warranted against all defects arising, solely from the use of faulty material or poor workmanship. Consequential liabilities will not be entertained. The warranty commences from the date of sale to the original purchaser.
- In the event of any complaint, the battery should be returned untampered and complete to the company's authorized dealer, wholesaler or depot in India. Delivery of the replaced/rectified/discounted battery will be F.O.R. to the same point.
- The defective battery arising out of free replacement or pro-rata settlement under this warranty will become the property of the company and no scrap rebate will be given for it.
- The warranty period on the battery being replaced free of cost shall commence from the date of sale of the original battery as stated in the original warranty card and not from the date of replacement given. For batteries purchased on pro-rata settlement discount under this scheme, a fresh warranty will be applicable from date of purchase.
- All liabilities under this warranty shall cease if the battery is transferred to a third party or any other vehicle.

[**Note:** This is controversial and could be challenged in a consumer court.]

- Recharging is not covered under the purview of this warranty and shall be billed as extra.

- This warranty does not cover damage to the battery caused by faulty electrical systems. Improper handling of the battery by unauthorized dealers/auto technicians, willful abuse, destruction by fire, collision, theft or recharging. The charging system and electrical circuit of the vehicle will be checked by the company authorized personnel or dealer before finalizing any warranty claim.
- Breakage of container and cover or breakage/deformation of terminal due to mechanical shock like hammering do not come under the purview of this warranty.
- In case of a battery model is phased out, the company reserves the right to provide another model of the same capacity and suited to the vehicle, as settlement of warranty.
- Any tampering/over-writing of serial number/manufacturing code on the warranty card or the battery will invalidate the warranty claim.
- Claims will not be accepted in case of wrong fitment or wrong usage of battery. Warranty would be applicable only if fitments are as per company's fitment chart.
- The use of additives or dopes is not recommended. If anything else other than distilled water is added to the electrolyte, the warranty will be null and void.
- In case a service battery is issued, it must be returned within 15 days, failing which a nominal charge per day will be levied.
- Please note that in case period between date of manufacture and date of sale is more than three months the warranty will not be applicable.

[**Note:** In what way a consumer can ensure this? It's up to the dealer to make sure this condition is satisfied, otherwise he should not sell the battery to any customer.]

No service needed

Life would be wonderful if all products/services work without any problem/maintenance till their life is over. This is nothing but a dream given the complexity of products/services as well as proper use by consumers. The best that could happen is that these work without too many problems/service calls/maintenance for a reasonable period of time. The consumer too is responsible for using these properly and without mishandling/misusing these. The warranty/guarantee is an assurance that the company that sells these products/services won't abandon consumers in the midstream but would give them services so that the consumers could go on using these. These, of course, comes with a price tag in the shape of service costs/spare parts and the like, though during the guarantee period it's likely that most companies would provide service without charging. Annual maintenance contract between the company and the consumer is designed to provide services to the consumer for a price agreed in advance.

Some companies take pride in advertising: "We are a quality company and make our products/services last long to give you complete satisfaction. So we are happy that you are a proud owner of our products and we are sure you will enjoy using these for a long time. However, if due to any reason you are not happy with it, you may return it any time and get it exchanged for a similar product or get a refund, and that choice is yours. We are sure you don't have to do either of these." Such statements build consumer confidence and goodwill. Any day a consumer would prefer a product/service which is trouble-free and continues to give him/her satisfaction day in and day out. That's the hallmark of a good reliable quality company. Instead of ignoring or considering it as a nuisance, a complaint should be seen as an opportunity for improvement, and if handled correctly and satisfactorily, it can lead to a committed consumer for the loyalty of that brand.

What a consumer wants is that he/she be believed and trusted and would like repair/replacement/refund of an unsatisfactory product/service is done without delay and without fuss. Any dealer/service outlet interested in retaining customers should note that a dissatisfied customer who complains is better than the one who is simply so disgusted that he/she decides to shop elsewhere. That person could damage the reputation of the company by word-of-mouth adverse publicity. That's why a customer's complaint should be attended to with politeness and that too promptly to the satisfaction of that aggrieved customer. If he is not trusted or not believed, or worse, humiliated by silly and damaging remarks about that customer, it's like adding insult to injury.

Service technicians and personnel should be polite with customers who might sometimes get so frustrated that they use loud, harsh words about the product or that company. An intelligent and polite service person would try to calm down that irate customer by giving him/her patient hearing and seeing that the repair/refund/replacement is done quickly to the satisfaction of that person. One could see a world of difference in the attitude of that angry customer when he/she gets a patient hearing and his/her work is done expeditiously. There is a need to impart training in human resource management to the service personnel who interact with all sorts of customers — polite to outright hostile and rude. The skill of that person lies in trying to convince the customer that he/she has made a point and that would be attended to quickly and satisfactorily. It's important that the service personnel educate the customer how a product/service should be used properly so that it gives a long trouble-free service. A set of do's and don't should be given the consumers orally and in writing about the usage of a product/service. Such tips are useful to customers and they would appreciate such efforts in informing the consumers how the product/service should be used longer without problems.

HINTS TO CONSUMERS

- Do proper and thorough homework on the product/service you have in mind before you venture out to make a purchase decision.
- Shop for competitive offer from reputed brands. Search the Internet, magazines and other information before investing in any product/service, especially if it is high priced.
- A dealer/retailer might not show you all the brands available with him because he gets a better commission on certain brands. It's in your own interest to insist that you see for yourself all the competing brands within the price range you have in mind.
- Insist on a cash memo/receipt/proof of purchase which establishes your *bonafides* as a consumer; otherwise you have no legal standing in any judicial/consumer court.
- Do not buy cheap and shoddy stuff because it's low priced. The end could be disastrous 'cheap and nasty'.
- Look for quality, reliability, safety and brand name. Do not buy imitation/duplicate stuff though very low priced
- Buy a certified product/service (like ISI, ISO, FPO, Agmark and International norms like ISO) of a reliable brand and that too from an authorized dealer/service outlet.
- Check out the product/service yourself. Do not go by hearsay or what the advertisements state. Try to find out if anyone known to you has used a similar brand/product/service and ask for his/her experience, both good and bad, including after-sales service.
- Look for longer warranty period.
- Check whether there are adequate service centres nearby.

- Read and understand the instructions for use booklet before attempting to use the product/service as well as terms of warranty/guarantee, including the fine print and what the 'conditions apply' mean to you.
- If you come across a spurious/duplicate stuff make a BIG noise with the dealer, whom you might suspect, as well as the government authority concerned.
- Do not try to repair a product/service yourself without knowing anything about it. Do not meddle with the factory set controls indiscriminately. This will go against you, if something goes wrong with the product/service.
- Do not allow unauthorized persons do the repair on your product/service during the warranty period or even after that to safeguard yourself against unprofessional work. The service outlet could charge you if it comes to know on checking someone has done some shoddy repair work.
- Your life and that of the family members is precious. So do not compromise on quality and safety and buy yourself cheap and unsafe products to save money that could prove very costly in the long run. Do not buy products of fly-by-night operators or door-to-door sales-person.
- Be polite and factual when you want to complain about a defective product/service. Cut out the dramatics as far as possible that is a waste of time and energy. If by mistake or inadvertently you have mishandled the product/service, say so. That would help the service outlet to investigate and it might condone a mistake that's not deliberate.
- Blacklist any dealer/service centre which cheats you or does not provide proper and prompt service or which charge exorbitantly for service as well as spare parts. Persuade your friends and relatives not to have any business with such unscrupulous business outlets.
- Do not take 'NO' for an answer from a dealer/service outlet when you want redressal of your complaint. If your case is strong go up to the higher levels for redress. Be patient and persuasive.
- If everything fails, you may approach a consumer court nearby for redress. But remember that it could take a long time before you get your complaint settled.

PRODUCT LIABILITY

In the advanced country like the USA product liability suit is big business. Here is the definition of Product liability that's commonly accepted:

"It's the responsibility of manufacturers, distributors, and sellers of products to the public, to deliver products free of defects that harm an individual or numerous persons and to make good on that responsibility if their products are defective. They include faulty auto brakes, contaminated baby food, exploding bottles of beer, flammable children's pajamas, or lack of label warning.

Examples: Beauty Queen products that cause loss of hair, a faulty gear in a truck that causes accident, a toy that hurts a child and so on. The key element in products liability law is that a person that suffers harm need not prove negligence, since the negligence is 'presumed' and the result is 'strict liability' (absolute responsibility) on the seller, distributor and manufacturer. An injured person need only to sue the seller and let him/her/it bring the manufacturer or distributor into the lawsuit or require contribution toward a judgment. However, all those possibly responsible should be mentioned in the suit as defendants, if they are known. When damage is required to be paid due to arbitrary or capricious behaviour then it loses its individual character and assumes social significance."

Despite the passage of the Consumer Protection Act (COPRA) in 1986, and with it the experiences gained over the years, there is little progress in India in introducing the concept of product liability like in the advanced countries. There the manufacturer who markets a product/service which causes injury or bodily harm or fatality is primarily held responsible and is liable to pay a hefty compensation and face punitive action. Deterrent fines are imposed running, sometimes, into several million dollars along with jail terms for the CEO of the company and some of his officers directly responsible for the shoddy/defective product/service. In sharp contrast, in our country, those purveyors of shoddy and dangerous products/services can escape with little or no punishment.

In the advanced countries like the UK and USA, product recall notices are routine though frequent recalls damage the reputation of the manufacturer and lowers the consumers' confidence in that brand. Such notices are still regarded as 'inevitable' to escape or minimize product liability suits later on but nevertheless a black mark on that company. It shows the company in poor light in the market for having sent out defective products out of their factories, despite strict quality control checks. Such notices about possibility of damage to the user should be studied by the consumers to safeguard against injuries. These notices urge the customers, who are saddled with defective products/services, to return these to authorized service centres to get free repair or replacement.

For instance, a particular lawn-mower manufacturer could have discovered at a later stage there is a potential problem if a customer uses the product. The product recall notice could read as: "If you have bought our model KBZ lawn-mower, be advised that the blades might hurt the fingers if accidentally they come into contact with the lower case. So you are advised to return these equipments, bearing serial numbers ABCxxxxxx to our nearest dealer/service station to get a free replacement or repair. We shall pay you all the charged involved." This is a warning to a customer that he/she uses the faulty equipment at one's risk only. However, it's worth noting that a product recall notice does not absolve the manufacturer from future liability cases, if and when these arise.

The best guarantee against a product recall/liability suit is, of course, make the product/service so good that it has no defect or fault likely to be injurious to the user. Paramount concern should be to eliminate all possible causes of defects that could prove hazardous/risky to the user. A certain amount of 'misuse' is inevitable and so it's wise to make the product/service foolproof, childproof and even idiot-proof. The 'buck stops here,' is true of a CEO confronted by a product liability suit. He cannot escape his/her responsibility by pointing a finger at his subordinates though such persons too are likely to be sued for their part in making a defective/dangerous product/service.

Obviously, no corner should be cut in matters of safety of any equipment/service. Any shortcoming at the design/manufacturing stage, could prove a liability to the company in the long run — a case of 'pennywise and pound foolish.' Product liability insurance is a measure to safeguard oneself from future litigation, though it comes at a high cost to an individual as well as the company. Liability insurance, not yet familiar in our country, is routine in the advanced countries covering professionals like CEOs, directors, engineers, management personnel, designers, doctors and lawyers. It's possible that service providers, who charge for their services, too take out insurance in case a client files a case against him/her for deficiency in service or malpractice. There is a big demand for attorneys who fight the malpractice or deficient in service cases commanding a hefty fee. It is stated that due to product liability the costs to the consumer goes up but mostly it's a small price to pay for injuries/damages to an individual due to product liability or malpractice.

Liability cases

A few examples of product liability/malpractice cases settled in the USA, are revealing as to what extent a company in the docks is forced to shell out a hefty amount to the consumers, directly or indirectly, who had filed cases against them.

- General Motors, World's largest motor vehicle producer, at least till recently, was asked to pay a record breaking (that record could have been broken again) $4.9 billion in damages to a family of six killed when their Chevrolet Malibu car fuel tank exploded severely burning the passengers.
- Ford Motor Company was ordered to pay $195 million to a family of three killed when their Ford Bronco rolled over on an interstate highway. The company had announced later on it was recalling 279,000 vehicles of a particular year of manufacture to correct defects in the deactivation switch. The voluntary recall affected Ford's the top end models with the defects.
- Dow Corning Corporation settled $3.2 billion, once the largest manufacturer of breast implants, with those suffers who complained of various problems with these implants. Under the deal, women who claimed the implants made them sick could receive up to $300,000 for the most serious medical condition.
- Exxon, the giant oil company, was fined millions of dollars for causing oil spill through their oil tanker Exxon Valdez that went aground, on the coast of Alaska and was also ordered to clean up the oil sludge that caused severe pollution affecting marine life.
- Phillips Morris, a tobacco company, was fined millions of dollars for causing death of several persons due to cancer by cigarette smoking. The company went on appeal and the compensation amount was reduced.

The above are a few examples to illustrate the vibrant state of product liability settlements that protect the consumers from hazards, sickness or injury, or death. These are the market forces at work that provide the much needed checks and balances for the consumers. While the matter of product liability is taken seriously, in India the government, the industry, business and the consumers have yet to realize the importance of product liability. We do have cases filed against the doctors and hospitals, nursing homes for wrong treatment that caused serious problems or death of the patients. However, the compensation amount awarded is small and there is hardly any punitive fine, with exceptions. Public notices in the media about potential problems with drugs are hardly noticed. Some of these drugs are still being sold across the counter. A few drugs banned in the advanced countries are sold in India. Product recall notices are still rare in our country. Timely warning saves lives but our business people believe in secrecy. "The problem is minor. So why should we warn the consumers? Why should we panic or over-react to a small problem? Let the consumers try it out and complain. Then we will take action, if needed," is the general apathy towards defective products. For example, if only timely warning was issued, many hundreds of victims of the Bhopal gas tragedy could have escaped to safety.

Recall of products/services for repair/replacement/refund is more of an exception than rule in our business milieu. The idea appears to be to hide a potential problem till the last from consumers with a hope such problems would disappear by themselves. When the problem gets hotter, pretend as if nothing has happened ('business as usual'), admit nothing and blame the media, government, and consumers for all the adverse publicity. Our judicial system is consumer-friendly, with exceptions, but the compensation and fines are too meagre and cannot act as deterrents. There are still a few fly-by-night operators and 'blade' companies who fool the gullible and vanish overnight duping many consumers who are left high and dry. Punitive action for peddling adulterated, inferior and hazardous product/service is rare. It seems life in India is cheaper as compared to advanced countries by noting the small pittance of a compensation awarded in case of injury or death of a victim.

Advance warning

'Fore warned is forearmed' and that's why it is always preferable to give advance warning, even if this proves to be not so serious as thought of earlier. For instance, the meteorological department issues cyclone/ tornado warnings to coastal districts in our country. Often the people concerned just ignore such warnings and stay put. Some of them get into trouble because they didn't heed the warning urging them to reach safer places. It's also true that sometimes such warnings prove to be innocuous. However, in the long run, it is helpful to give advance warning either of a product/service that could pose problems to the consumers or any hazard warning such as in case of a natural or man-made disaster. The advantages are:

- Alerts potential and existing consumers to be careful.
- Minimizes future liability suits.

However, the flip side to early warning is that it creates an adverse publicity for the company that has issued such a notification. The best insurance against product liability is a safe and sound design executed properly at the manufacturing stage, transported properly without damage and handled carefully till the product/service reaches the consumer. Even then there should be clear instructions, orally and in writing through technical booklet and demonstration. All pcssible precautions have to be taken at every stage to make the product safe, foolproof and childproof. There is always the possibility of misuse at the customer's end and that's why controls, which are not be supposed to be touched by the customer should be hidden and not easy to access. Sometimes only authorized person can operate the locking system and that too through special tool only. For instance, a clear warning is shown at the back of a TV set cover indicating that high voltage present inside can prove fatal if the cover is opened while the TV set is switched on. Consumers should be educated on the proper manner of using a product/service to ensure continued enjoyment.

Repeated product recall is a dampener as far as consumer confidence is concerned. That's why all possible steps are needed within an organization to make the design and all the other stages of manufacture *et al.* as foolproof and defective-proof as possible. The Chief Executive Officer and his team, that includes everyone in the organization, should be so motivated that the product/service comes out as flawless as possible to make product recall unnecessary and an extreme exception. 'Safety first' should be the motto of any organization. Prompt settlement of complaints and early warning when the company has come across a potential quality and safety problem will go a long way in avoiding product liability suits that could prove ruinous to any organization.

Reliable design→Sound manufacture→Proper quality control at every stage→Right instructions for use→Safe operation at consumer's end→Minimum complaints→Fewer product liability suits

We are into a globalized market. It's a question of time that some of the good practices like product recall/liability will come to us with a bang. It is necessary for the trade and industry to be fully prepared so that they are not caught napping. That applies to prompt settlement of consumer complaints too without hassles. Presently, we come across a situation where instructions and warnings are issued to the consumer to be careful. However, the responsibility of the dealer/manufacturer towards the consumer is not highlighted. In fact, it should have been the other way with the consumer treated as a king.

Here is an example, as printed on the ticket, how a state-owned ferry treats its passengers:

"Ferry service does not assume any liability in the event of any loss or damage to life and property of any passenger in the event of an accident."

Strange but true! But the ferry-service cannot get away by merely printing such a warning. It is supposed to safe to use the ferry and in case of accident the passengers are provided with lifejackets and rescue-boats so that the passengers can reach the shore safely. It is necessary for the company to take out insurance for each passenger, either part of the ticket fee or separately so that adequate compensation is given in case of injury or death. The ferry-owners and their employees cannot absolve themselves of their responsibility of what in essence is their physical and moral duty to carry passengers safely and save them in case of a mishap with all the means at their command.

'Errors and Omissions Excepted (E & OE)', 'Goods carried at owner's risk', 'No refund/exchange/replacement' are all consumer-unfriendly measures which we have been forced to accept as 'normal' so far. It is time the mindset of everyone, including tradesmen, businesspersons and the consumers, changes in keeping pace with the advances in the rest of the world.

Your dream vacation

CHAPTER 5

CONSUMER COMPLAINT REDRESS

There is no right way to do a wrong thing
—Anonymous

Consumer satisfaction is taken for granted for any successful business as its very existence depends upon the goodwill of consumers who patronize their products/services time and again. That's theory but the ground reality is, unfortunately, different. Sellers are keen to sell their products/ services to make a handy profit often forgetting the end user, the consumer who is actually paying for their output. We have not yet reached the level of consumerism of the advanced countries though after liberalization and globalization the availability of goods and services of international quality have improved dramatically.

However, we have not reached the American consumerism of "throw-away" culture. We would not like to throw any product/service that is working well. As long as spare parts are available, we would like to make the maximum use of a product/service. Nevertheless, there is now a tendency to change models every three to five years in our country, thanks to availability of newer and better models. Dealers are offering attractive terms like, easy loans with zero interest, exchange of old to new and installment schemes et al to induce consumers to exchange their older products/services to newer ones that have more features and more energy efficient. Now one can see brand new models of cars being introduced every year in our country too though the number of models are far less than what a consumer can choose in the advanced countries. Now it's rare for consumers to have cars older than 15 years, which have to be recertified for road-worthiness.

There are two ways of looking at a quality of a product/service. One is the initial quality that can be seen in the first few hours or days or weeks and the one that can be seen after a lapse of few years. The first one is "Quality" and the second one is "Reliability" aspect of a product/service. Consumers are looking not only for initial quality but long-term quality, which is defined as reliability. Any deficiency in the product/service performance becomes "unquality" which is a cause for not only unhappiness but for a complaint too.

Quality of a product/service = Short-term quality + Long-term quality (reliability)
Deficiency in short-term or long-term quality = Unquality→Unhappiness + Complaint

When a consumer has paid for a product/service, he/she has every right to expect it would give continuous satisfaction and would last long. The least thing on the mind of the consumer when he purchases a product/service is the problem of repair and maintenance. If he/she is denied happiness due to poor quality he/she is annoyed and curses the dealer/manufacturer for deficiency in service. The consumer expects the dealer/service outlet to see that the product/service is restored to working condition as soon as possible. That consumer would be unhappy and disappointed if he/she has to appear as if he/she was responsible for the fault, which is patently unfair. The consumer expects to get back the product/service after repair without delay and without having to pay for the repair. Though claims are made about 'free' warranty repair/maintenance, in our business milieu it's difficult to get anything done quickly without reminders and without delays. Often, some 'hidden' costs will have to be paid to get the product/service after repair.

Culture of '*chalta hai*'

A consumer has the right and duty to complain about a product/service that doesn't give him/her satisfaction to the manufacturer/dealer/retailer/service center. Unfortunately, an average Indian consumer has the attitude of '*chalta hai*' (will do). He/she would go to any extent to use that sub-standard product/service as long as possible. The consumer has stoically accepted his/her 'fate' to be saddled with it— "Oh, I will manage to use it somehow. Besides, who is going to take the trouble to telephone? Why take so much trouble and what's the use anyway? I know nothing would come out of such a complaint. So why waste my time and energy on such a futile exercise? Instead, let me put up with it as long as possible. Slowly, I will get used this sub-standard product/service." We are so used to accepting/receiving poor quality product/service all these years that consumers tend to ignore minor problems until there is a major breakdown that makes the product/service totally useless.

Confronted with little or no choice, Indians accepted substandard products/services without complaining too much for years. Not only there was a sense of apathy but an attitude of resignation and acceptance of the inevitable while dealing with poor quality of products/services. Such a meek acceptance of substandard products/services offered a fertile field for sellers to dump poor quality products/services to make a hefty profit at the cost of gullible and hapless consumers. Fortunately, after the regime of liberalization and globalization, there is hope for Indian consumers. Now consumers have a choice that gives them opportunities to shop for quality products/services of international quality at Indian prices. However, the attitude of sellers/dealers/retailers has not changed much. They are eager to sell but not all enthusiastic when it comes to complaint redress. They are expert at passing on the buck to everyone else, including consumers. They blame everyone, but themselves, for poor quality. They still think rectifying a product is a waste of time, which could be utilized well by selling and making money. According to them, service centers are a necessary evil, which they would like to dispense with if they possibly could.

"Consumer Rights Day" every year is on March 15th. Huge advertisements are taken out in the print medium by the Department of Consumers Affairs, Ministry of Food and Consumer Affairs, which gives helpful hints as indicated below:

"As a consumer, you should remember:

- It is your right to get standard goods and services free from defects/deficiencies and restrictive/unfair trade practices.
- You should insist on a proper receipt/bill/cash memo, warranty/guarantee card against all purchases. Seller/service-providers cannot deny issuing them
- You have the right to demand replacement/repair of defective goods sold to you. "Goods once sold will not be taken back/exchanged" etc., are not enforceable under the law."

In Latin, *Caveat emptor* means, "Let the buyer beware." Sellers were relieved of the obligation to tell everything about the product/service. That meant, the sellers couldn't be hauled up to court to redress consumers' complaints. However, we have come a long way from such a situation thanks to an open market situation where winds of change are blowing in. Now consumers are protected by '**contract law**' which he/she has entered into with someone, the seller, and the '**tort law**' which makes sellers responsible for injuries/damages caused to others. Consumer Protection Laws strengthen the basic legal rights provided by these two sources.

A consumer when faced by a poor quality product/service should not keep silent and accept it without complaining. It is the consumer's duty and responsibility to highlight the problem to the seller/dealer/ service outlet without fear. The encounter is not a pleasant one as the seller/dealer does not want to listen to any complaint. For him it's a sheer waste of time, which he could have utilized better. Attack is the best form of defense and so the first thing a seller/dealer does is to blame the problem on the consumer for misuse of the product/service. If this does not work, he will flaunt the notice before the consumer, "Goods once sold cannot be replaced or exchanged." A stouthearted consumer will have nothing to do with such a one-sided notice and he/she won't be dissuaded from pursuing the complaint till its logical end, politely but firmly.

A few consumers get rebuffed by aggressive sellers who ask the disgruntled consumers to leave their shops. They think getting rid of such a consumer who complains too much is more important than retaining him/her. In the face of such uncooperative, negative and hostile attitude of sellers/dealers, some consumers leave the shop unhappy and vow never to shop there. They would go elsewhere to get the product/service fixed by paying from their pockets. There are instances, where the sellers/ dealers after bluffing their way out, but finding such tactics don't work, change their strategy. They reluctantly agree to 'look into' the complaint but the concerned repairperson/technician is not there or they have to consult the higher ups. Such tactics might not work with a persistent consumer who knows what he/she is doing.

A consumer who has a genuine complaint should have proof of purchase — a cash memo, receipt, warranty/guarantee card. Without any of this, he/she has no locus standi as a consumer. A customer with a genuine grievance should marshal all the facts, be honest and open about it and talk politely and to the point with the concerned person in the shop from where he/she had bought the product/service. There is no reason to get frustrated or lose one's temper however provocative the action of the shopkeeper is. By no means he / she should accept "No" for an answer. The consumer should approach the next higher level in the shop so that his/her grievances could be heard loud and clear. Threatening the shopkeeper that he/she would go to the consumer court is not done before exhausting all the means available to get one's problem redressed.

A telephone call, FAX, e-mail, letter and personal: visit are the means of registering a complaint. Some organizations have a separate cell to receive complaints directly or through the e-mail or telephone. All details regarding the product/service, like nature of problem, date of purchase, model and serial number, year of manufacture and cash memo number should be given for registering the complaint — the fuller the details the better for tracing the complaint at the shopkeeper's/dealer's end. Normally, a complaint number is given for follow-up. Personal visits with the defective product/service becomes necessary if it's possible to transport the item easily. Service personnel do visit the householder's place of residence to check and verify the complaint, on a TV set, fridge, microwave et al, and often get the product/service in running condition by on-site repair/maintenance. If for example, there is a problem with the telephone or internet connection, the customer support personnel check the problem at their end and make necessary corrections. If they feel the problem lies at the customer's end, then they send a service technician to look into the problem and rectify it. However, your TV channel cannot be disconnected without notice, even if you have not paid the cable subscription fee for one month.

Patience and politeness take a customer long in getting his/her problem sorted out quickly. If there is a hot exchange of words, then the customer complaint gets sidelined till amicable relations are restored. A customer should be prepared to run from pillar to post to get the problem sorted out quickly. Of course, that person should be able to inform the higher ups the problem he/she encountered in getting the problem sorted out. Such a feedback is important for the higher levels of management to understand the ground reality and initiate steps to make the lower staff more responsive to consumers. When every persuasion and means fail, the consumer can approach the relevant consumer redress forum for redress as a last resort.

Helpline

Complaints about poor quality of consumer durables, telecom services and banks flooded the National Consumer Helpline (NCH) in September, 2006. The NCH, which is a consumer grievance cell instituted by the Department of Consumer Affairs to register complaints on the phone regarding quality of products and services, had received a total of 2921 calls in September, 2006.

The complaints were mainly against service providers like BSNL, MTNL, Airtel, Tata Indicom, Reliance, Idea, Hutch and Spice besides broadband service providers. The banking sector, which occupies third place with 8.13 per cent calls, received complaints against SBI, ICICI, PNB, Citibank and Standard Chartered.

Insurance related problems accounted for 3.03 per cent involving LIC, Tata Aig, ICICI Lombard and ICICI Prudential among others.

Of late there is a realization even at the government levels that good governance, which is actually keeping the people (consumers) happy wins votes. The better the governance the better chance for the ruling party to be reelected and consequently poor governance could throw out an inefficient government in a democratic set up. Thus a strong factor is the 'anti-incumbency' factor that can mar a government's future. There is thus an increased focus on keeping people happy by settling their complaints fast and to their satisfaction.

> *"Harassment of a common man by public authorities is socially abhorring and legally impermissible."* —Supreme Court of India

Service sectors too like insurance, telecommunications, railways, airlines, road transport, postal, et al are now having grievance cells in each department to settle consumers' complaints. A designated officer, of sufficiently higher levels, hears the public's complaints at specified timings each day and promises quick action cutting red tape. 'Lok Adalats' take place regularly where the complaints are settled en masse in a *mela* type of gathering where the required persons from the service sector are present to settle the complaints on the spot. Suggestion/complaint register/box is required to be kept in each office that is supposed to be seen regularly by a senior officer and action called for from the required department/officer.

Customer→Complaint→redress→higher up→Lok Adalat→Consumer redress forum (court)

"We trust you," is the motto in advanced countries when a customer complains and his/her complaint is settled on the spot without hassles or any redtape. If a customer goes to the consumer cell in any departmental stores, he/she is sure to walk away with a replacement/exchange/refund within minutes. We are miles away from such an approach. However, a few departmental stores in our country are better at settling consumer complaints. With more foreign tie-ups coming up in the near future in the retail sector, there is a hope that consumers would get a better deal as far as redress of complaints are concerned. Our business leaders should appreciate the fact that a complaint is like a time bomb ticking away. A satisfied customer is the best salesperson for the company. On the other hand, a dissatisfied person can damage the reputation of the company/ brand by word-of-mouth adverse publicity. A prompt settlement of complaints could well be a sales plus point for the organization that cares for customers and wants to keep them happy and satisfied. A responsive company that has a good service centre has an edge over another with poor or no service center worth mentioning.

Happy customer→Good salesperson for the company

CONSUMER PROTECTION

Consumer protection is not new. The first consumer protection efforts began with the early dawn of civilization. In ancient Egypt, laws governed the processing of meat for human consumption. Greek and Roman laws prohibited the adulteration of wine with water. It is interesting to note that in ancient India in 200 BC. punishment was meted out to those adulterating grains and oils. During the middle ages, "Inspectors of the Peppers Guild" were established to oversee the activities of merchants who tried to mix pepper with items like worthless seeds, barks and coconut shells. The first American Consumer Law was passed in 1798 AD. In the 1790's, the first set of American Weights and Measures Laws were passed to protect the integrity of the commercial transactions. The words of the Federal Trade Commission Chairman James Miller who stated in 1985.: "Our proper role is not to tell entrepreneurs how to run their businesses. Nor is it to impose our views on consumers in a fit of Big Brotherism. Rather it is to keep markets competitive and free of fraud and deception. That way, we serve the interests of honest trades-people and consumers alike," these remarks are relevant to us even now.

Consumer movement in our country is still young. It has not reached a state of maturity like in some of the advanced nations. A sheltered market, prevailing earlier, made consumer movement more difficult, with the philosophy of 'take it or leave it' attitude of the trade and business. Consumers got a raw deal and the consumer movement made a slow and painful progress with just a few NGOs trying their best to attract the attention of the decision-makers to do something positive for the hapless consumers. Lacking a charismatic leader like Ralph Nadar of the USA our consumer unions were too weak and their plea was like a cry in the wilderness.

With the passage of the consumer protection law, some of the NGOs working in the consumer field got disheartened. They thought their role in consumer related matters was over. Far from it! In fact their role should have been enhanced in view of 'problem of plenty' as far as consumer goods/services are concerned. They should be able to guide the consumers how they should be going about making a meaningful choice that's cost-effective and is worth the money they are paying for. There is a strong case for an independent consumer organization that's not supported either by the government or the industry, to maintain its total independence, on the lines of the *Consumer Union* of the USA with its popular magazine *Consumer Reports* which is the reference document for knowledgeable consumers before making a purchase decision. This magazine publishes ratings on most of the consumer durables, automobiles and so on. In our country, *Consumer Voice* published by *Consumer Voice Organization*, based in Delhi is trying to do just that though its reach is still limited. Such ratings on commonly used products/services serve as valuable guide for taking sound purchase decisions.

Role of NGOs

The following are some details of the role of NGOs:

- Guide/educate consumers.
- Interface with government/industry/business on matters affecting consumers.
- Assist consumers in getting complaint redress, when needed.
- Provide testing facilities and arrange for ratings of products/services.
- Participate in committees at government/industry/business/international level on consumer affairs.
- Coordinate with other agencies regarding standards/laws/rules concerning consumer matters.
- Increase awareness in the public on matters of interest to consumers.

Consumer protection is a form of government regulation, which protects the interests of consumers. For example, a government may require businesses to disclose detailed information about products, particularly in areas where safety or public health is an issue, such as food. Consumer protection is linked to the idea of consumer rights (that consumers have various rights as consumers), and to the formation of consumer organizations, which help consumers to make better choices in the marketplace.

Consumer protection law or consumer law is considered a public law that regulates private law relationships between individual consumers and businesses that sell goods (products) and services. Consumer protection covers a wide range of topics including, but not necessarily limited to product liability, privacy rights, unfair business practices, fraud, misrepresentation, and other consumer/business interactions. Such laws (especially in advanced countries like the USA) deal with bankruptcy, credit repair, product safety, service contractors, bill collector regulation, pricing, utility turnoffs, consolidation and much more.

Consumer protection laws often mandate the posting of notices in all automotive repair shops in California, USA. In the United States there are a variety of laws at both the federal or state levels that regulate consumer affairs. The Federal Trade Commission and the US Department of Justice enforce federal consumer protection laws. Most of German protection law has been enacted pursuant to European directives. A large part of the directive was incorporated into the German Civil Code. In the UK the Office of Fair Trading nationally enforces consumer laws, which is the UK's consumer and competition watchdog. At the International level the NGO Consumers International is active. In the USA, a few of the organizations working in the consumer affairs are: Better Business Bureau, Consumers Union, publishers of *Consumer Reports*, Public Citizen, Consumer Federation of America, Center for Science in the Public Interest. Apart from the legendary Ralph Nadar, the other prominent persons in the US connected with consumer affairs are Michael Vernon and Victoria Nahum. In India Consumer Education and Research Centre (CERC) is actively concerned with consumer matters.

Self-regulation by those who are producing/selling products/services is highly desirable though it looks like a Utopian dream in our business milieu. But experience, all over the world, suggests that such a hope is misplaced and more often than not a business is more guided by the profit motive rather than consumers' well being. Consumers and their representatives are skeptical, not without reason, the tall claims of business/trade/industry that they too are concerned with the consumers' interest. They describe such concern, rather cynically, as the case of a 'fox guarding a chicken coop'.

The time has come to rethink on a true consumer-oriented economy in terms of well being of consumers, that's how products/services enhance the quality of life, rather than measuring it in terms of production value (in rupees) of the total number of products/services. A point that needs to be noted is that our scarce resources should not be fritted away in producing products/services that have little value to consumers. There is no need for us to copy the capitalistic model of consumerism of advanced countries where market forces determine which products/services should be continued to be produced and which ones to be dropped because of poor consumer demand.

Consumer laws, rules and regulations

Our nation has the dubious distinction of having the largest number of laws, rules and regulations on the statute, most of which are either badly enforced or not at all. We have a law or rule or regulation for everything a common man is concerned. He needs a license to own a pet, he must get a permit to start a small business, a marriage has to be registered, sales tax/VAT/income tax has to be paid and so on. Some of these are, of course, needed to regulate a society. But people are breaking some of the rules with impunity and the law is slow in catching these culprits and even slower in punishing them, if at all. So essentially what we need is fewer laws that are enforced strictly rather than many laws loosely enforced or not at all.

"Common or case" law is based on major legal decisions made by judges. Lawyers refer to such a case as "land mark" decision. In such cases the judges state the legal basis for deciding a case in a certain way; they set precedents that latter courts follow to decide similar cases, though variations are possible from case to case. There are statutory laws, which are passed in legislature bodies from time to time, which are approved by the Governor of a State or the President of India. These laws affect the environment, functioning of the legislature, government, administration of services like banking, telecommunication, postal services, stock exchange, civic matters and so on. These are for regulating the society affairs, protection of the environment and the citizens (consumers) in general.

Some of the laws, rules and regulations, which affect the common man (consumer) have been enacted over a period of time and now are in the statue book. These are being amended from time to time after gaining experience while more laws, rules and regulations are being framed as per the needs of the society/environment. Certain International laws, rules and regulations have to be adhered as part of our commitment to the United Nations.

Some laws, rules and regulations framed over a period of time affect the common man (consumer). These are listed in the Table below:

- Drugs and Cosmetics Act 1954.
- Prevention of Adulteration Act 1954.
- Essential Commodities Act 1955.
- Standard Weights & Measures Act 1956.
- Monopolies & Restrictive Trade Practices MRTP Act 1969.
- Water (Prevention and Control of Pollution) Act 1974.

- Packaged Commodities Regulations Order 1975.
- Household Electrical Appliances (Quality Control) Order 1981.
- Air (Prevention and Control of Pollution) Act 1981.
- Consumer Protection Act 1986.
- Environment Protection Act 1988.

Understanding consumer terms

Consumer means any person who:

(1) buys any goods (Note: or service) for a consideration which has been paid or promised or partly paid and partly promised, or under any system of deferred payment and includes any user of such goods other than the person who buys such goods for consideration paid or promised or partly paid or partly promised, or under any system of deferred payment when such use is made with the approval of such person, but does not include a person who obtains such goods for resale or any for any commercial purpose; or

(2) hires or avails of any services for a consideration which has been paid or promised or partly paid and partly promised, or under any system of deferred payment and includes any beneficiary of such services for consideration paid or promised, or partly paid and partly promised, or under any system of deferred payment, when such services are availed of with the approval of the first mentioned person.

Service means service of any description which is made available with banking, financing, insurance, transport (air, rail, road and sea), processing, supply of electrical or other energy, board or lodging or both, housing, construction, entertainment, amusement, or the purveying of news or other information, cable/Internet services, telephone and telecommunication et al, but that does not include the rendering of any service free of charge or under a contract of personal service

Complainant means—

1. a consumer or
2. any voluntary consumer association registered under the Companies Act, 1956 or under any other law for the time being in force or
3. the Central Government or any State Government, who or which makes a complaint, or
4. one or more consumers, where there are numerous consumers having the same interest.

Complaint means any allegation in writing made by a complainant that—

1. an unfair trade practice or a restrictive trade practice has been adopted by the trader;
2. the goods (services) brought by him/her or agreed to be hired or availed of by him/her suffer from one or more defects;
3. the services availed of or agreed to be hired or availed of by him suffer from deficiency in any respect;
4. a trader has charged for the goods/services mentioned in the complaint a price in excess of the price fixed by or under any law for the time being in force or displayed on the goods or any package containing such goods with a view to obtaining any relief under this Act; and
5. goods (services) which will be hazardous to life and safety when used, are being offered for sale to the public in contravention of the provisions of any law in force at the time of the purchase, requiring traders to display information in regard to the contents, manner and effect of such goods (services).

Consumer dispute means a dispute where the person against whom a complaint has been made, denies or disputes the allegations contained in the complaint

Defect means any fault, imperfection or shortcoming in the quality, safety, quantity, potency, purity or standard which is required to be maintained by or under any law for the time being in force or under any contract, express or implied or as is claimed by the trader in any manner whatsoever in relation to any goods.

Deficiency means any fault, imperfection, shortcoming or inadequacy in the quality, safety, nature and manner of performance which is required to be maintained by or under any law for the time being in force or has been undertaken to be performed by a person in pursuance of a contract or otherwise in relation to any service

Unfair trade practice means a trade practice, which for the purpose of promoting the sale, use or supply of any goods or for the provision of any service, adopts any unfair method or unfair or deceptive practice including any of the following practices, namely:

1. Any of the following:

(i) Falsely represents that the goods are of a particular standard

(ii) Falsely represents that the services are of a particular standard

(iii) Falsely represents any second-hand, renovated, reconditioned or old goods as new goods

(iv) Represents that the goods or services have a sponsorship, approval, performance etc., which such goods and services do not have

(v) Represents that the seller or the supplier has a sponsorship, or approval, or affiliation etc., which seller or supplier does not have

(vi) Makes a false or misleading representation concerning the need for, or the usefulness of, any goods or services

(vii) Gives to the public any warranty or guarantee of the performance, efficacy or length of life of a product of any goods that is not based on an adequate or proper test thereof

(viii) Makes to the public a representation in a form that purports to be (a) warranty or a guarantee of a product or any goods or any service or (b) a promise to replace, maintain or repair an article, if such purported warranty or guarantee or promise is materially misleading or if there is no reasonable prospect that such warranty, guarantee, or promise will be carried out

(ix) Materially misleads the public concerning the price at which a product or like products or goods or services, have been or are, ordinarily sold or provided

(x) Gives false or misleading facts disparaging the goods or services or trade of another person

2. Permits the publication of any advertisement whether in any newspaper or otherwise, for the sale or supply at a bargain price, of goods and services that are not intended to be offered for sale or supply at the bargain price

3. Permits the offering of gifts, prizes or other items with the intention of not providing them as offered or creating impression that something is being given or offered free of charge when it is fully or partly covered by the amount charged on the transaction as a whole

4. Permits the sale or supply of goods/services intended to be used, or are of a kind likely to be used, by consumers, knowing or having reason to believe that the goods/services do not comply with the standards prescribed by competent authority

5. Permits the hoarding or destruction of goods, or refuses to sell the goods or to make them available for sale or to provide any service, if such hoarding or destruction or refusal raises or tends to raise or is intended to raise, the cost of those or other similar goods or services

Under the Act, The Central Consumer protection Council is the Apex body whose chairman is the Minister in charge of the Consumer Affairs in the Central Government. The objectives of the Central Council are:

- To promote and protect the rights of the consumers detailed in chapter 2 of this book
- To promote and protect the right to seek redress against unfair trade practices or restrictive trade practices or unscrupulous exploitation of consumers

Each state will have a State Consumer Protection Council chaired by the Minister in charge of consumer affairs in the State Government whose objective is to promote and protect the rights of consumers within the State laid down as above.

The most important matter as far as consumers are concerned is the setting up of "Consumer Disputes Redressal Agencies".

These are:

- **Consumer Disputes Redressal Forum** to be known as the "District Forum" (Forum) established by the State Government in each district of the State by the State by notification; provided that the State Government may, if it deems fit, establish more than one District Forum in a district.
- **Consumer Disputes Redressal Commission** to be known as the "State Commission" established by the State Government in the State by notification
- **National Consumer Disputes Redressal Commission** established by the Central Government by notification

The hierarchical structure of the three fora are given below:

National Consumer Disputes Redressal Commission ↓ State Consumer Disputes Redressal Commission ↓ District Consumer Disputes Redressal Forum

A few points on the constitution of the forum may be of interest:

District Forum: President, level of a District Judge, in service or retired; two other members, persons of ability, integrity and standing, one of whom shall be a woman. It has the same powers as are vested in a Civil Court.

A District Forum can issue an order directing the opposite party, in case the court finds the complaint to be genuine, to do one or more of the following actions:

- To remove the defect pointed out by the appropriate laboratory from the goods/services in question.

- To replace the goods/services with new goods/services of similar description which shall be free from any defect.
- To return to the complainant the price, or, as the case may be, the charges paid by the complainant.
- To pay such amount as may be awarded by it as compensation to the consumer for any loss or injury suffered by the consumer due to the negligence of the opposite party.
- To remove the defects or deficiencies in the services in question.
- To discontinue the unfair trade practice or the restrictive trade practice or not to repeat them.
- Not to offer hazardous goods/services for sale.
- To withdraw hazardous goods/services from being offered for sale.
- To provide for adequate costs to parties.

Any person aggrieved by an order made by the District Forum may prefer an appeal against such order to the State Commission within a period of thirty days from the date of the order, in such form and manner as may be prescribed.

The State Commission shall have the jurisdiction:

1. To entertain—
   (i) complaints where the value of the goods or services and compensation, if any, claimed exceeds rupees fifty lakhs but does not exceed rupees one crore, and
   (ii) appeals against the orders of any District Forum within the state.

2. To call for the records and pass appropriate orders in any consumer dispute which is pending before or has been decided by any District Forum within the State, where it appears to the State Commission that such District Forum has exercised a jurisdiction not vested in it by law, or has failed to exercise a jurisdiction so vested or has acted in exercise of its jurisdiction illegally or with material irregularity.

Any person aggrieved by an order made by the State Commission in exercise of its powers conferred may prefer an appeal against such order to the National Commission within a period of thirty days from the date of the order in such form and manner as may be prescribed. Provided that the National Commission may entertain an appeal after the expiry of the said period of thirty days if it is satisfied that there was sufficient cause for not filing it within that period.

Jurisdiction of the National Commission — subject to the other provisions of this Act, the National Commission shall have jurisdiction:

1. To entertain—
   (i) complaints where the value of the goods or services and compensation, if any, claimed exceeds rupees one crore, and
   (ii) appeals against the orders of any State Commission and

2. To call for the records and pass appropriate orders in any consumer dispute which is pending before or has been decided by any State Commission where it appears to the National Commission that such State Commission has exercised a jurisdiction not vested in it by law, or has failed to exercise a jurisdiction so vested, or has acted in the exercise of its jurisdiction illegally or with material irregularity.

Any person aggrieved by an order made by the National Commission in exercise of its powers conferred, may prefer an appeal against such orders to the Supreme Court within a period of thirty days from the date of the order. Provided that the Supreme Court may entertain an appeal after the expiry of the said period of thirty days if it is satisfied that there was sufficient cause for not filing it within that period.

Limitation period: The District Forum, the State Commission or the National Commission shall not admit a complaint unless it is filed within two years from the date on which the cause of action has taken. Not withstanding anything contained, a complaint may be entertained after the period specified, if the complainant satisfies the District Forum, the State Commission or the National Commission, as the case may be, that he/she had sufficient cause for not filing the complaint within such period. Provided that no such complaint shall be entertained unless the National Commission, State Commission, the District Forum, as the case may be, records its reasons for condoning such delay.

Enforcement of orders: Same manner as if it were a decree or order made by a court, such order may be passed on to the court within the local limits.

Dismissal of frivolous or vexatious complaints: Dismissal of such a complaint and make an order that the complainant shall pay to the opposite party such cost, not exceeding ten thousand rupees, as may be specified in the order.

The Bangalore Urban Consumer Forum has, in an unusual case, penalized a consumer for filing a fraudulent complaint and has directed him to pay up Rs. 5000 to the Karnataka State Small Industries Development Corporation. The complainant, Acharya ITI, had filed a complaint about an industrial site allotment against the Corporation. But, on examining the evidence, the Forum President and member H. S. Nalina and Muniyappa found that the complainant had by suppressing material facts in the case, had approached it for relief that he was not entitled to. They also noted in their order that the complainant had also tried to over-reach and get another site from the Corporation by suppressing material facts (Deccan Herald, Bangalore, 13 June 2000).

Penalties: Where a trader or a person against whom a complaint is made or the complainant fails or omits to comply with any order made by the court, the person shall be punishable with imprisonment for not less than one month but which may extend to three years or with fine of not less than two thousand rupees but which may be up to ten thousand rupees.

Important note: Consumer Protection Laws have been subjected to changes from time to time. That's why it's necessary to look at the latest edition of the act with all the amendments incorporated in it. For example, the various amounts stated above have changed over the years.

Changes

Since April 2004, consumers wishing to file a case in consumer forum (District Forum, State and national Commission) must pay the prescribed fee, as applicable under the rules. The Consumer Protection Rules, 1987, have now laid down a fee, by a crossed demand draft or postal order, as prescribed in the Table below:

Table 5.1

District Forum (w.e.f. 10-2-2005)	
Value of goods and compensation	*Amount payable*
Less than Rs. 1 lakh	Rs. 100
Rs. 1 lakh and above, but less than Rs. 5 lakhs	Rs. 200
Rs. 5 lakh and above, but less than Rs. 10 lakhs	Rs. 400
Rs. 10 lakhs and above	Rs. 500
State Commission (w.e.f. 10-2-2005)	
Value of goods and compensation	*Amount payable*
Rs. 20 lakhs and above, but less than Rs. 50 lakhs	Rs. 2000
Rs. 50 lakhs and above, but less than Rs. 1 crore	Rs. 4000
National Commission (w.e.f. 10-2-2005)	
Value of goods and compensation	*Amount payable*
Above Rs. 1 crore	Rs. 5000

When you file an appeal, the amount required to be deposited for making appeal against the order of:

1. District Forum to State Commission — 50 per cent of the decreed amount or Rs. 25,000 whichever is less.

2. State Commission to National Commission—50 per cent of the decreed amount or Rs. 35,000 whichever is less.
3. National Commission to supreme Court—50 per cent of the decreed amount or Rs. 50,000 which ever is less.

CONSUMER DISPUTES SETTLED

The following paragraphs give an idea of a few cases settled by the various consumer fora and other agencies. Most of them relate to cases settled in courts from the year 1999, though the actual filing of cases could have been much earlier. These have been taken up at random from the reports in newspapers and magazines. These are not complete or comprehensive but included for the purpose of illustration only. Cases are decided entirely based upon the evidence presented in the court. Each is unique and has to be treated as such. The cases presented in the following paragraphs are illustrative of the nature of the complaints that have been filed and the type of judgment on these by the various courts. The cases are grouped under various heads for easy reading and understanding.

Cars

1. Ford Motor Company, India Ltd., was ordered to redress the grievance of one Mr. R. Gopalnathan of Bangalore whose Ford Ikon car caught fire and destroyed the car as well as his luggage. The Karnataka State Consumer Redressal Commission (KSCRC) awarded the complainant: A new car as replacement, compensation of Rs. 2.5 lakhs for the luggage lost and Rs. 1 lakh for mental shock, hardship and punitive damage of Rs. 10,000 as compensation.

2. Maruti car catches fire while parked: The Commission ordered Maruti and its dealer to pay the customer a compensation of Rs. 15,000 and Rs. 5000 as cost of litigation.

3. Maruti Swift has posed a peculiar problem to consumers. It has provided a stepney that is of a different size from the rest of the tyres. So it's thinking of recalling this odd size stepney in view of complaints. (*2006*)

Education

The Karnataka State High Court ordered notice to be issued to the Rajiv Gandhi University of Health Sciences (RGUHS) and others on a public interest petition challenging the RGUHS's action in continuing affiliation to an Ayurvedic college at Dharwad, which was not affiliated to any other university.

Electricity

1. The Bangalore District Urban Consumer Forum (BDUCF) ordered the Karnataka State Electricity Board (KEB) [now known as Karnataka State Power Transmission Corporation Ltd. (KPTCL)] to refund Rs. 45,114 to a consumer and to pay him Rs. 2500 as compensation for making him suffer mental agony and inconvenience. The complainant had asked the KEB to replace his defective meter but they did not do so and continued to send inflated bills and also they disconnected his supply.

2. The National Human Rights Commission (NHRC) has directed the Uttar Pradesh Government to pay a compensation of Rs. 1,25,000 to an eight-year-old boy who lost his arms after receiving an electric shock from a transformer kept in a public place without adequate safeguards. The NHRC discounted the State Government's plea of contributory negligence of the boy saying, that the victim, by virtue of his tender age, was not expected to know the hazardous nature of the equipment installed nor to exercise due care and diligence while approaching such equipment.

3. The Karnataka State High Court sends a notice to KPTCL (formerly KEB) on a public interest petition challenging KPTCL's action in collecting three month's average bill amount as additional deposit from domestic consumers.

Farms, orchards and plantations

1. The complainants L. Manjula and C.V. Chaya had paid Rs. 27,000 and Respectively to Maxworth Orchards (India) Ltd., which had promised to develop and maintain orchards for them in a quarter acre of land each in the company's two projects. However, the company did not fulfill its agreement despite requests and even legal notices issued to it. The BDUCF ordered their amounts to be returned with interest and costs of Rs. 1000.

In another complaint filed by Leela, Maxworth Orchards (India) Ltd., had collected a payment of Rs. 1,26,001 from her and agreed to procure and acre of land. The firm was to develop and maintain a mango orchard for her, which would yield an annual income of Rs. 16,000 per acre, three years and nine months from the date of the investment. However, they never fulfilled their promise and gave various excuses for not doing so. The court ordered Maxworth Orchards (India) Ltd., to refund Rs. 1,26,001 with interest at 18 per cent and costs of Rs. 2500.

Finance

1. The BDUCF ordered a finance agency, Nandana Investment and Finance, Jayanagar, Bangalore, to pay up money for a Maruti van to a consumer Vimala Kumari who had won a Maruti van as a bumper prize under their benefit scheme in February 1994. The company had demanded 30 per cent of the value of the prize as commission. They also told her to pay the road tax, insurance etc. The Forum concluded from the available evidence, that the prizewinner is not required to pay money to the company as commission or to pay road tax, insurance etc. "The prize came with no strings attached," the Forum remarked.

2. The BDUCF ordered a finance company, The House of Maxworth, Chennai to pay back Rs. 4,95,000 to complainant C.S. Devarajan. The company had failed to make the payments due to him and the cheque they sent him was returned with the endorsement "account closed".

3. The BDUCF ordered another finance company, Asia Pacific Investment Trust (formerly Nagarjuna Investment Trust Ltd.), Hyderabad and the Asia Pacific Investment Trust office on Miller Road, Bangalore to refund Rs. 25,000 and Rs. 15,852 to two complainants.

4. The BDUCF found another finance company, Synergy Financial Exchange Ltd., Chennai and in Bangalore, Raheja Plaza, Commercial Street, guilty of deficient service and ordered it to refund (amount not stated) to two complainants.

5. The BDUCF directed the State Bank of Hyderabad on Victoria Road, Bangalore, to pay Rs. 2000 as compensation to a consumer for unjustifiably dishonouring a cheque issued by him.

6. The Karnataka State Commission for Consumer Grievances Redressal (KSCCGR) ordered an investment consultancy firm to pay up Rs. 1,13,120 to a consumer. The complainant Prajna Distributors was engaged in the purchase and sale of shares through Sagar Investment Consultancy Services in Udupi who were shareholders. The complainant told the court that shares of an aggregate face value of Rs. 2,30,233 purchased by the firm on his behalf were not delivered to him and he was forced to suffer a loss of Rs. 3,16,500. The Commission ordered the firm to pay the complainant Rs. 1,13,120 along with interest at the rate of 12 per cent per annum and Rs. 3000 as costs.

7. The KSCCGR found a city businessman and Sterling Tea and Industries Ltd., guilty of unfair trade practices and has ordered them to pay up sums ranging from Rs. 36,000 to Rs. 56,000 to four consumers. The four complainants Paul Raj J.V., Isiah Robert, Varalakshmi and

Sridhar T.N. had invested various amounts in Sterling Tea and Industries through Ashok Babu, Commercial Street, Bangalore. Instead of getting equity shares of Sterling Tea and Industries Ltd., they received by post undated letters from a certain Poonam Investments, a total stranger to them along with share certificates for 800, 500, 700 and 500 shares respectively. The broker Ashok Babu though he promised to get the money back failed to do so. Both Ashok and Sterling Tea Industries Ltd., did not appear before the District Forum, which ruled they were guilty of deficient service and ordered them to repay various sums of money due to the complainants. Then Ashok Babu appealed to the Commission, which upheld the order of the District Form.

8. The BDUCF ordered Prudential Capital Market Ltd., to return Rs. 10,000 each to complainants N. Hemalata, P. Jayalakshmi and N. Kailasanath along with the interest due on these. The company had not returned the fixed deposit after maturity despite requests for return of the deposit amount.

In another case the BDUCF ordered Synergy Financial Exchange Ltd., on Commissariat Road, Bangalore to return Rs. 16,780 with 19 per cent interest to one complainant, Rs. 16,788 to another, Rs. 10,000 to a third and Rs. 11,000 to the fourth complainant.

In another case, the BDUCF came to the rescue of Mr and Mrs Saty who had invested Rs. 3,26,000 with Shetty Leasing (India) Ltd., on Lavelle Road, Bangalore. The court ordered the firm to pay back security deposits with interest to the complainants, as they wanted the money to meet hospitalization expenses.

Another company, which treated the customers shabbily, was the Schematic Finance Ltd., which was ordered to repay its customers with interest.

9. Withdrawal of facility before "due date" deficiency in service. *(2006)*

10. Deficient service by Standard Chartered Bank—The National Commission ordered the bank to return Rs. 1,64,407 with compensation of Rs. 25,000. It held the bank guilty of deficient service in servicing the car loan cheques and also for threatening the consumer by sending emissaries to his house. *(2006)*

Health care

1. The Karnataka State Commission for Consumer Grievances Redressal Forum (KSCCGRF) has severely pulled up a homeopathy doctor, Dr. A.M. Mullah of Bijapur District whose medical treatment resulted in the blinding of a young boy Yaseen, ten years old. It directed the doctor to pay Rs. 2 lakhs as compensation to the boy.

2. The KSCCGRF has found the Sri Dharmasthala Manjunatheswara Education Society in Dakshina Kannada District and two of its doctors guilty of deficient in service and has ordered it to pay Rs. 1,03,200 as compensation along with Rs. 3000 as costs to a patient for causing him injury, agony and inconvenience. The complainant Ambalappa had gone to the Society's College of Dental Science Hospital in Sattur, Dharwad, for treatment of a dental problem. He was advised extraction of his right molar of the lower jaw. After extraction the patient was bleeding heavily in the mouth and Dr Rajashekar who was treating him, felt it was necessary to clean out the socket. The complainant told the Commission that the doctor, carelessly and negligently' put the syringe in the mouth without setting the needle properly. The needle got detached from the syringe and slipped into Ambalappa's throat. He immediately informed the doctor about this but the doctor did not do anything about it, he said.

At a later date, when persuaded by another doctor, Bhaskar Rao, Dr Rajashekar took the patient to an X-ray center where an X-ray revealed that the needle was stuck in his throat. He was then taken to a hospital attached to the X-ray centre where both the doctors tried their best to remove the needle but it slipped into his stomach. The patient then had to be taken to a Civil Hospital, Dharwad, where the needle was removed after surgery. He was forced to stay in the hospital for 25 days. After the operation, the patient could not eat properly, could not lift heavy objects and had suffered various disabilities. Dr Rajashekar claimed that the patient was not a consumer as the treatment at the hospital was free. But the State Commission found that though consultation and diagnosis were free, other items were charged for at the hospital. Hence the patient was a consumer who was entitled to complain to the court. Finding all four opposite parties guilty of deficient service, the Commission ordered them jointly to pay the compensation amount to Ambalappa.

3. "Doctors cannot be held guilty without medical evidence," stated the National Consumer Disputes Redressal Commission (NCDRC). It ruled that doctors cannot be held guilty of 'medical negligence' in treatment of patients in the absence of any 'medical evidence'. The NCDRC set aside a West Bengal State Consumer Disputes Redressal Commission's order asking two doctors of the Damodar Valley Corporation (DVC) to pay Rs. 2 lakhs each to the wife of a DVC engineer for allegedly giving her wrong treatment for her bronchial problem. The Commission observed that the complainant, Sanjukta Sengupta had failed to produce any expert medical opinion that the treatment given and the medicines prescribed by the doctors were wrong.

4. The Consumer Disputes Redressal Forum, Ernakulam, directed a private hospital in Kolencherry and one of its surgeons to pay a compensation of Rs. 2.23 lakhs within a month to the widow, children and mother of a man who allegedly died due to their 'negligence and carelessness'. It also asked them to pay the amount with 12 per cent rate of interest from May 3, 1997 the date of filing the complaint. The deceased C.M. Beeras, a driver with the Kerala State Road Transport Corporation, had met with an accident and suffered serious abdominal and liver injuries. The Forum held that there was negligence on the part of the surgeon in not conducting necessary investigations on the patient, in not performing the laparotomy operation for nearly six hours and failing to examine the liver injury. But for the negligence, the Forum observed the patient's life could have been saved.

5. Health insurance companies' argument to reject consumer claims on the grounds of a 'pre-existing disease' is thrown out of the window by the Delhi State Commission.

[**Note:** However, this may not happen all the time. Customer has to be open and honest about his/her medical problems if that person wants health insurance.] *(2006)*

6. Adopting a wrong procedure for treating a fractured hip joint of a bank employee proved costly for an orthopedic surgeon with the Karnataka State Consumer Disputes Redressal Commission directing him to pay Rs. 50,000 compensation to the patient. *(2006)*

7. The third additional Bangalore Urban District Consumer Disputes Redressal Forum has directed the Green View Hospital at Ejipura and its proprietor Dr. Balkis Ara to pay a compensation of Rs. 2 lakh to a woman who suffered due to a piece of sterile gauze that remained in her abdomen after a surgery. *(2006)*

8. The Karnataka State Consumer Disputes Redressal Commission has directed city-based Kidwai Memorial Institute of Oncology to pay a compensation of Rs. 1 lakh to a person who suffered due to the negligence of one of its doctors who had left forceps inside the abdomen after surgery. *(2006)*

9. The Commission directed Udaya Nursing Home, Chitradurga to pay Rs. 3 lakh compensation to a 7 year old girl, Deeksha, whose mother died as the hospital authorities tried to perform hysteroscopy without having ventilator facility, which was essential. *(2006)*

10. *Hospital pulled up:* The Commission has found the JSS Hospital, Mysore, and one of its doctors guilty of deficiency in service due to which a patient had to unnecessarily undergo operation four times for the removal of kidney stones. It directed the hospital to give a compensation of Rs. 1 lakh to the complainant, for negligence of the doctor who had conducted the first three operations. *(2006)*

11. The Delhi State Commission directs hospitals and nursing homes to furnish photocopies of entire record of treatment of the patient, admitted with them. Any violation of the direction would amount to deficiency in service. *(2007)*

12. The State Consumer Form has held Apollo Hospital guilty of deficiency in service as no clinical tests, including X-ray, were done before proceeding with surgery to fix the fractured right leg of the patient. The Commission asked the hospital to pay Rs. 50,000 compensation to the daughter of the patient who became invalid for life.

Housing/Real estate

1. The BSADCF ordered Brindanvanagara Socio-economic and Cultural Development Trust to repay Rs. 13,725 to complainant Padmavathamma who had paid this amount for a site, which she never got.

2. The BDUCF ordered a builder in Koramangala, Bangalore, to compensate a consumer by paying Rs. 1,11,950 and Rs. 5000 as costs and another Rs. 5000 as compensation. The complainant Nicholas had entrusted the builder the construction of his house in Sanjaynagar, Bangalore, which could not be completed and moreover the builder had demanded more than what was earlier agreed upon.

3. The Karnataka State Commission for Consumer Grievances Redressal has ordered the Bangalore Development Authority (BDA) to immediately grant relief to a consumer by removing the encroachments and obstructions around her house, which caused her inconvenience and harassment. It has also told the BDA to ensure that the complainant gets relief within four months failing which the BDA would have to pay her Rs. 50 as compensation per day till her complaint is redressed.

4. The Mumbai High Court ordered the Defence Ministry to release the emoluments to any army Colonel whose entire salary was deducted for recovery of house rent reimbursement claimed by the Colonel for four years.

5. The BDUCF has ordered Maxworth Home Ltd., at HAL II State, Bangalore, to compensate a consumer. The complainant, N. Maheshwaran,

had deposited Rs. 25,000 with the firm as registration fee for allotment of a house in its new township project. As per the terms and conditions, the amount was refundable if claimed within one year. In May 1997 he approached Maxworth Home for a refund with all the original and relevant documents. But the firm did not refund his money. The court ordered the firm to refund Rs. 30,000 to him with interest at 18 per cent per annum and costs of Rs. 1000.

6. The BDUCF ordered Vikas Enterprises in Block III, Jayanagar, Bangalore to refund Rs. 17,000 each to P.K. Parvathi and her daughter Beena. They had become members of this firm's scheme for allotment of sites near Chandrapura, on Hosur Road, in May 1997. Later they came to know that the layout was far off and not a good location and not suitable for residential purposes. However, Vikas Enterprises went back on their promise of refund. The court found the firm guilty of deficient service and ordered it to refund their amounts with interest of 12 per cent per annum and costs of Rs. 500.

7. In a landmark judgment, a consumer court in Mumbai has ordered a builder to pay compensation ranging from Rs. 50,000 to Rs. 3 lakhs to 288 flat-buyers who were deprived of shelter for eight years as they neither got possession of their tenements nor refund of the booking amount. Hearing 288 separate complaints filed by the Mumbai Grahak Panchayat, the Mumbai District Consumer Court also ordered on August 13, 1999, the Paranjape Construction Company to refund within two months principal amounts with 9 per cent interest per annum to flat owners of the proposed J.P. Nagar Housing Project in Suburban Virar, besides paying compensation of Rs. 5.45 crores. The builder has also been asked to pay costs of Rs. 200 each to complainant and Rs. 300 per consumer to the Panchayat.

8. The BDUCF has pulled up a housing society, Maxworth Homes Ltd., Bangalore, which has left several consumers in the lurch. It has asked the firm to pay Rs. 27,000 with 18 per cent interest per annum to D.K. Gundu Rao who had decided to withdraw from the housing scheme. Another consumer Shalla Seetharam too got relief when the Forum ordered Maxworth Homes Ltd., to pay back Rs. 30,000 with 15 per cent interest per annum. Another consumer Soumya was asked to be paid Rs. 30,000 with 18 per cent interest per annum with costs of Rs. 1000.

9. The BDUCF has come to the help of two consumers who were shabbily treated by a firm, which offered sites to consumers. M. Kausalya and S. Ganesan had paid Rs. 21,000 and Rs. 17,500 to Shivapriya Farms and Resorts in Kodia Arcade, Infantry Road, Bangalore. They had joined a scheme sponsored by this form for allotment of sites at Bidadi. But the firm failed to allot these and instead offered to give them sites near Nelamangala for a higher price. The two complainants refused to accept this offer and complained to the court, which found Shivapriya Farms and Resorts guilty of deficient service. It ordered the firm repay money due to both the complainants.

10. *Real estate:* Investing in property, and seeing the investment result in profits many times more than the money invested ranks high on every investor's wish list. Consumers are pre-sold apartments even when construction has not even started. What is missing from the scene is a regulator that will keep frauds under check, and give consumers some basic assurances of safety of investment and timely delivery.

Precautions while purchasing land: Purchasing a property/land requires utmost care. For details contact website: http://www.mpb.co.in/images/precautions.pdf

11. A Consumer Court in Delhi has directed a builder to pay Rs. 7 lakhs as refund and compensation to a consumer who was not handed possession of a flat in time in West Delhi's Palam area. The State Consumer Commission held the builder guilty of deficiency in service for over-shooting the completion deadline by six months and refusing to refund the consumer's money paid in instalment by the consumer.

Insurance

1. The BDUCF has told the National Insurance Company to pay up Rs. 91,639 as compensation to complainant Yashoda Subash who had insured her lorry with the firm for third party, for property damage and theft during the period. The lorry was stolen when it was parked in front of her house. It ordered the company to pay interest at 12 per cent per annum from March 11, 1993 till the date of payment and costs of Rs. 1000 to her.

2. The BDUCF ordered the Life Insurance Corporation of India (LIC), Civil Station, Bangalore, to pay up Rs. 5000 to a consumer for causing her mental agony and loss. The complainant Madhavi K. Amin had applied to the LIC for a Jeevan Shree Policy for Rs. 5 lakhs, which had a maturity period of 15 years. She paid up Rs. 26,121 the first yearly instalment. But the LIC issued an endowment policy to her for Rs. 1,50,000 with a maturity period of 15 years without her consent. The court ordered the LIC to refund her Rs. 26,121 along with Rs. 3000 as cost.

3. The KSCCGR ordered the Life Insurance Company of India (LIC) to pay money due to a consumer for two insurance policies of Rs. 50,000. The complainant is the widow of Nagi Reddy who had taken out two insurance policies for Rs. 50,000 each with the LIC, Raichur Office. Nagi Reddy's wife was the nominee. When Nagi Reddy died due to a heart attack, the LIC refused to pay the sum covered under the two policies claiming that Reddy had got the policies revived under a false declaration. Nagi Reddy's wife complained to the District Forum, Bellary, which had over-ruled the LIC's argument and ordered them to pay up the money due to her under the two policies. The Senior Divisional Manager, LIC, at Bellary appealed to the State Commission which upheld the order of the District Form and found no reason to intervene.

4. Insurance firm to pay Rs. 4 lakhs to relatives of mishap victim as compensation in New Delhi. *(2006)*

Products

1. The BSADCF ordered Jaipur Corporation, a shop in Jayanagar, to pay back Rs. 475 to complainant P.V. Prasanna who had bought a net from the shop, which turned out to have defective weaving.

2. The BDUCF compensated a consumer Dr. B.L. Bhandari, who got a defective computer from Rockwell Systems Pvt. Ltd., R.T. Nagar, Bangalore. Finding the company guilty of deficient service, the Forum ordered the company to repay Rs. 62,400 with interest at 18 per cent per annum to the complainant along with costs of Rs. 2000.

3. The BDUCF ordered the Standard Chartered Bank, Mumbai and the Managing Director of PAL Peugeot Ltd., to jointly refund the booking amount of Rs. 27,700 with Rs. 1000 as costs to complainant A. Sridharan. He had paid the amount but the company neither delivered the car nor refunded his money.

4. The BDUCF has pulled up a firm for deficient service and ordered it to take back defective door-frames supplied to a consumer. Complainant Y.M. Anandavardhan had ordered ten door-frames and 100 door-shutters from Benwood in Yeshwantpur and paid Rs. 15,000 in advance. The shop supplied nine door-frames, which did not conform to measurements of the order, and three were defective. So he cancelled the order and asked the shop to refund his money. Benwood refused to refund but asked the consumer to take back goods worth that amount. But he refused to do so as he did not want any material from that shop. The court found Benwood guilty of deficient service and instructed the shop to refund Rs. 10,591 to the consumer and take back defective goods.

5. The Supreme Court has imposed a penalty on auto major Hindustan Motors Ltd. (HML) for selling a defective car. A division bench comprising Justice S. Saghir Ahmad, Justice B.P. Wadhwa upholding the Madras State

Consumer Disputes Redressal Commission's judgment, directed the maker of 'Ambassador Nova' to return to the buyer Rs. 1,17,200 the price of the car, and pay 12 per cent penal interest from the date the complaint was filed before the forum. The court also ordered the company to pay Rs. 50,000 as compensation for mental agony suffered by the buyer along with a litigation cost of Rs. 3000.

6. The BSADUCF gave compensation to a consumer R. Venkateswara who had bought a black carved sofa set for Rs. 7000 from Sajawat Furniture in R.T. Nagar, Bangalore. The consumer was annoyed and embarrassed by termite boring into his new sofa set within three months of purchase. The proprietor, instead of taking back the sofa set or refunding the money, threatened the consumer with police action. The court found the shop guilty of deficient service and told the proprietor to replace the sofa set with a new one free of cost or refund Rs. 7000 within four weeks of receiving the order.

Guard your furniture

7. The Monopolies & Restrictive Trade Practices Commission (MRTPC) has restrained BPL from advertising its LPG stove cooked much faster than others on the ground that it was a 'false claim'. The advertisement, which had appeared in various newspapers, claimed BPL's gas stove appliances manufactured in a technical tie-up with Sanyo, Japan, cooked 40 per cent faster than other brands.

8. Foreign particles found in sealed bottle. Coca Cola disowns responsibility. *(2006)*

9. Cadbury recall in UK: Cadbury has recalled seven of its flagship products in the UK because of a salmonella scare. Will the company ever do the same in India if a similar situation arose? *(2006)*

10. The Karnataka State Consumer Disputes Redressal Commission has found Pune-based M/S Frito-Lay India, the company manufacturing Lays branded potato chips, guilty of 'unfair trade practices' as the weight of the contents of chips packets found to be less than the weight claimed on the sealed packets. The complainant claimed that the packet weighed about 15 grams each instead of 60 grams printed on the sealed packets. The Udupi District Consumer Redressal forum had directed the company to pay Rs. 500 to the complainant as compensation. However, the State Commission enhanced the compensation to Rs. 50,000 observing that it would send a message to all those indulging in such unfair trade practices. *(2006)*

11. *MRP on packaged products*: Hotels and restaurants, not even 5 or 7 star, can charge more than the maximum retail price (MRP) for products like packaged mineral water. This is a clear message that the Delhi State Commission has given to business and entertainment establishments that charge an exorbitant price for products that very clearly have the MRP printed on them. *(2006)*

12. *Advertising aimed at children to be regulated*: **Ofcom** — the independent regulator and competition authority for the UK communication industries has put forward rules that will apply to programming that appeals to children under the age of 16 at any time of day or night on any channel. *(2006)*

13. A bread worth Rs. 10, which did not carry its date of manufacture, has cost its producer Rs. 15,000, Rs. 5000 as compensation and Rs. 10,000 as fine to the Government by South Delhi District Consumer Forum. *(2006)*

Railways

1. The BDUCF ordered the Chief Commercial Manager of Southern Railway, Bangalore and the Western Railway, Mumbai, to pay up Rs. 32,035 to a passenger whose baggage was stolen during a train journey from Mumbai to Bangalore. Though the complainant, Subhasani Katkar went as soon as she noticed the loss of her luggage to the Railway protection Force (RPF) personnel who were travelling on the train, they did not help her but went back to sleep. The court rejected the contention of the railways that the court had no jurisdiction and that the passenger herself was responsible for her luggage. The court held the railways responsible for the loss of luggage. It ordered the railways to pay Rs. 500 as costs.

2. The BDUCF ordered the Bangalore Railways Authorities to pay Rs. 1 lakh compensation to a passenger Prakash Vittalrao Patil Who lost part of his thumb while trying to close a window in his coach while he was traveling from Belgaum to Bangalore by the Rani Chennamma Express on June 1, 1997. When he tried to close the glass window near him the shutter slammed down hard on his left thumb and chopped off his thumb phalanx. He bled profusely and also suffered shock and trauma. He had incurred medical expenses of Rs. 3000. The claims by the railways that the Forum had no jurisdiction and the complainant was negligent were rejected by the Forum, which awarded a compensation of Rs. 1 lakh to the passenger.

3. Delhi Consumer Disputes Redressal Forum VI directed the Indian Railways to pay Rs. 1000 as compensation as well as litigation cost of Rs. 500 to a traveler for its failure to clean up a coach having a lot of cockroaches. The complainant Maj. Pankaj Awasthi who traveled from Nagpur to Hazart Nizamuddin, New Delhi by air-conditioned sleeper class on January 8, 1997 alleged that there were innumerable cockroaches in their coach as a result of which they could not sleep. He lodged a complaint with a TTE and also wrote down the complaint in the prescribed book. However, despite the written complaint and numerous oral protests, no remedial action was taken. The railways initially took objection to the complaint and stated that the court had no jurisdiction over the matter. Later on it claimed that the conductor took action to spray the coach at Bhopal. The court did not accept the railway's contentions and awarded a compensation of Rs. 1000 and costs of Rs. 500.

4. The BDUCF has ordered Southern Railway to pay Rs. 5000 as compensation to two consumers who were put to great inconvenience and harassment on a journey. Vinod Jain and his sister Leela Devi had bought tickets on July 30, 1993 for a journey from Bangalore to Sojat Road via Ahmedabad. They boarded the Ahmedabad Express at Ahmedabad and occupied berths number 46 and 47 in coach S 3. But another passenger came there and asked them to vacate those berths claiming they had been allotted to them. The TTE came there and asked them to check up and verify on the notice board. They were shocked to discover that their confirmed reservation had been cancelled and only one berth given to them in some other coach. Jain and his sister were put to great hardship and inconvenience. The court awarded a compensation of Rs. 5000 with Rs. 500 as costs.

5. When Railways fails to confirm booking: Railways to pay Rs. 10,000 and refund the difference in fare between I class and AC. *(2006)*

6. Deficiency in service by railways: Poor maintenance. The railways to pay Rs. 3000 as compensation with Rs. 1000 as costs. (*2006*)

7. The Commission has held that a poor AC functioning in an AC compartment of the railways amounts to deficiency in service and a consumer can seek redress. (*2006*)

8. The State Consumer Forum has directed the Northern Railway to pay Rs. 10,000 as compensation to a passenger who was forced to travel by 3-tier sleeper while he had ticket by 2 tier AC. The Commission ordered Northern Railway to refund the fare with 18 per cent interest per annum (*2006*) apart from the above compensation.

Services/Repair

1. The BSADCF ordered Sri Vinayaka Electronics, Gandhinagar to pay a compensation of Rs. 1000 to complainant Venkatesh who had given his camera for repair but it was returned without the flash. The court also told the shop to repair and return the camera with flash.

2. The BSADCF ordered Konica Shop, Miller Road to pay Rs. 2500 to a complainant B.S. Shetty as it lost a film, which contained invaluable snapshots of his family.

3. The BDUCF censured Kanishka Gas Agency, Hindustan Petroleum Corporation and National Insurance Company Ltd., for gross negligence, callousness and deficient service towards two consumers who sustained severe burns in a gas leakage accident. It has ordered all the three parties to pay Rs. 20,000 as compensation for 'mental shock, injury, agony, suffering and physical discomfort.' Besides the compensation the Forum ordered the three agencies to pay up the medical expenses of the complainants totaling Rs. 9058 with 15 per cent interest per annum from July 1, 1992 and costs of Rs. 3000 within one month of receiving the order.

4. The BDUCF ordered a shop in Hanumathnagar, Bangalore to compensate (amount not specified) for deficient service. The complainant B.N. Narayan Rao had given his film roll for developing and printing to Satellite Town in Hanumanthnagar. But the roll was not returned as it was damaged during printing. The proprietor had offered to replace it with a free new roll, which Rao refused.

5. The KSCCGR ordered a Supreme Court advocate to pay up Rs. 10,000 as compensation to a client for deficient service. The complainant Sathyanarayana had engaged the services of a Supreme Court advocate Padmanabha Mahale for filing a special leave petition before the Supreme Court. However, Mahale did not give him a copy of the petition and other relevant documents in time and caused him great inconvenience. The court found Mahale guilty of deficient service and ordered hi to pay up the money with Rs. 1000 as costs.

6. The BDUCF ordered a Courier Service, Professional Couriers, Cassia Complex, Hosur Road, Bangalore, to pay Rs. 18,670 to a consumer, Neptune Travels, for failing to deliver four airlines tickets to their customers with consequent loss to Neptune Travels. It also ordered costs of Rs. 200 to be paid to the complainant.

7. The BDUCF ordered BWSSB to refund the excess water charges collected from the complainant B. Basvana Gowda.

Telephone

1. The BDUCF ordered the Bangalore Telecom Department to pay Rs. 1600 to a consumer within four weeks of its order for disconnecting his telephone without prior notice, causing him inconvenience.

2. The BDUCF has ordered Bangalore Telephones to restore the telephone connection of a consumer within 15 days of receiving its order, failing which it would have to pay Rs. 50 per day as compensation to the complainant till the connection was restored. Dr. C. Shivaramiah had complained that he was charged for ISD calls he had not made for which his telephone connection was disconnected. The Forum directed the Bangalore Telephones to refer the dispute for arbitration under section 7(b) of the Indian Telegraph Act and to decide the dispute within four months.

3. The BDUCF decided in favour of a consumer in a case involving Bangalore Telephones and complainant J.P. Singh who had filed a case urging the court to direct Bangalore Telephones to revise his telephone bills and refund the excess amount of Rs. 4080 and pay him compensation for having arbitrarily collected Rs. 70 as STD charges. The court found Bangalore Telephones guilty of deficient service and ordered it to refer the dispute relating to two inflated bills for arbitration. The court told Bangalore Telephones to decide the dispute within four months failing which it should refund Rs. 3080 to the complainant along with Rs. 70 collected as surcharge and costs of Rs. 200.

4. The BDUCF ordered JTM Mobile Phone Ltd., (renamed Airtel) to refund Rs. 7758 with costs of Rs. 1000 to complainant A. P. Jain who had a problem of getting calls but despite complaints the firm collected charges from him.

5. The Karnataka State Consumer Disputes Redressal Commission (KSCDR) has asked Spice Communications to give compensation for wrongly giving the mobile number of a subscriber as customer service number. Paul G. Brahmakulam had to pay Rs. 31,500 as the incoming calls were charged. It directed the service provider to pay a compensation of Rs. 40,000 within two months. *(2007)*

Tours, Transport and Travels

1. The Bangalore Second Additional District Consumer Forum (BSADCF) ordered Venkataramana Travels to pay up Rs. 1000 as compensation to a tourist S.R. Mohanty who endured discomfort and agony during a bus journey from Vijayawada to Bangalore.

2. The BDUCF ordered the KSRTC to pay compensation to a consumer for causing him inconvenience and injury. Complainant C.N.A. Gupta had hired a KSRTC bus by paying and advance of Rs. 9650 for taking a marriage party from Bangalore to Pondicherry on May 1, 1997. But the bus broke down and the complainant had to make alternate arrangements. The court concluded that the bus was not maintained properly. It ordered the Depot. manager and the General Manager (Traffic) of KSRTC to pay Rs. 2000 as compensation to Gupta along with Rs. 300 as costs.

3. The BDUCF ordered Excelsior Travels on Hare Krishna Road, Bangalore, to pay up Rs. 9758 to a consumer and it has found it guilty of deficient service. Though the complainant had a confirmed ticket by Sahara India Airlines, the flight did not operate that day from Bangalore to Delhi.

4. The BDUCF found the Kuwait Airways and its agent Travel Tours on J.C. Road, Bangalore, guilty of deficient service and ordered them to pay Rs. 26,000 as compensation to a consumer. The complainant Van den Berghe Jan had bought a ticket for Rs. 26,500 for travelling from Mumbai to Amsterdam via Kuwait and back by Kuwait Airways on March 4, 1997 from Travel Tours. When he went to board the flight he was told that his flight was not confirmed. For the next two days he was denied a seat and so finally he had to buy a fresh ticket costing Rs. 40,000 for travel by another airlines. When he returned the unused ticket for refund, Kuwait Airways refused and asked the consumer to get the refund from its agent who too refused. When he served a legal notice, Travel Tours returned the money but kept Rs. 830 as tax deduction. The court found both Kuwait Airways and Travel Tours guilty of causing the consumer inconvenience and financial loss. It ordered them jointly to pay him Rs. 26,000.

5. The BDUCF pulled up a city travel firm and Hotel Goa International in Panaji, Goa, for deficient service and has found them guilty of unfair trade practices. B. P. Chatterjee, a resident of Sanjaynagar,

Bangalore, had approached Sangam Travels on Tank Bund Road, Bangalore, for a four-day package tour to Goa. This package included travel fare from Bangalore to Panaji and back, in an air-conditioned luxury bus, as well as three days and two nights deluxe accommodation at Hotel Goa International. The tour also included sightseeing for a total of Rs. 1650 head. On arrival in Panaji they were given ordinary rooms without AC. On returning to Bangalore the consumer asked Sangam Travels for refund of Rs. 250 collected as excess. But the firm neither refunded the money nor did it respond to the letter. The court ordered Hotel Goa International and Sangam Travels to refund Rs. 1250 to the complainant with interest at 15 per cent per annum from September 1996 till the date of payment with damages of Rs. 1000 and costs of Rs. 1000.

6. The Department of Legal Metrology, Government of Karnataka, conducted a special drive from July 21 to 23, 1999 to check the accuracy of auto-rickshaw meters in Bangalore City. 3500 auto-meters were inspected and 423 cases were booked with Rs. 98,725 fine collected. Drives were also conducted in Belgaum, Gulbarga, Hubli, Mysore and Tumkur where 4296 meters were inspected and Rs. 45,000 fine amount collected in 342 cases.

7. The Karnataka State Commission for Consumer Grievances Redressal has found the Indian Airlines, Bangalore, to be guilty of deficient service and has directed it to pay Rs. 12,000 as compensation to a passenger whose luggage was tampered with.

8. Cox & Kings asked to compensate a couple that did not get the agreed number of days of cruise. The National Commission ordered the company to pay a compensation of Rs. 50,000 and ordered the misleading advertisement to be withdrawn. *(2006)*

9. Jet Airways prevents a bonafide ticket-holder from travelling to accommodate film actors. National Commission provides relief to aggrieved consumer by way of compensation of Rs. 15,000 with 12 per cent interest from the date of the complaint in addition to the ticket fare and cost of Rs. 5000. *(2006)*

Summing up

The examples given above are a few consumer complaints that have been settled from time in various consumer fora. A few conclusion s that could be drawn from the consumer redress cases are:

- In general, the consumer courts are consumer-friendly which means the cases are settled in favour of aggrieved consumers provided these are genuine.

- The complainants do get relief by way of return of money/exchange of goods/services.
- Compensation amounts are modest.
- Costs incurred in litigation are not much and mostly recovered from the opposite party.
- Heavy deterrent fines are not levied.
- It is rarely that the courts sentence the opposite parties to jail terms.
- Rarely the courts order all defective goods/services to be removed from the sales outlets.
- It takes two to three years after filing cases that redress is obtained. However, in a few cases these are settled within months.

Backlog of cases

The government is aware from time to the large number of pending cases as these amount to 'justice delayed, is justice denied'. On a few occasions the presidents of State Consumers Commissions and District Fora meet to review the pending cases and action plan to reduce these are discussed. The National Commission gets into the act and plans to monitor the cases through better overall administrative controls. With interlinking of these consumer courts through the Internet it should be possible to monitor the progress faster. The government is urging the consumer courts time and again to speed up their disposal rate of cases. Infrastructural bottlenecks too are cited for the heavy backlog of cases—not sufficient courts especially in urban areas, space for courts, adequacy of number of judges and finance. In general adjournments are not too many like in civil and criminal cases and lawyers are not required to argue cases, with exception, if the case is legally complicated. The Centre as well as State governments grant amounts to the courts to operate efficiently. However, the funds would have to be utilized better to deliver verdicts faster. Salaries and honoraria to members of consumer fora are revised from time to time. What is needed is, "Quality judgments and speedy disposal of cases will make a mark in making consumer courts meaningful to consumers," observed Justice M.N. Venkatachaliah. Another judge, Justice V. Balakrishna Eradi, observed "Constant monitoring and avoidance of unnecessary adjournments of cases will make the consumer courts more popular."

Actions taken to reduce pending cases in Consumer Courts:

- Computerization.
- Computer networking with other consumer fora.

- Increase in the number of posts in the National Commission from five to nine to facilitate the constitution of more benches.
- More funds from centre to the states to set up more commissions.
- National Commission to set up 11 circuit benches at notified places outside Delhi.
- There are 35 state commissions and 607 district fora in the country.

The Consumer Protection Act, 1986, was the first step in independent India to address consumer complaints specifically. It was to ensure that consumers were not foisted with substandard goods and services as well as restrictive and unfair trade practices. To achieve these objectives, a three-tier quasi-judicial machinery was set up at District, State and National level for inexpensive, simple and speedy redress of consumer complaints. The government, by various amendments have sought to make the consumer protection Act in tune with the times – enlarge the scope of 'unsafe' goods, more trade practices to come under the scanner as unfair, award of higher punitive damages as deterrent, enforcement of a rule for 'corrective advertisement', and empowering consumer courts to pass interim order to take care of miscarriage of justice.

The government is aware of the fact that there are too many backlog cases due to various reasons. It wants to strengthen consumer redress courts and also set up alternate means to dispose off cases faster trying to clear the backlog of cases. *Lok Adalat* type of *melas* could help clear backlogs without compromising on the quality of redress.

Tips for filing consumer case

- Send one copy original (preferably typed) complaint along with two copies and other copies of all relevant documents to your nearest District Forum that has jurisdiction over your complaint.
- Do not send original bills, letters etc. till called for by the court. Pay the relevant fee by DD or postal order as specified (see above). You can type the complaint on ordinary paper, letterhead etc. and not on stamped paper, unless it's an affidavit or as required by the court. Send the documents by registered post or courier. You should get an acknowledgement from the court as proof of receipt.
- You may or may not inform the 'opposite party' that you are taking the complaint with the consumer forum. Sometimes if you inform the party the settlement of complaint, out of court, is quicker
- Remind the Forum if no acknowledgement is received within a week of sending the complaint by registered post/courier service.

Take up with the Forum after about a month to find out, if possible, when your case would come up. This may not be easy given the large number of pending complaints with any Forum.

- Meanwhile if the 'opposite party' approaches you for a compromise, be ready to discuss and settle out of court to your reasonable satisfaction. This is quicker than through the Forum.
- Attend the court on the date and time given. Do not ask for an adjournment unless really needed. The more adjournments mean your case goes on getting postponed.
- However, if the Forum decides to have an adjournment so that all the parties have sufficient time to prepare, do not grumble. Accept it with grace.
- You do not need the service of a lawyer or an expert, unless the matter is complex
- Be prepared to present the case yourself with all relevant facts and details
- If due to some valid reason, you cannot attend to the court, you may depute a person with all details. Provide that person your authorization in writing.
- Be honest and open. Do not exaggerate the claim. Be polite and humble. Do not lose your temper, however, provocative the situation could be. Be respectful while addressing the judge or the members of the Forum
- Accept the verdict of the Forum with grace and humility. You can always appeal to the State Forum or National forum, if your case is strong and you are convinced about it. Note that there are a few cases where the verdict is delivered against the complainant, as that's the considered judgment of the honourable court.
- Remember to preserve all documents even after the case is closed. The 'opposite party' or yourself could go on appeal.

Making the best out of Consumer Protection Law

We have gained some experience while working with the Act when it was formulated in 1986, with amendments from time to time. There is no place for any frivolous complaints or bogus complaint or something to defame and put someone into trouble. Without any doubt, such misuse goes against the letter and spirit of the Act. There is scope for improvement of the Act, which would come after study and gaining experience. It should cover more and more services as our nation too is going 'service oriented'. It would be nice if government and semi-government services too come under the ambit of the Act to make these more consumer-friendly and responsive. The punitive damage, in terms of jail/fines, should be enhanced, especially where goods/services result in serious accidents or fatalities. Fly-by-night operators and those selling dangerous drugs/equipments should be penalized heavily to safeguard the citizens against such activities of a few black sheep.

A need has come where information with one Forum should be shared with others within the State as well as outside, depending on the individual case and the seriousness of the issue that could have a national ramification. Periodical newsletters/website of the Forum, district, state and the national, could be helpful for the citizens. The Forum should incorporate the concept of product liability, where applicable and award compensation or punitive damage accordingly. It should encourage responsible sellers of products/services to be open and honest about any shortcoming that could cause a potential problem with the consumer. Early warning about any deficiency in goods or services could help consumers to guard themselves against any future problem.

The Consumer Protection Act should be dynamic and a useful link between the government/seller/consumer for better relations and ushering in a consumer friendly society. The Act should be treated as a tool for improvement in quality of goods and services. By making products/services of international quality we would gain new export markets and at the same time our consumers too would be benefited. The role of the consumer activists/NGOs should increase in the new regime of consumerism. It seems some consumer organizations have started enrolling members so that the consumer movement could be strengthened in the country. They are bringing out magazines that are helpful to consumers on various matter of interest.

We need a fruitful partnership between the government, business and consumers for the common good. Governmental help and commitment is needed in making the consumer movement meaningful. Unlike in the advanced countries where the government does not interfere directly in the market, unless absolutely necessary, the market in a developing country like ours, should be regulated, to some extent al least. That would give the market a proper direction for consumerism so that resources are not frittered away under the guise of a 'free market economy'. The government as well as the business is morally bound to uphold the rights of consumers. On the part of consumers, they should act responsibly so as to patronize products that are eco-friendly and energy efficient, use products / services as long as possible to conserve resources and encourage recycling as far as possible.

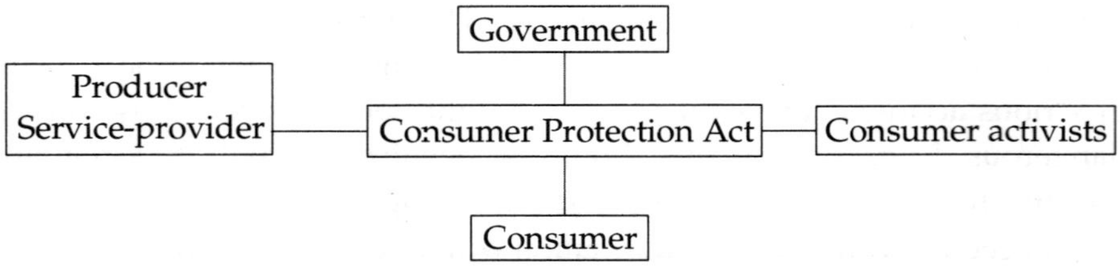

Consumer education is another aspect of the Act that needs to be addressed to. More consumers, especially the weaker sections of the society and the rural masses, should derive benefits from the consumer Act. Periodical newsletters on the complaint settled as well as quality aspects of goods/services would be welcome to increase consumer awareness in our country.

Consumer Protection Act is not a panacea for the ills of poor quality and service. It is a tool to make the sellers and service-providers 'behave' and become consumer-friendly. We have miles to go make the consumer King in our country. There is mindset with the sellers and service-providers that their job is over when they sell the goods or services. The culture of service is missing to a large extent. Hopefully, with more foreign brands and outlets coming in this would change for the better. There is a big market for quality goods and services. Take the example of the mobile phones whose use has become almost universal in our country, be it urban or rural. Liberalization and globalization are welcome news as the harassed Indian consumer could hope to have world-class goods and services right in our country without leaving our shores. With the coming years we should expect a better clout of the consumers who will have multi-choice market place. Government too is expected to play a proactive role in making consumer movement a success as we are entering a world where the national boundaries are crumbling, at least as far as trade and commerce are concerned. It is also the time for consumer organizations and activists to accept the fact world is changing and they have their role cut out in a multi-choice environment for goods and services.

CHAPTER 6

THE ROLE OF CONSUMERS

Knowledge is power
—Francis Bacon

Customer Satisfaction Index (CSI), is a term used by the producer to estimate how happy and satisfied a consumer is with the product or service he/she has purchased in comparison with the other products/services of comparative value and features in the market. The aim of such a study would be to find the factors that make a consumer happy and loyal to the brand he/she is satisfied with. Such a study of 'brand loyalty' is an important business strategy. The objective is to create a 'benchmark' to assess that elusive factor that gives a consumer satisfaction over a period of time. It is standard against one's products/services could be compared with, whether these are domestic or foreign brands. Consumer feedback, oral or written or through surveys is an attempt to get consumers reactions to products/services so that actions could be undertaken for improvements in existing or future items. Thus, consumer feedback, via consumer satisfaction index or any other, is a valuable tool in quality improvement.

'Brand Asset Evaluator' is another term which is a measure of the health of the product/service, its strengths and weaknesses. Brand reputation is the perception of overall quality associated with the name. For example, we associate excellent/luxury quality when we speak of Mercedes Benz cars. Rolls Royce is another brand that has a very high reputation of quality and excellence. Such attributes do not come easily for any brand. Take our own example of Tatas who have established their name in various fields. Infosys is another brand name that is heard everywhere, thanks to the phenomenal success it has achieved in the IT field all over the globe. Such a high reputation associated with a brand helps to sell products/services though higher priced. A brand of a company means that a consumer expects that whatever that company makes has the same excellence associated with the brand. It is thus a selling point – you sell a brand not necessarily a product, that's the advantage of a high brand reputation. Some brands develop stature on the basis of their strengths. If a brand is relevant to consumers, the response is esteem.

In buying a product/service, consumers move through four stages:

- Awareness
- Interest
- Desire
- Action

A consumer develops an attachment driven by faith in a particular brand he/she has been satisfied over the years. Even when he/she wants to go in for another product, the first thing the consumer does is to check whether his favourite brand sells that product/service. If the answer is no, he/she shops for some other brand. That's known as brand loyalty developed over continuous use and satisfaction. A brand loyalty could easily lead to 'esteem value' for that company's brand image. In other words, a customer feels pride in possessing a brand that enhances the esteem value. Hence, the consumer is interested to know more about a product/service that reveals its 'soul'.

Sometime back a beauty product known as Pond's Dream-flower talc powder captured the imagination of the fashion conscious and it could outsell other brands on the sheer momentum gained by the product's widespread acceptance. Buoyed up by such a resounding success, the company tried to cash in on the goodwill by venturing into the toothpaste segment. Alas, there were no takers for its brand of toothpaste. It couldn't breach the formidable brand leader Colgate Palmolive, which had successfully nurtured its image of a good toothpaste despite stiff competition from other brands.

MARKET SURVEY

Producers would like to measure consumer satisfaction of their products through well-designed scientific market research employing competent persons. This is especially important when a company is about to introduce a new product. Understanding the 'needs' of the market (people) is the first step towards planning for a new product/service. However, there are others who 'create' a need for products—instant coffee, instant ready mix food / snack items, disposable syringe, brush-less shaving, disposable shaving blade, electric shavers, portable stereos (*Walkman*), compact disc (CD), DVD, mobile phone and so on.

Despite market research sometimes a product launched with fanfare falls flat due to lukewarm response from the consumers. Take the case of the multinational Coca Cola which invested millions of dollars in bringing out a new soft drink, the 'improved' fizz drink which showed great promise in test marketing some years ago. However, the market reaction to the new 'improved' drink was a disaster as far as the company was concerned. Loyal consumers had no place for the 'new' fangled drink, as they preferred to consume their good old *Coke* brand. In no time the 'new' drink had to be withdrawn from the market, with a loss of face to the company, at least temporarily. What went wrong? It was a case of hasty introduction of a new brand that had no additional features or merit in it as also the poorly conducted test market that had raised false hopes of good sale. It was clear the feedback on the new drink from its test consumers was not realistic, which had misled the company.

A few multinationals that thought India was a good market had to beat a hasty retreat, after suffering loss and face, had to wind up shop sooner than expected. One had to understand the culture of the local people as people differ from one region/one country to another. Hence what was good in one place might not work elsewhere unless local features are incorporated innovatively. One has to study consumers' preferences carefully before jumping into conclusions. Take for example, the ubiquitous pizza that is so popular in western countries. Except in a few big cities and towns, the pizza 'culture' has yet to seep into our society. After all, we have our own snack/food items which we are so used to for generations. Consumer preferences are fickle; you like something today but reject it tomorrow. Hence to manage in such a changing situation is difficult and it takes all the skills of a good management to woo and retain customers. We have to understand and appreciate the fact that Indian consumers have to be treated, as a separate entity with their own likes and dislikes.

The management guru Tom Peters has put it succinctly: "Customers perceive services in their own unique, idiosyncratic, emotional, irrational, end of the day and totally human terms. Perception is all there is!" That makes any market leader's work so challenging.

'Old is gold,' sometimes is not true. Take the example of one of the longest running car models, which the German company Volkswagen had built, the *Beetle*. For years, this cute car was the rage of many satisfied customers. The company buoyed up by such brand loyalty of customers never thought of improving this model or bringing newer models to keep pace with the trend in the market. Meanwhile, the other car manufacturers went ahead, brought newer designs, marketed aggressively and talked about safety, mileage, features and so on that attracted customers in large numbers. In course of time, the *Beetle* sale plummeted and it had to be withdrawn ultimately, as the market had no more use for this tiny car. Our own Hindustan Motor Company that is producing their brand Ambassador had to fall in line and come out with newer models, but other car manufacturers have surged ahead as they went on introducing newer and better cars. Hindustan Motor's near monopoly in the car segment is a thing of the past. More car manufacturers believe that to have a tie-up with foreign companies is a sure recipe for customer satisfaction. This is true as automobile sector is technology driven. The success of Maruti that entered into collaboration with the Japanese giant Suzuki Motors is a case in point. Even today Maruti has a big share of the car market, thanks to its numerous state-of-the-art models.

In brief:

New product/service→Test marketing→Advertisement→Release of bulk quantity→Customer feedback→Corrections and Improvement→Newer models

We have in our country, examples of big producers who relied on their brand image to push other products. Due to capacity and other limitations a big MNC farmed out its domestic product, mixer-grinder, to a third party some years ago. Design, technical inputs and supervision, marketing and sales were undertaken by the MNC. Test market results were encouraging. The product was introduced with great fanfare as if the product was a breakthrough in the line of brands available till then. The market reaction was slow in coming. However, when it came, it was a shock to the senior executives who had pinned so much hope on the success of their maiden brand of their domestic appliances range. Customers returned the first100 units sold due to one problem or the other — gets hot soon; cup does not sit well; vibrates too much; makes too much noise and the complaints were endless. What went wrong pondered the chief executive and his team.

Conclusion: Hasty introduction without proper homework and with no prior experience in a new field. It had to recall all the other mixer-grinders off the shelves. It took several years before the company could stage a come back from such a disastrous launch.

Moral: Don't have the ego to think you can sell anything under your brand. It's the customer who finally decides the acceptability or otherwise of a product/service.

It's but natural for an average consumer to be totally confused with a plethora of high-tech products/services which are on display in posh air-conditioned showrooms with smart sales boys and girls hovering over you to make you feel more self-conscious. In such a situation, one could easily be stampeded into a buying decision because you dare not ask too many questions with an odd feeling 'what will the salesgirl think of me!' However, patience and caution are the watchwords in a situation where the choice appears to be tough with many competing equally good products/services staring at you on shining counters. The psychology of not wanting to miss the bus when everyone is getting on to it should be avoided; that's 'keeping up with the Joneses'. It depends entirely on what you want not what others have it. Of course, it helps to know what others have bought it and their experiences, good or bad. For example, consumers invested in VCRs a few years back while others did not do so. However, when the technology change brought out the DVD a few consumers, who had not bought the VCR, now jumped on to it while the others who already had the VCR had to junk it or use it sparingly.

It is not always "Neighbour's envy, owner's pride" when it comes to keeping up with your neighbour, friends or relatives. Now practically every middle class family has at least one computer. There is no doubt this invention is fantastic and the sooner people invest in a computer the better as it opens up windows to the latest developments all over the globe. A knowledgeable and intelligent consumer will neither be swayed by advertisements nor because someone else has bought a product/service.

MAKING A GOOD CHOICE

A few of the latest gadgets have all sorts of features. A customer might wonder what exactly is 'Golden Eye' in a TV set and whether he/she should invest in such a high-tech product at that high price. In fact, the customer should be able to judge whether that particular feature advertised, he/she can discern easily, otherwise why spend so much on some fancy feature which one cannot even see? That applies to many other 'modern novel' features in products/services. It's a question of one's choice—whether to invest in a car that has 'power windows' which operate by the touch of a button or not. On the other hand, power-drive steering has features that make driving easier. It's how a feature helps or makes the life simpler or better without having to spend too much money on initial or long-term repair and maintenance. For instance, 'remote locking' in a car has many takers. Well, it's a good feature, when it works properly. The flip side is it gives trouble now and then that calls for a qualified mechanic to come to one's aid in disabling the feature. What happens when the door cannot be operated because the remote locking facility is not working?

Ultimately, any purchase decision has to be taken keeping in mind one's own needs and requirements. However, it always helps to get a feedback on the same product/service or brand you have in mind. Needless to emphasize the fact that one has to be in tune with the latest trends in products/services so that a customer may make a meaningful and cost-effective decision. One should be aware of terms like 'Smart technology', 'Tumble wash', 'Magic vision' which are high-sounding. However, one has to judge whether such features are so desirable, at the quoted price that you can make out the difference. Glib sales talk can sometimes impress a confused consumer who might be conned into buying a product/service that's of dubious quality.

Customers should be wary of salespersons who go overboard in praising a particular product/service inspite of the fact it has no any outstanding features compared to other brands. May be a good talker is paid to promote a brand that couldn't be sold otherwise. But mere talks won't carry an average product/service far when compared to a superior product/service. A knowledgeable customer might ask a few important searching questions about the product/service that a salesperson is promoting to find out how much truth is there in those advertisements or claims he/she is making. Now-a-days it's difficult to fool a customer with so much information available from various sources. It's only the naïve and gullible that can get fooled by tall claims, which cannot be proved.

Quality of product/service is assuming greater importance than before. Our daily life revolves around so many product and services. We expect these to be of acceptable quality day in and day out without fail. If electrical supply is cut off in the morning, the day's programme gets disrupted and alternatives will have to be planned. "Indeed, quality is not for the elite alone," sums up the importance of quality to each and every person, that's the universal truth. Consumers expect value for money, trouble-free service, durability and reliability and at the right price. Unfortunately, a few door-to-door to sales-persons and fly-by-night operators palm off shoddy goods and services on the gullible and those who go by price alone. Some people are attracted by 'second sales', 'every day low prices', 'half-price', 'export rejects' and 'discounts', 'buy one and take one free', 'freebies', 'lottery and prize' schemes *et al.* But no organization worth its name could sustain for long on consumers' gullibility and simplicity. Its true worth would be known one day or the other and would be blacklisted sooner or later. Moreover, market forces would act effectively to drive out shoddy products/services, in these days of easy availability and plenty of choices.

In the regime of a market-driven economy, no organization could sustain for long without a *full commitment to total and continuous customer satisfaction*. This can happen only if it delivers on quality, which encompasses: product quality, delivery commitment, price, service after sales and final disposal of product after end of life. Without a clear understanding of what consumers want, it would be a case of a person chasing a black cat in a dark room.

What quality means?

- Right specification
- High product quality
- Right delivery on time
- Correct price
- Prompt service
- Correct disposal/recycling

It's the problem of abundance for consumers! From a limited or no choice marketplace, we have a multiple-choice environment each of good and often of international quality at reasonable prices. Even payment options range from instalment to credit card and loans to buy products/services, cars to homes. An intelligent customer would arm himself/herself with all the details and information of the proposed product/service he/she is intending to purchase. That consumer would make a survey of the available brands within a price band for serious consideration. Of course, brand royalty would play an important part in a purchase decision. Consumer brand surveys, Internet search (by Google and other search engines), information from newspapers and magazines, inputs from family and friends would be considered for better decision-making.

A consumer prefers to shop at a 'single window' for his/her requirements. For example, if a student wants to buy stationery he/she would like to get all the requirements like notebooks, drawing sheets, carbon paper, file, clips, pens, pencils, gum/glue, pencil sharpener, erasers, punching machine, stapler with staples and so under one roof. Similarly, a person who wants to go in for a computer should have access to—monitor, CPU, keyboard, CD, floppy, speakers, printer, tape, printer cartridge, service-providers for Internet/Broad band connection *et al.*, that shop should have the facility for servicing/technical support too. A good salesperson would maintain a friendly and cordial relation so that the customer would come back again. There is nothing like a one-to-one relation for furthering a business relationship. There are few nice salespersons who make it a point to enquire about a customer's family and well-being. That customer would receive small gifts to celebrate birthday, anniversary, as well as festival greeting cards. Such a personal touch is welcomed by customers who feel important.

A wise customer always goes for a standard branded item despite the fact it's more expensive. If a company is engaged in export business all the better. Such companies, in general, have two standards of operation — one for the overseas market and the other for domestic. However, such a distinction is disappearing, as domestic customers too are demanding higher standards. One can reasonably be sure that export-oriented company products meet international standards. With such a choice, the customer has assured himself/herself of continuous satisfaction. On the other hand, there are others who shop for low prices but end with low quality. That person, obsessed with low prices, is in trouble from day one. Spare parts, repair and maintenance, technical support and service are conspicuous by their absence in those outfits who assemble standard parts and sell as complete equipments.

What to look for?

Certain companies make customer feedback an important feature of their product development as well as continuous upgrading of quality standards. Some customers too could be invited to take part actively in product innovation. Comments and suggestions by customers are taken seriously and actions taken to incorporate as many of these in present or future designs. Such an interface gives the customers a sense of involvement as well as achievement that their ideas have been put to good use.

Customers are advised to study magazines, newspapers and surf the Internet when they have some product/service in mind. For instance, students seeking higher education would do well if they go through in detail the report published in magazines like *India Today* ('Top ten colleges of India') that rates colleges and institutions of higher learning. This could be a valuable guide for those who plan to go in for higher studies. Each of the top ten colleges have been rated for various parameters of interest to prospective students.

A new product/service could have teething problems to be overcome after use and corrective actions. That's the reason a cautious customer wouldn't rush to buy a new product/service unless it has established its reputation over a period of time. One should study how a market reacts to a new product/service. Moreover, it's a good idea to know the quality policy, quality objective, customer care policy of a company whose product/service you intend buying. Some customers are keen to know what a company does for social causes, their attitude to environmental issues and the way they treat their employees and stakeholders. Concerned customers would have nothing to do with a company's product/service if it has a poor track on environmental and social issues. This is a way of protesting against a company that is environmentally and socially unfriendly. Sometimes such boycott could have a salutary effect on a company, which is forced to change its ways of operating through customer pressure.

In India we have awards for recognizing excellence in the field of quality by the corporate sector. Some of these are:

- Rajiv Gandhi National Quality Award
- Golden Peacock National Quality Award
- CII Award for Business Excellence
- IMC Ramakrishna Bajaj National Quality Award
- IMC Juran Quality Award
- NIQR Awards

There are awards for excellence in exports by government and business. These recognize the excellence in quality and management as well as exports and serve as benchmark for others to follow. Customers who keep a track of such excellence in quality would buy products/services from such outstanding companies whose excellence has been recognized nationally/internationally.

Customer expectation vis-à-vis actual performance can be seen from Fig. 6.1 below:

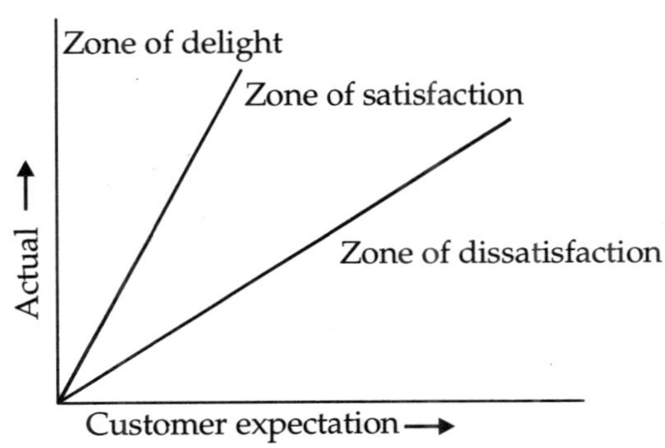

Fig. 6.1

A few companies have devised questionnaires to get a feedback on the way their customers react to their product/service. This is especially so in case of the hospitality industry to receive feedback on customer satisfaction through "Quality Focus Questionnaire". This is used to rate employees too so that at the end of the month a person(s) could be declared as the 'outstanding' person of the organization. In some other instances, like the airlines, customers are asked to identify those who have given them service 'beyond the call of duty' so that they could be recognized as such. All these depend upon customers' inputs.

Some points that could be included in the questionnaire are:

	Strongly agree	Agree	Disagree	Strongly disagree
1. We have a clear understanding of who our customers are				
2. We know their expectations				
3. We provide a good standard of service				
4. We match this standard to the customers' expectations				

A responsible customer would base his/her buying decision on a few important factors as given below:

- Reputed company/organization
- With ISO/BIS or other certification
- Ethical products/services
- 'Green' products with responsible recycling policy
- Companies, which are ethical and socially committed

After a general discussion in the above paragraphs, it would be interesting to get an insight into various topics of general and particular interest to customers selected at random. *These are in the nature of general information and so are neither comprehensive nor authoritative. These are in the nature of broad guidelines that could help customers in making better and informed decisions*. The information is taken from various sources, too numerous to mention. However, a word of caution is in order. It's better to get the latest information as matters are changing fast and so something that was important could be of no consequence and *vice versa*. There is nothing like a well-informed customer for a good purchase decision, which gets value for the money spent.

'Green' products

Environmentally friendly products are labelled 'Green' products in stores. They have pride of place but unfortunately do not get wide patronage due to their higher price as well as lack of knowledge and interest shown by customers. Industry has taken some initiatives in making their products/services environmentally friendly. Air-conditioners using chemical chlorofluocarbons (CFCs), which are linked to the destruction of the protective ozone layer in the upper atmosphere, are being phased out and replaced by substances that are less harmful to the ozone layer. Those customers who are aware of the need to protect our environment tend to purchase eco-friendly products only.

Use of recycled materials to replace, at least partially, virgin material is gaining momentum. For example, paper that is used once could be recycled and used for various purposes including packaging. Some books/greeting cards are printed only from recycled paper. A feeling of satisfaction arises when a customer uses recycled paper: "I am happy I have used recycled paper and saved so many trees from being cut." In some advanced countries, where the consumption of everything is so high as compared to the developing world, a few concerned citizens are spearheading recycling in a big way. What was once a 'throw-away culture' society is slowly, but surely, realizing it needs to conserve resources by recycling. Some companies take pride in their greening efforts. For instance, an advertisement by the Indian Oil Company states, 'Committed to a clean environment.' It has become necessary for more companies/organizations to show their commitment to the conservation of the environment by deeds and actions and not mere platitudes.

A few consumers are determined to consume fruits and vegetables grown by the 'organic way', which contain little or no chemical fertilizers, pesticides or herbicides. This is a way of demonstration that shows one's commitment to the cause of the environment that's getting an overdose of chemicals from various man-made activities. Another social commitment is not to use items, like carpets, jewellery, fire-crackers, made in small/medium size units employing child labour who are exploited by paying them a pittance for their efforts. Moreover, they are forced to work under hazardous conditions that affect their health. A few importing countries, have already banned import of carpets and the like from India, which use child labour.

The USA took another step by banning import of leather and leather goods from India due to pressure form Animal Rights Activists who protested against the ill treatment meted to animals during their life time and the crude and cruel methods of slaughtering them. It is interesting to note that even children are getting into the protection of children from exploitation. A band of school children determined that they would not buy firecrackers for Diwali as a protest against employing children in that industry. It is expected that there would be more awareness among the customers as well companies and organizations on environmental as well as social issues. Only customers' pressure, through their refusal to buy environmentally unfriendly and socially unethical products, could make companies and organizations become more proactive on environmental and social issues.

Shelf life of products

The rules for packaged items include the Maximum Retail Price (MRP) and date of manufacture/date of validity for use, among others. Most perishable goods, like milk, butter, bread, medicines, with limited shelf life, must be dated and marked on the package. The consumer should check the 'Expiry date' of the product carefully before buying it. There are a few shops/stores, even in the advanced countries, where the products that have expiry date approaching are offered at a discount. In our country, only a few consumers take the trouble to check the expiry date and refuse to buy it if it is over. Some traders, who want to get rid of such outdated products, with expiry date over, offer a hefty discount. "Oh, it's only a few months that have passed after expiry date. There should be no problem in using it," is the 'logic' of the trader as well as the consumer who knowingly buys it trying to save money. But others would have nothing to do with 'expired' products that could pose a health hazard. The reduction in price is of no consequence for those who value their health and life.

Some shops do follow the 'first-in first-out' rule by arranging that newer products are kept at the back of the rack so that older products get sold earlier. There are shopkeepers who do not sell old stuff but give them away or just scrap it. It's better that consumers do not shop at places where old stuff could be passed off as new. Some of them do not take back old stuff once these are sold to a customer. But you must make a noise and threaten him/her that he/she could complain to a court if such practices are not stopped. It's your right to get such bad stuff exchanged or replaced or money refunded. When items like ice-cream cups/packs are stacked in a deep freezer it's difficult to check which is new and which is old stuff. Of course, one has to make sure the expiry date is checked before buying such items. Check always for date of manufacture/date of expiry/marked price before buying packaged items. There is a need to make these markings bold, clear and unambiguous so that even a layperson could easily check these before purchase.

In developed countries like the USA officers from each country health department visit grocery stores at least once in three months. Inspections include checking food temperatures and floors, walls and ceilings for cleanliness. Coolers are checked to see if they are keeping food items at the correct temperatures. Meat displays are checked and examined to see if packaging has been damaged. Shelves are also inspected for dented cans and bags are checked for signs of weevils, pests or leaks. The principle of 'first-come-first-out' rule is also checked for items like dairy products.

Beauty is a big business with beauty queens being discovered every now and then at various platforms, domestic as well as international. Inspired by such 'rags to riches' stories, even ordinary people in small towns have taken to beauty treatment in the hope of looking good for marriage, job or to win at any local beauty contest. It has become fashionable, from the poor to the rich, to get beauty treatment, whether one could afford it or not. Even men-folk are not far behind women in taking to beauty treatment. Massage parlors, ayurvedic treatment centers, spas, hair stylists, beauty parlors, and gyms are sprouting all over the place to entice people to join these at a hefty fee. The wise and intelligent customers would check these for competence, staff, equipment and fee before joining these. The experience of others who are using these parlours or those who had left also should also be taken into account before joining these. Sometimes, a simple 'grand-mother's' recipe for looking young and beautiful would do the same trick as an expensive treatment with all kinds of modern and expensive gadgets.

Women's magazines have whole pages devoted to such home and traditional remedies and beauty aids to kitchen shelf to which every woman will have access. Here are a few tips which consumers might find useful. Tips are taken from various sources but are neither complete not comprehensive but given here for information as useful tips:

Know your fruits and vegetables

Bananas: Eat a ripe banana and follow it with a glass of milk for a quick, well-balanced, instantly energizing meal. Eat bananas to soothe an acidity-prone stomach and to ease constipation. To re-hydrate the body especially in case of children during a bout of diarrhoea, make a meal of mashed ripe banana mixed with cooked rice.

Calorific value: 116 calories in one large banana.

Beauty bulletin: Apply a paste of mashed ripe banana mixed with a teaspoon of honey to over-dry lifeless skin, leaving it soft and supple. Strap a piece of banana skin, soft side down, on newly appeared wart and leave it overnight. Try the treatment for a week to get rid of it, and if you cannot, consult a doctor.

Kitchen economics: 'A penny saved is a penny gained,' is an old adage. A wise consumer will device various ways of saving money whether it is shopping for groceries or keeping the kitchen clean and hygienic.

Great taste products: Crystal salt and free flowing salt, great taste pastes are some of the new introductions that should be tried to assess the quality and taste oneself. Only iodized salt is recommended for general use with exceptions where one could use non-iodized salt.

Buying food is not a 'routine' activity as it affects one's short-term as well as long-term health. It would be better not to be compromising on quality by going for cheap stuff as it might affect the health of your family. In general, use of fat and salt should be kept to the minimum as they have long-term health effects on people. There is an effort to indicate the salt, fat and salt content on food items, including packaged food items. One need not start calculating the calorie, fat or salt intake but care should be exercised not to indulge in any of these but to have a balanced healthy food. We in India have not achieved such a sense of health care as demonstrated in advanced countries. A new idea is to have a food audit system, which like other audits, is pro-active, positive and a constructive process, which should be taken up by professionally competent persons.

An informed consumer keeps himself/herself abreast of the trends in food and other matters that affect one's short/long-term well-being. For example, a few years ago in the USA, a chemical Alar was used to ripen apples uniformly and to make them stay fresh in storage. Researchers came out with an alarming finding that this chemical was carcinogenous and consumers were at risk of developing cancer. Hence, due to consumer protest, Alar was withdrawn voluntarily at a whopping loss of US$ 50 million to the chemical company, a small price to pay to safeguard the health of a community and well-being. A careful study of such developments enables a consumer to make intelligent and informed decisions.

Fast food joints are springing up even in small towns. Packaged food/snack and take-home food/snack items are on the increase. Traditionalists would have nothing to do with such fancy food items. For them, it's the home cooked food that's best. However, with working couples, it is increasingly becoming difficult to devote time to preparation of food. Here comes the easy ready-mix, and ready-to-eat food. Roadside joints, and the *dhabas* have their own devoted clientele. For them cleanliness is a small concern as long as the food tastes great and it's cheap. However, one should be careful in eating cut fruits and drinking juices sold on the pavements as these could lead to sickness during vulnerable seasons. A word of caution on packaged water: Do not think or assume all packaged water is 'mineral' water or it's safe. But for a few reputed brands, the other being vended in the market could be of doubtful quality. There is much money to be made in a bottle of water and so some unscrupulous persons get into the act and supply even tap water as mineral water at Rs. 10 a bottle. So beware of such tricks and do not fall a prey to all sorts of packaged water. It's recommended that you buy bottled water only from authorized outlets. There is always the danger of fakes being sold as genuine stuff as the profits are very high in this packaged water business. A simple water filter removes dirt and suspended particles and nothing else. However, filtering and then boiling the water for five minutes at least makes the water safe for drinking when cooled.

"Make your kitchen a safety zone (Issued by Indian Oil Corporation, Indane)"

Doís: Always close the burner and regulator valve/knobs after use and before retiring at night. Use only a BIS approved gas stove as well as an approved rubber tube and replace the same every two years. Check periodically the rubber tube for holes, cracks and softness. Keep the rubber tube from fire and flames. Keep the gas installation at least one metre from electrical outlets. The length of the rubber tubing should be a maximum of 1.5 metres. Put out all the flames and immediately close burner and regulator knobs if you smell gas. Use only a cotton apron while cooking. Put out all open flames while changing a cylinder. Always keep the gas stove on a platform above the cylinder level. Keep the windows of the kitchen open as a safety precaution.

Donίts: Never allow open flames and inflammable material near the gas installation. Never leave vessels unattended on a burning gas stove. Avoid use of electric switches while changing a cylinder. Never place a cylinder inside a closed compartment. If you do so, have ventilation holes at the floor level as well as the top. Don't attempt self-repair. Always call your distributor for help. Don't allow children to play inside the kitchen. Don't keep vessels etc. on top of a cylinder.

Safety begins at home.

Tips to save energy

- Buy energy saving appliances.
- Turn off lights and fans whenever they are not in use.
- Open curtains and blinds till you have natural day light.
- Switch to CFL lights wherever possible. A 40 W tube-light is equivalent to 100 W bulb.
- Keep bulbs, tubes clean. Dust can decrease lighting levels by 20–30%.
- Set water heater at optimum temperature level.
- Avoid frequent opening and closing of refrigerator and air-conditioned rooms.
- While maintaining safe lighting conditions for work areas, remove lamps where you have more lighting than you really need.
- Providing the right lighting can save up to 15 per cent on your lighting bill.
- For really big energy savings, replace the incandescent floodlight bulbs with new fluorescent lamps.

Home remedies

Despite so much progress in medicine and medical practice, the use of home remedies has not diminished. For simple ailments some people try the time tested home remedies. If these do not work then only they seek the help of a qualified doctor. The inadequacies of our health care are well known. Wrong diagnosis, wrong treatment and inadequate after care are all matters of concern as well as the increasing cost of medical care. Just like advanced countries, health care insurance has come to stay in our country, especially for those who are employed or even self-employed. That's because misfortune may strike anyone anywhere anytime.

An intelligent consumer doesn't rush to seek medical; help the moment he sneezes. There are time tested home medicines/treatment, which generally are harmless and might do so some good. There are people who believe in simple and inexpensive home remedies and treatment to treat simple ailments like stomach upsets, colds, coughs and mild fever.

A wise consumer would first give these home remedies, and of course, one's own defensive mechanism to work till he/she seeks help from doctors. If these do not work after a reasonable period or the condition worsens he/she would consult a doctor. There are those who drink one liter of water every morning to start the day. Others swallow a spoonful of oil as a preventive medicine. There are others who drink fresh fruit juices for health reasons.

The home remedies, often handed over from generations, are mostly harmless without side effects. A sore throat, for example, might need only simple treatment of warm salt-water gargling three to four times a day. But wisdom dictates that these simple remedies have their limitations and so one shouldn't go overboard to the exclusion of modern treatment. Over the counter drugs for pain relief, stomach upset, headache and sleeplessness are available. Again one has to be careful in using these over a long-term due to unknown side effects. For instance, using eye-drops over a long period might cause cataract of the eye. Again, using painkillers for long could damage the kidneys and so on. Hence an intelligent consumer would go slow in using any medicine over prolonged periods.

Here are some home medicines, which you might like to try:

Headache: Make a simple paste of ginger and apply to your forehead.

Constipation: Take five parts rose buds, four parts *senna* leaves, three parts pulp of *amaltas*, five parts turmeric, with *triphala* and make pills out of them. Drink lot of water and eat plenty of fruits and vegetables.

Indigestion: Chew a piece of ginger with powdered rocksalt before meals.

Coughs: 250 mg of black pepper ground with honey, ghee and sugar candy makes a pleasant medicine.

Common cold: Inhale smoke from a piece of burning turmeric.

Caution: Do not continue to use these home remedies if the situation gets worse.

Asafoetida has a number of curative properties, which form part of home remedies. Some of these are:

Asthmatic problems: Mix a little asafoetida powder in 2 tsp honey. Add to this a little juice of white onions and betel leaf. Sip thrice a day.

Stomachache/Liver problems: Fry equal quantities of asafoetida, fenugreek, (*methi* seeds), mustard seeds and turmeric powder in ghee. Powder them. Take 3-4 tsp of this powder with a little rice.

Gas problems: A small piece of asafoetida with a banana.

Diabetes: Mix a little asafoetida powder in 2 tsp in *Karela* juice.

Toothache: Mix a little asafoetida in limejuice. Warm this mixture slightly. Soak a piece of cotton and place in the painful tooth cavity.

Heartburn: (Not to be confused with heart attack) A glass of water to rinse off the acid taste off the esophagus. Avoid food items that trigger off heartburn and above all avoid hitting the bed soon after meals.

Caution: Home remedies should be discontinued if there are no signs of improvement after three to four days of treatment or if the condition worsens. It is wise to seek professional help if the symptoms continue or the situation gets worse.

ALTERNATE SYSTEMS OF MEDICINES

There are alternatives like Acupressure, Acupuncture, Ayurveda, Homeopathy, Naturopathy, Reiki, Tibetan system, Yoga and Unani *et al.* Some of these are gaining popularity not only in our country but outside too. For example, yoga has entered in a big way to foreign countries and there are many votaries of this form of body and mind control. One has to accept, whether one likes it or not, that allopathic system of treatment is ahead of others in diagnostic methods. Moreover, it has potent medicines thanks to much investment in drugs, treatment and research on diseases. However, costs of health-care are increasing steadily in this system and many cannot afford costly treatment.

One has to choose the type of treatment one has faith in. A combination of some of these could prove beneficial. For example, diabetes may not have a cure but manageable. Yoga, it appears, can help the patient in controlling the diabetes, with or without medication. However, it's important not to abandon any system one is used to. For example, a blood pressure patient cannot stop medication overnight and take up yoga as a cure. There is a place for these alternate systems of treatment. However, the patient has to be careful to see that his/her condition does not go from bad to worse when that person is experimenting with various systems in the hope of a miracle cure. Homeopathy works on the basis of treating the symptoms without actually checking what causes the ailment. Sometimes this is like hit-and-miss treatment — if one medicine does not work, try another. To some extent that's true of allopathy too. By all means, a patient has freedom to try another line of treatment, taking care that the condition doesn't become so bad that emergency treatment would be required.

Ayurvedic drugs are becoming like any other modern allopathic drugs. Pop it and elicit a standard response from the body. It becomes irrelevant who dispenses it — vaidya, general practitioner or chemist. Some new drugs of ayurveda have potential of controlling disease like high blood pressure (BP) but field trials will have to be more extensive over a longer period to justify the claim of some of the new drugs touted as cures for certain diseases. An ayurvedic drug is claimed to improve the condition of mentally retarded children. However, there is no hard evidence to prove such a claim. What is lacking in ayurveda are the field tests and trials that could prove or disapprove certain drugs for specific diseases. One cannot merely vend drugs stating these are ancient ayurvedic drugs. We need solid proof through properly designed trials to prove the potency of drugs. No one can sell *Brahmi* herb, which was used for centuries, as something novel and revolutionary. Such claims are patently cheating the gullible.

Beware of advertisements like: 'Cure short/long sight by yoga.' This might sound too good to be true. Do not give up your glasses to try yoga to cure your sight problems. Unless proved by scientific means, claims that yoga cures all sorts of illnesses should be taken with a pinch of salt. If you want to try yoga to benefit you, there is no doubt it does, go about it slowly with the help of a trained yoga teacher.

As people are getting more and more interested and concerned about their well-being, more 'novel' health care methods are coming up to meet the demand. A suffering individual would try anything to get well. "Magnified healing through pure higher vibrations of divine love, power and wisdom," sounds exotic. One might argue that there are things beyond the scientific and the rational world that the human mind does not comprehend and these healing techniques may belong to such a realm. However, caution is the word when one is trying such techniques. Do not expect instant and easy cures for any problem. A health care clinic that advertises, 'instant computerized slimming, innovative cure,' should be viewed with suspicion. There is no magical formula that would ensure 'instant' slimming. In fact, such a cure could be worse than the disease. If some clinics claim, 'no invasive treatment for any disease,' there is something wrong. It's too good to be true.

It is interesting to study the various systems of medicine vis-à-vis a patient's participation in the treatment:

Acupuncture: No participation, some contact.

Reiki: No participation, no contact.

Pranic healing: Some participation, no contact.

Allopathy: Fair amount of participation, high contact, single frame of reference, easily verifiable and reproducible.

Ayurveda: High participation, fair amount of contact, no single frame of reference, not easily verifiable and reproducible.

Yoga: Same as in Ayurveda.

"It would be easy if all specialists can offer their services under one umbrella, with a commonality of philosophy. If this is done, there will not be any hostility or antagonism," states an expert. We need doctors, health-care specialists and healers to take a holistic view of a human being and not just treat individual parts that might need attention from time to time.

The quest for alternate system of treatment never stops. People in the advanced countries are turning to India and developing countries to find cures. Yoga has become a big business, with variations, which our ancient masters never dreamt about. Meditation is being prescribed for stressed executives and patients suffering from various diseases. Traditional knowledge of healing, including use of herbs and the like, is waiting to be discovered.

Caution: Proceed slowly and with caution when you want to switchover or to try alternate systems of treatment.

Health fads

Not all health fads should be dismissed as being fetishes. For example, a low cholesterol diet is proved to be easy on the heart. A total of LDL + HDL cholesterol level under 200 is considered good, between 200 and 240, a potential problem and over 240 is a cause for concern needing urgent medical attention. Heart diseases are due to many factors: risk factors like smoking, alcohol, drug abuse, obesity and genetic factors. However, a moderate intake of red wine is claimed to be good for the heart in elderly people. Health conscious consumers use low fat milk like skimmed milk instead of full cream milk, avoid fat and high salt intake. In packaged food items, in the advanced countries, calorific information is given along with details of salt, fat, mineral content and other relevant information on the product / package. It is not to suggest that one should be paranoid of eating counting calories and being stressed in the process. Moderation in eating and drinking are good along with physical activity to burn the calories, say, a brisk walk in the morning or evening or visiting the gym regularly for a workout.

Awareness about one's well being is important amidst all the stresses at home and at the workplace. Since we cannot control the external factors, we have to live with stress and manage it within limits. A weekend with the family is what the doctor will order. Spending quality time with the spouse and children can bond the family better. Benefits of vegetarian food are not overrated. In fact, more westerners are turning vegetarians due to the beneficial effects. Tobacco in any form is harmful and so its use should be stopped. Awareness of the health problems due to abuse of drugs, alcohol and tobacco should be improved targeting especially the youth. Also, certain precautions are important. For example, pregnant women should not consume alcohol or smoke in the interest of the unborn. Another example is smoking affects the non-smoker too — passive smoking which is as dangerous, if not more, compared to actual smoking.

Buy more

The marketing technique adopted in advanced countries is slowly seeping into our marketplace. In USA and other advanced countries, 'big is beautiful'. There are stores like 'Sam's' which deal with bulk quantities only. One normally cannot buy a small quantity for love or money! If you want to buy a pair of socks — you cannot! You have to buy a pack of at least six pairs, whether you like it or want it or not! The bigger and the larger the better — you are supposed to get a good deal by such purchases. But in our country, the masses, some of whom who eke out a miserable existence of hand to mouth such bulk purchases are out of the question. However, those who could afford such bulk purchases do so. For example, some families think it's better to buy a year's requirements of items of daily use like rice, dhal, and tamarind when it's a cheap season for such items. However, there are others who are frugal and believe in buying what they need once a month or once a week. In the USA consumers buy big milk cartons that lasts at least one whole week. We, on the other hand, buy milk every day and we like the fresh taste as a bonus.

Dealing with fakes

How to deal with counterfeits and fakes?

Remedies available under the law: At present actions against spurious products are being taken by various enforcement agencies on the basis of various acts such as Copy Right Act, 1957, Trade Marks Act, 1999, Customs Act, Central Drugs and Cosmetics Act, Prevention of Food Adulteration Act, BIS, etc. In a country like ours there is enough scope for those duplicate fast selling goods and offer these to gullible persons as real. There is a market for such illegal products. For example, there is a thriving market for pirated books and popular CDs, which are available on the pavements/ shops. Enforcement agencies do catch the culprits and destroy the fakes but they do rise up and resume their nefarious activities once again. It's only an alert and honest consumer/shopkeeper who will shun such products that cost the economy crores of rupees every year.

The unfortunate fact is any popular 'fast' selling product can be 'duplicated' and passed off as original. It could be liquor, CD, cassette, designer shirt, jeans, electric bulb and so on. Sometimes, the label and material look at a glance exactly as the original. There are some clever crooks who make a slight alteration in the name/logo to stay away from trouble if and when caught. When even currency notes can be duplicated, despite the stringent and most complicated design, there is no wonder anything and everything could be faked. An unwary buyer can easily mistake a fake for a real one. Moreover, there is always the price difference that's attractive enough to a buyer. It's a long and hard battle, all over the world, to trace and crack down on the persons/agencies involved in producing duplicate stuff. The punishment, in terms of jail term and fine, is not deterrent enough to prevent such illegal activities, which can gross huge profits. Companies who have invested much money by way of design and manufacture are the sufferers when someone easily duplicates their stuff and causes immense loss to the genuine sales.

There are organizations like the Silk Board and Wool Board that issue notices to protect genuine silk and wool manufacturers. They have their own logos that are registered. For example, Silk mark: Your assurance of pure silk.

Leading companies/organizations issue warning in the print and electronic medium against fakes. They try to protect their patent rights and their official logo against misuse by unscrupulous operators. Here is one such advertisement by Grasim suiting:

"Genuine Grasim Gwalior and Grasim suiting have GRASIM on the border. Gwalior suiting is now available only under the labels GRASIM SUITING and GRASIM GWALIOR SUITING. Genuine fabrics bear either of these two names woven/stamped on the border and/or the fabric top. Persons engaged in manufacturing, dealing in or selling of imitation fabrics with the label Grasim suiting and Grasim Gwalior suiting or any similar sounding names are liable for criminal prosecution. Insist on genuine Grasim suiting."

Reputed companies use better quality yarn, high grade chemicals, better quality dyes, combination like 70/30 correctly depicted, mill cloth softened at a later stage of production, full number of pick required per weight, processing cost about Rs. 17 per metre(This could be more now). On the other hand, those who duplicate the cloth use poor quality yarn, low-grade chemicals, sub-standard dyes, combination falsely depicted, cloth is soft from the start, less number of pick done, processing cost 70 paise per metre (This could be more but far less than genuine product). The effect on finished textiles in fakes can be summed up: Durability and appearance of cloth is affected, quality of finish and colour are inferior, colour fades fast, shine disappears, low weight in strength and fuzzy appearance, uncomfortable to the skin.

Suiting from well known mills range from Rs. 500 to Rs. 1000 upwards per metre and fake ones Rs. 100 per metre. While Gwalior is the most exploited of all brand names, two other favourites are Vimal and Siyaram. This list varies from time to time. One thing is for sure, no brand (especially that sells well) can escape from being duplicated.

If you want to make sure of genuine stuff, then shop only at factory outlets and their authorized dealers/agents. Do not buy from roadside vendors or door-to-door salespersons however attractive the price could be. Do not be tempted by freebies, gifts and lotteries.

A few reputed companies have registered their hologram logos and stick these on packages/products/documents. For example, UTI, IDBI, tickets by road transport corporations as well as other agencies have started using holograms that are difficult to fake. "Hologram is that colourful sticker which shines in light." The enforcement agencies do have some success in catching the culprits, which is nothing but the tip of the iceberg. Reports like: "The CCB have arrested a businessman for allegedly selling fake bearings in the name of a reputed company and seized fake bearings worth Rs. 74,000 from him," are few and far in between.

Trade mark caution notice: You may see such notices in newspapers from time to time. Do make a note for your reference in case you deal with such companies/organizations. Here is a press release issued by the legal adviser of 'Duckback' trade mark owners:

" 'Duckback' is patented for various products including rubberized water-proof raincoats, air-pillows, gum boots, snow ankle boots, hot-water bottles, rubber sheets/clothes, travelling bags etc. Conscious customers are requested to refrain from purchasing counterfeit products and cooperate by bringing such misuse of trademark so that strong action can be taken against offenders."

Here is another advertisement to guard against fakes. 'Oriflame': "Natural Swedish cosmetics, also available at the wrong places. Please don't buy Oriflame cosmetics from retail shops. They may not be genuine.

Worse, you lose out on the 'Oriflame' distributor's beauty advice, assistance in selecting cosmetics suited to your skin type. Trust only the Oriflame Distributor. For she alone can pamper you."

Here is another caution note. "Notice is hereby given that our clients LOGITECH S.A. Switzerland are the proprietors of the following trade mark, both in India and overseas (two sketches shown). Be warned that our clients shall resort to appropriate civil or criminal action or both against any party passing off or intending to pass off their goods as our goods."

Bottled water: There is much easy money in faking bottled water that has entered practically every household in our country. It is purchased for use during travel, in office, and in homes too. Sometime back a consumer magazine '*Insight*' found that only 3 out of 13 brands tested conformed to standards. One brand revealed high arsenic, another high aluminium and another floating particles. This is not surprising, as those who make fake bottles as genuine, simply fill up discarded bottles of reputed manufacturer, fill it up with tap water and use seals just like the company's original. The label too is 'genuine', as it is simple to duplicate. For an effort of less than Re. 1 there is Rs. 10 to be made by selling such fakes. Hence caution is needed in buying bottled water from shops, which might be tempted to sell fakes to get a share of lucrative fake market. In fact, a cup of hot tea or coffee in a strange place is better than a 'bottled water' of unknown quality.

Package tours: Sometime back a magazine listed some problems with the popular packaged tour within the country as well as foreign location. Some of their actions are not in the best interests of customers. So if you are planning a package trip check for the print and the 'conditions apply' carefully before signing on the dotted line. A 'free air ticket' may not be after all free! 'There is no free lunch!' Packaged tour operators, to save costs, undercut each other with the result the customers suffer due to all sorts of compromises. It is estimated that the dollar component of a ten-day European tour, on a twin-sharing basis for rooms, should not be more than a certain amount of dollars but the tour operators collect about twice that amount. Some of them charge visa fee, fee for entrance to attractions like museums and art galleries and so on. Some of the best sightseeing options are kept 'optional' which means the customer has to do these by spending his/her own money and that too if time permits. Tour operators are cutting costs unabashedly—overnight flight, stay in cheap hotels outside big cities, fewer meals, and tourists sometimes taken directly from the airport to sightseeing destinations — never mind the jet lag! There is little time for relaxation and taking things easy on a packed packaged tour. Some of them promise a lot but end up with providing fewer amenities than promised. There are advantages on taking a packaged tour, especially for those who do not want any hassles anywhere. However, there could be glitches in any tour and hence it's advisable to book with reliable operators who have experience of such conducted tours over a long period of time.

Caution: Do not fall a prey to cheap unreliable tour operators who promise the moon!

Frequent flyer programme: This is to award/reward passengers who choose the same airlines for many trips. Such passengers accumulate points that could be converted to (a) upgrade (b) free ticket for self (c) free companion ticket. However, a few conditions apply while using such 'free' tickets—blackout dates during peak seasons, tickets not confirmed till the last day. Frequent flyers have other benefits too: staying in hotels that would give additional points. Shop in fashionable stores at discount, free gifts and so on. Some airlines offer hotel accommodation, subsidized sometimes as part of the deal, car rentals, escort service and so on. A point that needs to be noted is that the airlines do not hold themselves responsible for any deficiency in service by any of their partners in this arrangement. A wise frequent flyer chooses more than one airline for his/her frequent flights so that there is always an alternative when that becomes necessary.

Door-to-door selling

Door-to-door salespersons are a tough working lot. They do not take 'no' for an answer. They are persistent and sometimes are rewarded when someone buys their products. They are charming glib talkers promising the moon. It's tough to chase them out. 'Beware of dogs', 'we do not buy from door-to-door sales-persons,' and other notices do not stop a salesperson from ringing the bell at all odd and even hours of the day. They ooze with self-confidence and extend a warm handshake whether you want it or not. They reel off what they have been tutored. Sometimes they express a surprise that you are so far behind the times and that you do not have that product which he is about to sell it to you. They always state that it is a new product and so you are lucky to get a hefty discount. "If you buy at the regular shop you will have to pay Rs. 600. Sir, I am giving it for you for Rs. 400; it's a good bargain."

It's not easy to get rid of these charming persons nattily dressed with a command of language. They have an answer for everything, right or wrong only time will tell! Their business is to sell and that's their bottom-line. After all their livelihood depends upon how successful they are in selling as many products as possible—from disinfectants, toilet cleaners, soaps, detergents, games, books, torch-lights, CDs, water purifiers and the like. Obviously, they get a commission for every product sold or booked. Then there are others who want to make a 'survey' on various matters—insurance, banking, investment, club membership and so on.

The sales-persons, boys and girls, can be very persuasive. Often they have a sob story to sell — how they are studying hard and the money from the commission is all that they have to continue to study and so on. You have to be decisive otherwise anything vague or hesitant behaviour on your part opens another window to continue their hard sell. Be firm but polite. Don't shout and shut the door — after all they are doing their job, which is tough walking and listening to hostile talk and sometimes abuses too. Products vended at the door may not have any quality or safety standard. Normally, there is no repeat order coming from you. So you buy the goods out of sympathy but do not expect much from such products, which could be cheap and nasty.

Sometimes you might be moved by the plight of the person who is begging you to buy an item. Well, that could be charity but don't expect anything from such a product. Of course, for that young man it means a lot, at least he is getting a commission, thanks to your generosity. Then there are some women who have sob stories to tell. "Madam, my child is sick and my husband has no job. So I have to feed the family. Please help me by buying at least one soap. I shall be grateful for your help," and she would breakdown to shed copious tears. One need not be cynical all the time. There are occasions such stories could be genuine. If you are in a mood to help, you may think you are donating to a good cause, then go ahead and do not complain afterwards about the poor quality of the product someone has foisted on youi. Some pose as students and try to sell agarbattis, biscuits stating that they have to pay for their fees with the money they earn as commission. You should ask for more details, including their ID before you part with your money.

A **few tips** in dealing with door-to-door sales-persons:

- Do not buy a product, which you don't want.
- Be polite but firm.
- Go ahead and oblige the person if you believe or moved by the sob story.
- Beware of aggressive salespersons who could be nasty.
- Do not argue with these persons but politely tell them you are not interested in buying.

- A firm 'no' helps.
- Try not to buy any food items whatever might be the reason.
- Beware of persons who pose as salespersons but who could have ulterior motives.
- Do not disclose your assets, bank accounts, insurance policies, and investments details to anyone.
- If you are alone and especially if you are a woman, do not open the door without peeping through the peephole and preferably talk to that person from a window.
- Do not hand over your jewellery to any outsider for polishing or exchange. You might lose your valuables without even being aware of the tricks of conmen.
- Don't encourage soothsayers, godmen and others to come in, who want to pray for you or tell your fortune, especially when you are alone at home.
- Don't encourage donation seekers who often are fakes without any ID.
- Be wary of strangers and play SAFE.

Door-to-door/telephone surveys

With the widespread use of cell phones, the common man is being targeted for surveys of all kinds. There are those who want you to go in for credit card of a certain bank/organization. Without bating a breath, the young lady would reel off the advantages you would get if you go in for that particular brand credit company. Then there are telephone calls soliciting you to open an account in a bank that gives you lots of advantages and benefits. Others might ask you to join a club or enroll as a member of a vacation resort. They generally do not take 'no' for an answer. If it's a recorded voice, then it's simple—just disconnect! A young man dressed in a suit and tie would ring the bell and greet with you a 'good morning'. He would then open a notebook importantly and ask you a number of questions. You are not obliged to answer any of them.

However, if the person is from any government or civic agency, with a proof or ID, then you are expected to answer the survey questions, taking care not to disclose your bank or financial details. Do not sign any questionnaire unless it's official. Some householders the moment a person says, 'Survey, Sir,' would state firmly 'No surveys, please' and close the door. Often, the moment you state, 'I am a senior citizen,' those calling on the telephone soliciting your membership of a club/credit card/vacation club would stop the conversation as the general policy is not to enroll older people but target the youngsters and middle-aged persons. That's the advantage of being a senior citizen!

There is another trick employed by organizations to con you into joining a club/vacation plan. "Sir, you have been selected to be an honoured guest at a presentation at a prestigious hotel. You and your spouse are welcome," trills a sweet voice over the phone. You are mighty pleased to be one of the few persons who made it to their list. You are in high expectation of sumptuous dinner and a free gift that's supposed to be a surprise. You are received at the desk politely, "Sir, I shall take you to the presentation room shortly. Sir, I hope you have brought your cheque book," she asks. You are surprised that you were supposed to take a cheque book for that presentation. She expresses surprises but nevertheless takes you to be seated in the presentation room, which is nearly full of eager couples waiting for the presentation and more importantly for the dinner and free gift.

The presentation, is nothing but a sales pitch, for selling vacation membership to customers. It could be a film or a documentary highlighting the features of the club. This is generally impressive and professionally done. After forty-five minutes you heave a sigh of relief that's over. However, you are mistaken. Your ordeal has just begun! A junior assistant approaches with a broad grin. "Sir, I am sure you like the presentation. It's the right thing for you and madam. Don't you think it is one of the best in the world? There are so many novel features, which many don't have. Just think of how much money you would be saving if you join our club right now. You might vacation at any of our vacation places scattered around the world, just for a pittance. All that you do is to invest Rs. 1.75 lakhs, a one-time payment, so that you enjoy a life-time holiday." He will make a quick calculation and come with a figure that's astounding. "Please accept our package now and enjoy your holidays for the rest of your life. Simple, isn't it, Sir" he will go overboard. However, your patience is wearing thin. You had enough of such a sales talk. All you want is to get out have a dinner and grab a gift and go home quickly.

'Sorry, I am not interested in your offer,' comes as a surprise to the young man. He appeals to you to use your better judgment and not to miss out on such a fantastic opportunity.

When everything fails, he requests you to wait for a minute. He brings his boss, another smartly dressed person with a confident stride. He launches into a flowery speech stating advantages of their scheme and how many eminent persons are enjoying their vacations and what a lot of money they are all saving, thanks to the novel vacation plan launched by his company. That talk doesn't cut much ice with you and you are prepared to get up and walk out. He comes with his trump card. He takes out his calculator and does a quick check. "Sir, as a special case, I can offer the package at Rs. 1.50 lakhs, saving you Rs. 25,000. This offer you cannot refuse, Sir," he grins and hopes you have fallen into the trap. However, you are not moved by such a reduction; you know this is one of the sales gimmicks to hook a customer. Disappointed, he lets you go with a cold stare. It's clear, from that moment, no one wants to have anything to do with you after your failure in not enrolling yourself in their scheme. You feel highly let down. You have become a *persona non grata* by then.

The girl at the counter stares at you coldly. You ask her where the dinner table is. She points a finger at a table where there are a couple of sandwiches and a few pieces of cake still left. Both of you grab a piece before they too vanish. You look at each other and a slow smile comes back. 'So this is the dinner,' you joke. 'Where can we collect our gift?' I ask. She glares at you as if you are asking for the moon. 'Please wait,' she replies curtly and goes inside to consult her boss. She returns unsmilingly and thrusts a small package into your hands. You are in a hurry to leave that place. You open the gift-wrapper with high expectation. "Oh, it's a cheap nasty perfume bottle. I have to simply throw it away," replies the spouse disgustingly. So much for the free gift!

Such enticements for getting something out of customers by arranging presentation followed by lunch or dinner and gifts are not uncommon. However, the response of those who arrange such meetings could vary — from being polite, despite a negative outcome, to downright hostility.

Investment decisions

Where to put saved funds: The undermentioned are some of the factors to be considered:

1. Safety
2. Liquidity
3. Return
4. Tax liability

There are publications like 'Making mutual funds work for you', issued by Association of Mutual Funds in India, written in layperson's language which one could study before investing.

Tips on life insurance policies

[Issued by the Life Insurance Corporation (LIC) of India]

- Pay your premium (monthly/quarterly/six-monthly/yearly) regularly. Salaried people could opt through their salary to pay premium.
- Nominate the beneficiary or assign the policy.
- Get your age admitted as early as possible.
- Intimate change in address promptly.
- Ensure safe custody of your policy.
- Review your insurance cover from time to time.
- Transfer the policy to the branch of your choice.
- Make sure you revive your lapsed policy.
- State claim on maturity of policy. On the death of the insured, the family members should lodge claim for the amount insured along with bonus, if any.
- Take advantage of grievance redress cell to get your problem attended to early.

Cell for redress of complaints Reserve Bank of India (RBI)

The RBI has set up a 'Complaints Redress Unit' under Shri P.K. Biswas, (or the latest officer), Regional Director for Karnataka, for prompt satisfaction/ settlement of complaints from the members of the public against the RBI. Any person who has a grievance against any department of RBI may lodge his complaint at the cell at the above address, in Bangalore.

The Reserve Bank of India has set up the Banking Codes and Standards Board of India which can take far reaching action like making public the names of banks that breach the Code of Conduct, and imposition of penal action.

Railways citizenís charter on passenger services of Indian railways

This charter is a commitment of the Indian Railway Administration to:

- provide safe and dependable train services.
- set notified standards for various services wherever possible.
- ensure adequate passenger amenities in trains.
- provide courteous and efficient counter services.
- set up responsive and effective Grievance Redress Machinery at various levels to ensure time-bound resolution of complaints and grievances as far as possible.

Buying a flat

A few factors to be considered before investigating in a flat are:

- Location
- Freehold or lease
- Reputation of the builder/promoter
- Type of construction
- Investment
- Finance/loan
- 'Hidden' costs (such as development, registration, maintenance, society registration, provision of emergency generator, landscaping, fire-escape, gym/swimming pool/club)/clauses
- Maintenance (lump sum or monthly)
- Car/two-wheeler parking space/charges
- Registration/transfer of ownership

Key questions to ask while buying a flat

(Issued by Alacrity Housing Limited, Chennai)

- Title deeds
- Undivided share in the property
- Permissible Floor Space Index (FSI)
- Allotment letter
- Comprehensive agreement of construction
- Authorized approved plan and planning permit by competent authority
- Post delivery commitments

In the advanced countries like the UK and USA buying land/flat/condo/townhouse or building your own house/flat is easy. There are a number of regulations and laws governing each of these activities but if everything is in order, the work goes on and completion is assured within a few months after starting the work. Getting a loan is easy, if the customer is creditworthy and has a steady income. It is a matter of hours, rarely days that a loan is sanctioned against mortgage. One can choose any plan suiting one's convenience. It is possible to renegotiate mortgage loans depending upon the market loan interest rate. One can repay and then negotiate a fresh mortgage at lower rates. These are all simple and routine matters that could be completed within a few hours. There are hardly any housing societies like what we have. Most are independent houses.

Promoters build flats and sell them as condos or townhouses, which are 'row' houses looking alike. Most of the times the activity of buying a land/constructing a house is negotiated through the help of a realtor, most of whom are women. They do charge a commission for their assistance and act as a go between the purchaser and seller. Normally a contract would state when a house would be completed after all the paperwork is completed. This is honoured, failing which a small penalty is levied for every day of delay. There are a number of checks/inspections by authorized town council personnel who are charged with certifying construction at various stages. These are all completed in a routine manner without having to bribe any one.

Planning to buy a new car (Issued in the public interest by Hyundai Motor Company India Ltd.)

Run a quick check with documents. *Sheergenius* and his six point checklist to help you choose the right car. He lives and breathes car technology. He will tell you what to look for; what questions to ask; how to evaluate in his friendly, delightful way. So, when you go for the big buy you can live happy and breathe easy for having made the right choice. Now check for all the six checkpoints together. The car that comes closest to meeting them all is the car for you! For more priceless tips on car buying ask *autoexpert@docsheergenenius.com.* In addition, certain newspapers like THE HINDU bring out 'auto supplements' every week that contain tips for car/two-wheeler purchase and maintenance.

Here are some more tips on car buying:

- Buy the most contemporary design.
- Get the best technology — how many cylinders it has; is it carbureted or multi-point fuel injected (MPFI); is there a computer controlling the engine; is it a multi-valve engine; finally look at all the figures; higher the torque higher the acceleration, lower the RPM better the fuel efficiency; go for a five speed gearbox with overdrive gears.
- Don't go for glitter. Go for gold! It lasts.
- Warranty must cover components.
- Spares must give you peace of mind.
- Service is about quality, not quantity.

In the USA the land of automobiles, the economy depends upon the sale of cars, trucks and other vehicles. There is a saying, "If Detroit (home to the world's largest manufacturers of cars, with General Motors and Ford Motors dominating the scene) sneezes then the entire USA may catch cold!" Dealers go out of the way to induce people to buy new models and trade in older cars. Used (pre-owned) car sale is big business with dealers displaying the used cars for sale. Easy financing is the rule than exception with attractive terms being offered to consumers, with good credit standing. Every facility is provided for the car owners. They can do shopping, conduct business at post-office, use ATMs, order food from fast-food joints without getting off his/her vehicle. Each motor company launches its own models every year or sometimes twice a year.

Apart from domestic production, the USA allows a number of imported cars, Japanese, German, Korean and so on. Petrol (called 'gas') is cheap compared to other countries. Any hike in petrol prices is resisted as the lifestyle of any average American depends solely on the use of his/her own car. 'Car-pooling' is encouraged to save petrol as well as ease congestion on highways. Those carrying two or more passengers are allowed to use a designated highway where there is less traffic rush. Parking is big business but there are adequate parking slots, some of them in multi-storied buildings. However, car parking in big cities like New York, San Francisco pose problems. People use the public transit system, bus/metro. 'Park and Ride' is encouraged so that congestion in central areas is less. Cities like London charge a fee 'Congestion tax' to reach central London, in an effort to discourage people driving to the congested areas in big cities and at the same time reduce air-pollution.

Futuristic fuel cell car

Personal loans

Professionals and non-professional are offered loans for various purposes such as: (1) renovating home/office (2) financing children's education/

wedding (3) buying household consumer durables and furniture (4) sudden health related costs like emergency hospitalization.

A list of conditions for a loan by a bank, Citibank is given below:

- Loan can be used for any purpose
- No security or hypothecation of assets required
- No guarantors need to be provided
- Competitive interest rates calculated on a monthly reducing balance
- Free International credit card with the loan
- Flexibility in repayment

Generally,

Loan amount = Two times gross annual income but this is flexible. Loans are also given against shares, fixed deposit, insurance policy, gold and house property. One can shop around for interest rates and other terms and conditions before taking a personal loan. The loan amount depends upon one's needs and payback capacity.

How to buy a personal computer (PC)?

Most homes now have a P.C. whose use is getting more and more widespread as it's a window to the outside world through e-mail and Internet related websites. It's wise to consult experts before buying a computer as you can discuss your specific requirements so that a suitable model could be selected which is cost-effective too. There are newspapers and magazines, which give you guidelines as to how to choose the right computer for the application. The speed/storage capacity, features, tasks it can do, upgrading possibility and other useful features will have to be considered before investing in a computer. You need a virus protection too, which now-a-days needs to be paid for regularly. Prices of PCs are coming down and it's the right time to buy a computer with as many features as you can. You can play a CD, DVD, use a floppy/CD to copy, set up long distance telephone conversation and chat with your friends and relatives within the country and overseas. There are various printers right from the (outdated) dot matrix, inkjet to the laser printer. Some of them have FAX and copying facilities too—a three-in one machine.

Here is one company that claims to be customer-friendly by playing on its name: CASIO

C — Communication with customers
A — Attentive to our customer needs
S — Speedy reliable service
I — Integrity always
O — Ongoing commitment to our customers

Companies have been trying to project an image of being customer-friendly that needs to be experienced. More companies are using the web to advertise their products and services, which means you are just a click away from accessing such information free of cost without leaving your home.

Bureau of Indian Standards (BIS), [formerly known as Indian Standards Institute (ISI)] is doing a good job in issuing standards on various matters of interest to the industry, business and consumers. These standards are now available on the CD-ROM format making their accessibility easier. These are cheap and affordable. The CD-ROMs contains over two lakh pages of 17,000 Indian standards and special publications on a compact disc format. Consumers can take the CD-ROMs on an annual lease charge of Rs. 2.5 lakh for a full set, which is about 30 per cent of the cost price of the hard copies of the Indian Standards.

Consumer organization

A list of consumer organizations is given in the Appendix. This list is not complete or comprehensive but given for guidance only.

SUGGESTED READING

A list of suggested reading/reference material of interest to consumers in included in the Bibliography in the Appendix. This list is neither complete nor comprehensive but given for information and guidance only.

CHAPTER 7

WHAT THE FUTURE HOLDS FOR CONSUMERS

"The market needs a place, and the market needs to be kept in its place."

—Anonymous

We are nowhere near the consumerism of some of the advanced countries where the consumers are treated as King. Our over one billion population makes any business profitable. Our middle class population is more than some of the fairly large countries like Australia. There is gold in the mine to be discovered in India as far as business opportunities are concerned. The last ten years have seen frenetic activity when reputed foreign companies have shifted base to India. Inflow of foreign capital has never before so much as of now. Global players are making a beeline to India, as they do not want to miss the bus of opportunity that's visible to anyone who has seen the phenomenal progress we have made these last few years in every field. This trend is likely to continue given the vast pool of trained persons available with the added advantage that we understand and speak English well. Moreover, our salaries and wages are still much below the advanced countries' standards.

Companies/organizations have to be 'customer-driven' to stay competitive. It's not what a company can do but what a customer wants to buy. It is expected that with such kind of focus customers will be treated as individuals to be cared for, and not as mere numbers in statistics to show the volume of business. Mr. John A. Young, President of Hewlett Packard Corporation, remarked a few years ago, "Satisfying customers is the only reason we are in business."

Our Father of the nation, Mahatma Gandhi, has put it succinctly:

"A customer is the most important visitor on our premises—
He is not dependent on us.
We are dependent on him.

He is not an interruption on our work.
He is the purpose of it.
He is not an outsider in our business.
He is part of it.
We are not doing him a favour by serving him.
He is doing us a favour by giving us an opportunity to do so."

It would be nice if every person, especially a seller, reads these lines carefully and acts accordingly to understand and appreciate what a customer is.

A few companies keep customer satisfaction as a measure of their success. The future is bright for Indian consumers. They can expect more products/services of international quality. Once a customer gets used to a certain higher level of quality, he/she would not choose a lower grade one whatever might be the incentive. Also good quality, in general, drives out bad quality products/services sooner or later. To be a world-class quality company it is essential to be a world-class customer. That fakes/duplicates still have a market in our country makes sad reading. Unless the customers are more alert and choosy such poor quality products/services continued to be sold. The government has to root out this menace that affects adversely genuine and honest business as well as customers.

Compared to the past, products/services now have more features than before. This means the value for money has increased as far as consumers are concerned. However, products/services that are time-tested will continue to be made as these will fulfill the needs of consumers so used to these over time. But there is always the possibility that products/services would improve with add-on features to the delight of customers. Presently, a portable radio is no simple thing. It has features like: clock, FM/AM radio, cassette player. Thanks to a competitive market, there would be further push for improvement, which can happen only in quality, which means quality in every sense of the word. More products have been developed to meet the ever-rising expectations of customers. A simple gramophone player that plays vinyl records is almost extinct. In its place, we have now cassettes, CDs and DVDs that have better quality and more compact. The cumbersome heavy frame bicycle is replaced by light frames and provided with multi-gears for easier riding. A revolution is taking place in the every day life. A radio is now a standard item in most homes, including the underprivileged. Even slums sprout TV antennas, and now cable TV, as part of the widespread use of electronic gadgets, which have become cheap and affordable.

INNOVATIVE PRODUCTS/SERVICES

A computer mainframe used to occupy a huge hall. Now it could be easily put inside a small room. Personal computers have revolutionized the use of e-mail and Internet. Now desktop publishing is catching on. Web-designs and animation are no longer strange words for Indians. More career opportunities have spring up due to globalization. 21st century will see more jobs in the entertainment and hospitality industry. India could as well be a BPO centre given the fact that there are many smart English speaking persons willing to work on reasonable salaries through the night shifts. Some of the prestigious Multi National Companies (MNCs) have brought their Research and Development (R & D) Centres to India as they find it cheaper and more efficient than overseas. One could never imagine that one day our country could be the production centre for cars of reputed makes. Those with vision and a capacity for innovation are likely to make handsome profit by bringing quality products that enhance the quality of life of consumers.

'White goods' are those domestic appliances like refrigerator, mixer-grinder, washing machine that reduces household chores. There is a rush to get these into as many homes as possible by providing affordable instalment schemes and by offering 'loans' for individuals. Products are getting more and more sophisticated.

TV sets come with 'remote' as an accessory, washing machines with washers and dryers, music systems that can play cassettes, CDs and DVDs. Multi-channel (over 100 channels) TV, cable or dish antenna, is a reality what with satellite TV channels making inroads into homes. These TV channels provide information, entertainment and education. One can read a web-based newspaper at one's leisure from home. There are now a number of 24 hours news channels that provide instant news with their 'breaking news' stories as events are unfolding elsewhere thousands of miles away. TV as a tool for education has been long recognized. Cable operation is one aspect and the other is having individual set-up boxes and or dish antennas that provide quality pictures and sound. Television sets are getting bigger and flatter with various features such as Picture in Picture (PIP) where one can watch another channel simultaneously.

Worldspace Organization provides 24 hours crystal clear music, classical to jazz, on a monthly rental. Internet connection to homes, through broadband connection is proving advantages to consumers as they have access to messaging, chat, talk as well as information through Search Engines like *Google* and *Yahoo*.

The consumer of the present age has to become IT savvy for survival. He/she should start using ATM facilities that provide 24×7 banking throughout the year. Electronic Clearing Schemes (ECS) is a convenient means of paying bills without the hassles of paper work or standing in long queues. E-commerce is coming up in a big way to provide instant transactions error free. For example, booking of hotels, airline tickets, train and road transport tickets, tickets for concerts and shows, cinema, tour and excursion can all be bought 'online'. The advantage of online booking is that it's without the intervention of any human being. E-mail has revolutionized communication, which is free and instantaneous. However, those who still relish handwritten letters are unhappy that we have forgotten how to write letters received through the ordinary post, known as the 'snail mail'. For these diehard letter writers, it's the personal touch that is important. But the world is changing slowly but surely whether one likes it or prepared for it or not.

> 'Network society'→Revolution in information/communication→Faster/reliable→Availability at the click of a mouse→Lacks personal touch

TECHNOLOGY SAVVY

The consumers of this century and beyond have to be technology savvy if they have to survive. Slowly, certain banks have introduced the Automated Teller Machines (ATMs) and they want their consumers start using these rather than use the chequebook and teller facility. Paperless transactions are the order of the day. Instead of pass books one can get a print out of the bank transactions at any time by accessing one's account with an ID and secure password. What we used to see piles of files stacked in racks in offices might become a relic of the past. More offices have realized the need for switching over to computer to store and retrieve data on various matters of people's interest. Of course, important and sensitive information would be kept away in backup CDS and floppies for use in any emergency. Banks are becoming user-friendly with a host of services: cash transactions, fixed deposits, mutual funds, stock market access through 'stockinvest' and the like, settling various bill like utilities through ECS, LIC premium payment, assistance in investment decisions, provide easy credit/home/consumer/car loans, inter-city/bank transfer of money, foreign exchange transactions. Thus, they act as friend, philosopher and guide to assist you to get various things done in an effortless way. It's likely more foreign banks would start their operations, either directly or with tie-ups with their Indian partners. We could see a sea change in the manner banking is done in future.

Health care

It's no surprise India is becoming part of health-related tourism. Already some of the ayurvedic centres in Kerala cater to the needs of foreigners who come to de-stress and rejuvenate. Then there are those who want to learn yoga the proper way and meditate under the guidance of a yogi or guru in Rishikesh and other Himalayan centres renowned for their spiritual activities over the ages. Super-speciality hospitals have come up in various parts of the country. By and large, these cater to the affluent section of our society. However, a few charitable institutions provide affordable health-care even to the underprivileged, either subsidized or almost free. There have been many developments in the technology of health-care. Ultra-sound, X-ray, MRI, angiogram have become almost 'routine'. However, a disturbing question arises whether these are being misused to make money. Negligence of doctors will have to be proved by experts before they could be sued.

A patient or his family has to exercise caution and should not be stampeded into taking action under pressure. In the advanced countries, pros and cons of any line of treatment are clearly explained to a patient and there is a choice. In our country, the doctor-patient dialogue hardly takes place. A doctor gets irritated if the patient or his family members ask many questions. The doctor thinks that's waste of time. He has better business than explaining to a patient, he/she thinks. With the Internet useful information on health-related issues are available by surfing. For example, *www.webmd.com* gives valuable information on diseases, their symptoms, causes and cures with treatment and medicine details. It is always better, 'Forewarned is forearmed.' A second or even a third opinion about an illness is desirable. The family doctor is getting to be an endangered species. There are now experts for every disease.

Home medicines and alternate system of medicines have their place in health-care. We need doctors to take a 'holistic' view of the patient rather than any ailing part separately. Prevention rather than cure should take precedence. Moderation in eating and exercising are important in every day life. Fitness of body and mind should get importance in these days of hectic activity and busy lifestyles coupled with stress at home as well as at the workplace.

Fake drugs

It's estimated that 20 per cent of the drugs sold in the country are fake. This means the consumers are at great risk consuming these with or without knowledge. The government has to act to unearth these illegal manufacturers who manage to sneak in bad/dangerous drugs along with good medicines. There have to be more stringent checks and fool proofing of packages with pilfer-proof packing of drugs. More stringent punishment, with hefty fines and longer jail terms should be awarded to drug peddlers and their bosses and manufacturers. Consumers should always be aware of the possibility that what they consume might not be genuine. It is better to shop only at reputed dealers and authorized outlets. The menace of dangerous fake drugs needs to be tackled much more seriously. Adulteration of food and oils is another aspect that too has to be given top priority by the government and the people in general. Even petrol, diesel and kerosene we buy are subject to adulteration. Quantity (weight or volume) of any item is another aspect worth taking note. In other words, the actual quantity contained in the container/package should match with the quantity mentioned on the package. Maximum Retail Price (MRP) is an important aspect a customer should be watchful. Generally, a consumer expects the actual price to be less than the MRP and certainly not more. All packaged items are expected to be marked with MRP and the date of manufacture.

Insurance

Indians, in general, do not pay much attention to taking out insurance policies. This is slowly changing with many insurance companies, domestic as well with foreign tie-ups, have come up with innovative insurance packages suiting various types of needs. Insurance is not only to cover risks (of course, the very basic purpose), and as a tax saving option but also as an investment option. Competition would bring down the premium and at the same provide interesting insurance packages for persons to purchase. A point that needs to be addressed to is that senior citizens get a raw deal as they advance in age. Some companies stop the coverage after 80 years. Entry age is generally restricted to about 65 years. Overseas medical insurance is not available for those above the age of 70 years. However, some foreign-based companies do provide such insurance coverage for those above 70 years. This is a hassle free insurance policy obtained on the Internet using a credit card that charges in foreign currency.

It is expected that Indian based companies too follow suit and reduce the discrimination against senior citizens who need health-care more than anyone else. Healthcare insurance is an important segment of insurance. Innovative programmes like 'cashless' medical treatment at hospitals and nursing homes have been introduced for the benefit of consumers. There is a vast potential for insurance in our rural areas. Crop insurance, cattle insurance and other rural-focused schemes could benefit a large number of rural folk. Suicide of debt-ridden farmers is a cause of worry that should be addressed to by the government, the banks, financial institutions as well as the insurance companies. This is a social problem that is a matter of serious concern in a democracy.

Insurance→Innovative packages→Life + Health + General purpose + Tax benefit→International standard→Consumers to benefit

SERVICE-ORIENTED SOCIETY

In keeping with the trend in the advanced countries, our economy too is being driven towards a service-oriented one. In other words, manufacturing sector is now behind the service sector in terms of gross national product. Just notice the phenomenal growth of the telecommunication industry. The mobile phone has entered many homes in the country where earlier owning a telephone was difficult with long waiting periods. We have access to pay phones on every street of the city, town or village. STD/ISD booths are springing up like mushrooms everywhere, including villages. Owning a phone has never been as easy as now and this trend would continue, as we are likely to become one of the largest network societies in the world. However, such a communication trend should not be at the cost of a personal touch so essential to build a personal relation with people.

Cell phone

The use of a mobile phone (cell phone) is widespread. It is certainly a breakthrough in connecting people. A person is reachable 7 × 24 days a year, provided the cell phone is not switched off, the battery is charged to make it operational, there is a network connection at the place the person is there and the person cares to answer the call. A flip side is the deterioration in certain aspects of human behaviour. For example, mobile phone users disturb others while talking endlessly. They disturb peace and quiet loving people by getting calls during cinemas, theatres, and shows. Some of them use these phones while driving which is a traffic offence. Then there are others who flaunt their mobile phones even while relaxing or taking a walk. Some doctors make patients wait while they attend to some other 'urgent' case.

The effect of small children using cell phones is a matter of concern as the radiation could affect their developing brains. Hence caution has to be exercised in allowing small children use the cell phone. The use of these phones in various criminal and illegal activities need not be elaborated. So, as with any invention, there are good and bad aspects of it. It is for the people to use such innovations the right way that needs to be encouraged. An individual (consumer) has to decide, before investing in any new product/service, to what extent any innovation improves the quality of life.

Internet has revolutionized the way we communicate, do business, receive and exchange instant information, chat/see each other while speaking, use 'blog' as a tool for information exchange and so on. "I have a simple but strong belief. How you gather, manage, and use information will determine whether you win or lose," so stated Bill Gates, the founder of Microsoft Corporation. His book 'Business@ the speed of light' reveals how expanding technology is propelling the business world into an exciting new economic era... how every manager can and must stay ahead of the curve...and how integrated information systems can help every organization achieve." Any one can benefit by reading such a book, which can provide valuable inputs to his decision-making.

INFORMATION FLOW

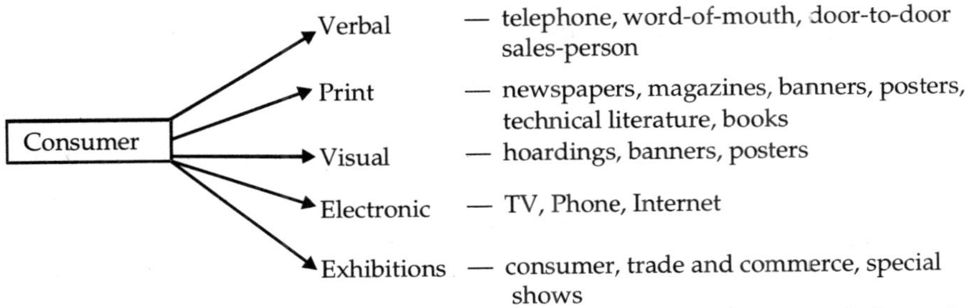

Here is an example of the kind of information, reports and data that can be had by accessing the Internet, using the Search Engines like Google and Yahoo, download and print or save on the hard disk for future reference.

Consumer Reports online: Website: *http://www.consumerreports.org*

1. Information on magazine subscription. Site subscribers can login. Subscription update.
2. Details of current issue of the magazine, *Consumer Reports,* and what to expect in the future issues and how to find a report.
3. Ratings/Reports on cars and trucks, appliances, electronics, house and home, money, health and food, personal, leisure.

   "Be informed before you click and buy. Our exclusive evaluations of online shopping sites help guide you in the web market place.

Just added: book, music, and toy sites. Start with our e-shopping tips, then visit our new Forums where you can tell us all about your e-shopping experiences on selected sites. Free!

4. *Other information:* Safety alerts, recalls. A few important such as: "Seeds of change: The global food supply is being genetically altered. Here's why you should care," information is there just a click away — FREE!
5. *Shopping online*: Do buyers' clubs and shopping agents really work?
6. Infant pacifiers recalled.
7. Is an HMO for you? Two new surveys compare HMOs with PPOs to help you figure out the tradeoff between choice and cost.
8. *Keep you cool:* Use your interactive worksheet to find out what size air-conditioner you'll need to stay cool when the heat rises.
9. *How to ruin a restaurant meal?* We asked our site visitors, and they told us their pet peeves about dining out.
10. Medicare ratings.
11. *Virtual health and beauty:* In our exclusive e-ratings: Online shopping guide, we tell you the best sites to shop for cosmetics, vitamins and more.
12. *Consumer issues:* Keep your eye on the issues affecting your wallet, your health, and your safety. Visit our Consumer Advocacy website.
13. *Another legal victory for consumer union:* A Federal Court, in the USA, throws out Suzuki lawsuit against Consumer Union (CU), after CU was cleared of liability in a similar suit filed by Isuzu.
14. *Features:* (1) The unknown risks of new drugs (2) Save big at off-season beach resorts (3) Healthy ideas for healthier living (4) Travel wisely using government warnings (5) Cold-Eeze: Can you believe the claims?

Here is a sample of features, information that one can glean from our own Consumer Magazine, *Consumer Voice,* published in Delhi available on the web. In the January issue of *www.consumer-voice.org,* read the following:

1. 14 brands of domestic pump-sets were tested and rated. Find out about the best brand.
2. Drug alert.
3. TV by conditional access.
4. Why do you need an optometrist?
5. Share your pets with us.

6. What is Yoga?
7. Sacred groves.
8. *Insurance:* Tips for consumers, for stolen cars.
9. *Products:* Tips for lodging complaints against selective durables.
10. Drinking water in four metros.
11. Chemicals in personal products.
12. Interactice space:
    (a) Are you being cheated? Have you been at the receiving end of a fraudulent deal? Talk to us.
    (b) Do you think consumer polls are important indicator of consumer concerns? Stand up for what you believe in!
    (c) Take part in our survey so that we can keep you informed on market trends.
    (d) Send us information that you think is relevant to the consumer cause.

Are you planning to buy any of the products in the near future? (a) Refined soybean oils (b) Fluorescent lamps (c) Flat screen colour TVs? Wait for upcoming test reports.

More such useful websites will come up to make selection of products/services easier. From online play games, to selection of products/services, these websites would give the consumers of tomorrow a greater choice. In fact, online shopping is expected to be popular. Retail would blossom out with reputed foreign retailers setting up their shops either directly or through collaboration with Indian partners. More consumer organizations would be coming up with their test reports and ratings that would serve as guidelines to consumers for their purchase decisions. An unbiased and independent test report is what a consumer wants to decide a product/service he/she is interested. This would become necessary as the products/services of tomorrow will have more features, more technology-driven and with a multi-choice environment.

Those who are used to written/printed matter, might find the electronic medium a little more complicated till that person gets over the initial problem of adjustment. The Internet provides information that can be saved and or printed for record. Retrieval of such information is easy once the consumer organizes data into easily identifiable files. Consumers, who are knowledgeable, would be the driving force in making the products/services of better quality. A well-informed and choosy customer is the best bet against spread of spurious/fake/duplicate items that harm honest consumers, the reputed companies/organizations as well as the economy of the country. Moreover, the reputation of that country that allows duplicates of foreign brands has a lot of explaining to do. They have to answer how the Intellectual Property Right (IPR) is getting violated.

Target→Produce higher quality products/services→ More information from media/Internet→Consumer gets more informed→Better decisions by consumers

'Give me any damn product and I well sell it,' used to be boast of some advertisers. Companies/organizations are allocating lakhs of rupees for advertisement. Whether mere advertising is enough to push a product/service has been settled in a competitive market of multi-choice. "You can fool some people some time but not all the people all the time," is true. Advertisement is one of the tools to make a product/service known to consumers. As far as selling is concerned, the product/service has to stand on the platform of quality, reliability, safety, performance, costs and so on for a consumer to decide whether he/she has to invest his/her money in it. "A good quality product/service will sell by itself," is not true either.

A brand has to be 'visible' all the time. No one can take consumers for granted. They have to be made aware of the company that produces good quality/service of international standards. While advertisements tend to be catchy and attractive, some are offensive. They are too bold. Some of them resort to cheap gimmicks and crude visuals with vulgar songs. Though there is a code of ethics in advertising, the thin line that divides the tasteful and the vulgar is being exploited. Companies and organizations have found devious ways of circumventing the code of ethics. For example, 'surrogate' advertisements are used to sell products like alcohol and tobacco. Public must be vigilant to expose advertisements that are in bad taste. Celebrity endorsement is a way of pushing a product/service. Such endorsement may or may not work. A consumer is an individual with likes and dislikes. He/she is not bothered whether a big celebrity has endorsed the product. It's up to that individual consumer to take a decision — buy or not to buy. Ultimately, the product/service has to prove it is worth being bought by consumers for their enjoyment or for their service without problems.

Culture of service

Winds of change due to liberalization and globalization have ushered in a market that is competitive with the availability of a variety of goods and services, of international standards. There are many foreign brands that are easily available in the country, a sharp contrast when tourists and visitors from overseas made it a point to bring some fancy goods or the other and some of them sold these at very high prices. There is now a choice to be made from plenty.

Unfortunately service sector lags behind the sales and marketing of goods and services. People are keen to sell but not at all keen to 'service' that means after sales service remains a problem. This kind of poor after-sale service interferes with the enjoyment of a product/service after investing one's hard earned earnings. While dealers/traders/retailers are keen to sell, they show less enthusiasm to attend to complaints, be it within warranty or outside it. The arrangement is the dealers and others have nothing to do with the service component of their business but they set up separate customer service cells to attend to problems post sales or post warranty. Though this is a good strategy, it also means the dealers are freed of their responsibilities to service and they can always point a finger at the service cell. More often, the pressure of selling products/goods and services is more than the pressure to 'service' (that's render customer oriented service to attend to complaints) as this part of a business activity is still considered to be 'non-productive' as it generates no income to the company. The experience of customers trying to get their complaint redressed through customer support cells, so far, has not been customer-friendly.

A good customer/technical support→prompt/friendly/cost-effective→Good sales point for the brand/company/organization

In the free market (capitalistic) economies of the advanced countries, availability of good quality products/services is taken for granted. Shortages or waiting for an item is very rare. The government generally follows a 'hands-off' policy towards the market allowing market forces to operate freely. For instance, a substandard product is driven out due to sheer consumers' protest — by not buying the brand/item, however, attractive the price could be. Only in exceptional cases, the government might intervene to stop sale of products/services that harm human beings or the environment. There are federal agencies like the FDI, which regulate drugs and related products.

In our country, we need government to be pro-active since the response from the industry/business is not matching with the aspirations of the consumers. Their regulatory agencies have to act as watchdogs to keep an eye on the market, example, SEBI that keeps a watch on the stock market and acts if the trading on any day is not in the investors' interest. Our drug controls have to be more stringent and prevent spurious and dangerous drugs harming the consumers. However, a wise consumer will not fall a prey to cheap and imitation stuff. He/she also will not waste his/her investment on dubious dealings that promise a lot but fail to deliver.

Then there are unscrupulous traders who hoard goods in a crisis so that they can jack up the prices and make a fast buck. Such illegal activities need to be curbed with an iron hand in the interests of consumers. In case of genuine shortage, due to natural causes, the government should import items in short supply in order to meet the demand. Another aspect that needs to be looked into is a fair return price for farmers and others engaged in agriculture and horticultural activities. It also happens that they get a low price when there is a glut in the market. Then it becomes so uneconomical to sell that they simply throw the produce away. In such cases, the government agencies should step in and give the farmers a fair return to their produce. More cold-storage facilities should be at the town/district level so that perishable stuff is kept safely and released gradually when the demand arises.

Market forces→Consumer awareness→Drives out poor quality product/service

Quality focus

Quality will be the number one factor in any purchase decision. This means, as discussed earlier, quality of product/service has to be right, delivery should be as promised, price should be right and competitive. Moreover, there has to be good and efficient customer support too. There are other matters that have to be looked into: environmental compatibility, energy efficiency, recycling, end-of-the-product cycle disposal of product/packaging. Independent quality certification like ISO (ISO 9000 set of standards) and BIS would be routine to assure consumers of an independent judgment of quality in all its aspects. More companies have obtained ISO's (ISO 14000 set of standards) environmental certification to assure consumers that the company is concerned with environmental matters.

ISO 9000: Offers guidelines.

ISO 9001: Model used in a company that develops and deigns own products.

ISO 9002: Covers the production and installation aspects.

ISO 9003: Simpler model than ISO 9002.

ISO 9004: Non-contractual model for a more advanced stage.

Certification is big business. More companies/organizations will, in future, voluntarily go in for independent certification that would give them an edge over those who don't have it. There are consultants/agencies who help a customer in taking the certification route, for a fee. One such organization is the 'Quality Council of India' (QCI), which is a non-profit autonomous society in a joint initiative of the Indian industry, and the Government of India. It has set up Accreditation Boards — National Accreditation Board for Certification Bodies (NABCB) and National Accreditation Board for Auditors and Training (NABAT). There are also private, domestic and foreign certification agencies that can help a company to be certified. They go through the company's systems, procedures, rules and the like and advise them how far they are in line to get the certification. It takes one to two years to get a certification provided the company is already doing something about it. A point that needs to be noted is the certification is valid for a limited number of years, 3 years or so, and it is to be renewed. Moreover, at any point of time, independent auditors could pay surprise checks to verify whether the company is following the rules laid down to be certified. So it's not a one-time exercise but has to work hard to obtain it and harder to retain it for years to come.

In course of time more companies will have ISO/BIS certification so that they have level playing field when wooing any customer. A fall-out of this certification is the awareness of companies and organizations to strengthen their internal quality organizations/systems and procedures and institute their own internal audit just to make sure everything is in order.

Sometimes a consumer is confronted with a situation where the products/services offered are just the same, but for the brand name and minor cosmetic changes. Let us take the example of health insurance where there are four government-sponsored organizations. The consumer finds that all the four have identical rules and conditions and the premium is just the same for any age group, for a typical set of benefits. In such a situation, what does a customer do? Well, he chooses the one he thinks good and nearer to his place of residence. Perhaps he has also learnt from various sources the reputation of the insurance companies. This is where an independent survey of the insurance sector could have helped the consumer to make up his mind. With more private insurance companies doing health and related non-life business, the situation for a customer is slightly favourable. Here again, one could find similar terms for any particular business. A customer is confronted with a little choice situation in some cases. For instance, senior citizens above the age of 70 years cannot get overseas medical insurance cover. Fortunately, there are foreign companies who provide insurance cover on payment in foreign currency.

The need is there to update the Consumer Protection Act to bring more services into its the jurisdiction. It should also enhance the compensation and fine/jail term when the opposite party is found guilty of deficiency of service. Moreover, products found defective in one State should be banned from circulation in other States, from the same producer. This is a 'recall' procedure, which is well known in the advanced countries but yet has to seep into our consumer scene.

Product liability

This concept is likely to be introduced in our business milieu in the near future. Such a practice is well established in advanced countries. Liability insurance is a means of covering any claim/litigation that could arise due to deficiency in product/service. There are lawyers who specialize in product liability cases. We too are likely to have such experts when product liability becomes a reality. The sooner we make the industry/business realize its responsibility towards the consumers the better. They have to inform the consumers in advance of any potential problem that could affect them. Such openness should be the norm in future.

Government→Proactive role→Protect consumers' interest→Consumer Protection Act→Bring progressive and relevant laws to protect the interest of consumers and environment→Checks and balances on business→Consumer education and creating awareness→Keep in touch with International laws on consumer related matters

Consumers want the government to be actively involved in consumer affairs. It has to show that it cares for consumers directly under its control. For example, the Public Distribution System (PDS) that now serves mostly those below the poverty line (BPL) families needs to be strengthened and at the same time make the quality and availability of quality and quantity of goods better. Unfortunately, these food grains are of substandard quality though priced low. Kerosene, the fuel mostly used by the poorer section of the population, is hard to get and its supply is limited and erratic. Though the price is subsidized. Some of the areas where the government can set examples of being caring for the consumers can be demonstrated in these areas where they are directly involved. For example:

- Basic health facilities in towns and villages.
- Quality of education in village and municipal schools.
- Quality of life in the slums.
- Potable water to millions in towns and villages.
- Environmental issues that affect the environment and the people.

- Protection for consumers against fakes and dangerous drugs and adulterated food and oils.
- Transparency in governance and upholding democratic institutions
- Punishing the corrupt.
- Making governance transparent and within easy reach of consumers.
- Delivering justice to consumers fast and affordable.

Accreditation

Announcing accreditation for food safety management systems certification NABCB as per ISO 22000, incorporating HACCP by National Accreditation Board for Certification Bodies (NABCB) Quality Council of India (QCI), 2nd floor, Institution of Engineers Building, 2, Bahadur Shah Zafar Marg, New Delhi-110 0092, e-mail: *nabcb@qcin.org, info@qcin.org*, Website: *www.qcin.org*

EXPORT INSPECTION COUNCIL OF INDIA
(Ministry of Commerce & Industry, Govt. of India)
3rd floor, NDYMCA Cultural Centre Building
1, Jaisingh Road
New Delhi-110 001
e-mail: *eic@eicindia.org* Website: *www.eicindia.org*

Work done by EIC

- Certification of product quality
- Product testing
- Training and technical assistance to industry
- Issue of Certificate of origin; health for food and other items; inspection for all commodities; authenticity for Basmati Rice.

Patient safety and quality of care accreditation

Mark of Excellence in Healthcare. Contact: C.E.O., National Accreditation Board for Hospitals (NABH) and Healthcare Providers.

(Member body of International Society for Quality in Health Care (ISQua)

2nd floor, Institution of Engineers Building,
Bahadur Shah Zafar Marg,
New Delhi 110 002
E-mail: *nabh@qcin.org* Website: *www.qcin.org*

Customer complaints and redress

QUALITY COUNCIL OF INDIA
Institution of Engineers Bldg.,
2, Bahadur Shah Zafar Marg, New Delhi-110 002
Tel No. 011-2337 9321, 2337 9621,
e-mail: *sg@qcin.org*, *nrbpt@qcin.org*

Mass transport

There have been a number of car manufacturers who have entered the market in the country. The range and the availability of cars of international quality have never been seen in the past. Practically every middle class family can now afford a car of their choice. Unfortunately, the masses are forced to travel in overcrowded trains, bus and ferries endangering their lives. Roads are in a poor state of development though there is now a move to improve the national and state highways. The connectivity with the remote villages is also being taken up though various programmes. Yet we have to go miles to make our roads anywhere near the standards of advanced countries.

The concept of quality of service and accountability for poor service has yet to take root in the railways, which move millions of passengers and millions of tonnes of goods every day on its vast network. No doubt more trains have been introduced to serve the people but overcrowding is the norm than exception. Certain innovative measures like Internet ticket booking have been introduced and faster trains are put into operation to cut down travel times. We need to pump in capital to modernize our ageing tracks, bridges, buildings, signalling and telecommunication to make rail journey comfortable and safe. Catering on the railways has to improve. Of late, Internet kiosks, shopping centres, and fast food joints have come up in a few stations, which serve the needs of passengers.

Both the government and the private sector have to understand that pleasing consumers is a sure way of increasing business. For example, the state-controlled airlines, Air India and Indian (there is a proposal to merge these in the coming months) have to compete with the many private airlines that have come up. Such healthy competition is good for the economy and makes the choice before consumers more meaningful. In a country like ours, the government has a more important role than in the advanced countries for safeguarding the interests of millions of consumers who could otherwise get a raw deal despite changes in the market environment. Since private sector is still profit minded, but for a few whose motto is to please consumers, some regulations to control business to prevent exploitation of consumers is in order. The government has to act as a watchdog to keep an eye on inflation, shortage of goods, price rise and cheating by financial and other organizations. Minimizing pirating of books, CDs, DVDs, and movies and strict control of fake drugs are needed in our market place to safeguard the interests of consumers.

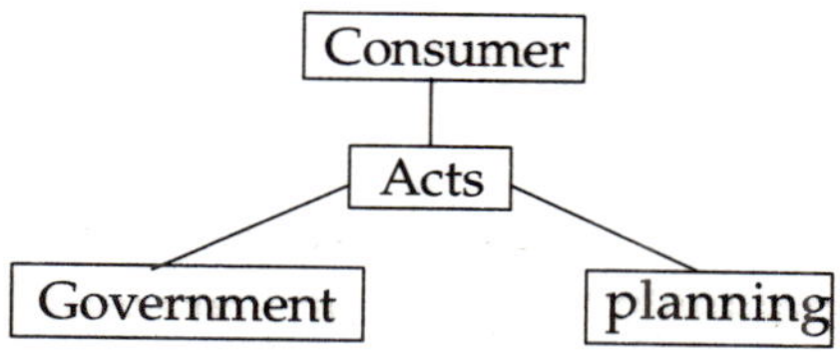

CONSUMERS BEWARE!

A sense of complacency has set in ever since, due to liberalization and globalization, the availability of goods and services has improved tremendously. Though a multi-choice market with goods and services at affordable prices is welcome, consumers cannot relax their guard lest they be cheated by glib talks and tall promises. A host of goods and services are entering the market everyday and this trend would continue. A wise consumer would invest where he/she gets value for the money. That consumer is not easily swayed by celebrity endorsement, attractive gift/prize/lottery schemes, easy finance or glossy advertisement. The more knowledgeable about the product/service he/she is Business to invest the better. Then hype can be set aside and the consumer gets a clear picture of the product/service he/she is thinking of buying.

Business/industry/company/enterprise/organization is in business to make money and not for charitable purposes. They are of course forced to pay attention to customer, the raison d'etre for any business worth its name. It's said, "Managing only for profit is like playing tennis with your eye on the scoreboard and not on the ball." The fierce competition among the players in the market is a mixed blessing for the consumer. Often he/she has a strange sense there is 'no real choice' among the competing brands. That's because everything looks alike, including the price tag. This is an unresolved dilemma of a situation of 'plenty' to choose.

Despite the presence of good brands, given the sheer size of the market, there is always space for duplicate fake brands undercutting the genuine stuff, which often look alike with standard brands. We need not endorse all products just because they are popular somewhere else. One should really think twice before investing in markets like powered backscratcher, electric toothbrush, powered-windows, which do not enhance the product, value much, but consume much resource, which could be better used elsewhere. Though it's a free market, we, still being classified as developing, should give a proper direction to consumerism that does not waste resources for producing goods that are redundant and of little use to ordinary consumers.

It's unfair to compare consumerism of the affluent countries with that of India. We live in a different world. Our values are different. We have always prided ourselves on our thrift and care in spending. Our goods should last longer and would like to get these repaired so that they could be used as long as possible. We do not like to waste or indulge in splurging. Many do not subscribe to the concept of a 'throwaway culture', which encourages conspicuous consumption and is wasteful. We adopted recycling as a way of life long before the advanced countries started adopting it. Despite attractive offers, except for a few who could afford, we do not yet subscribe to the idea of changing models every now and then, despite attractive financial incentives. Moreover, mere cosmetic changes in a car should not be the reason for trading in an existing model with another. But, if a model is fuel-efficient that is good enough reason to go for the new model. Energy efficient goods should be bought while discarding old energy guzzlers. An aspect that should be stressed in any purchase decision should be its impact on the environment. Availability of spares/service facilities should be considerations while continuing to use older models. As discussed earlier sometimes, 'old is not gold.'

Concern for our environment is minimal. We think it's not our concern but someone else. That's the reason we continue to pollute the air, soil and water. Our 'holy' rivers have 'unholy' waters. It's dangerous to bathe in these 'sacred' rivers. Our water-bodies are not clear or clean. Compare this to the situation in the advanced countries where environmental concerns are much more than in ours. Their water-bodies are a joy to behold, though tourists do enjoy boating and picnicking. Littering is unheard of whereas we continue to litter, spit and ease in public, that's the abysmally low level of civic sense prevailing in our country. Another problem that's being faced is the dichotomy in our culture. We tend to keep our premises clean while throwing the rubbish outside because somebody else is paid to clear it. Dumping of garbage around cities and towns is causing tension amidst those who live near these dumps. Their life is miserable having to breathe foul air, emanating from burning garbage, ground water is getting polluted and the soil in around the garbage dump is unfit for anything.

Need to keep rivers clean

MEGA PROJECTS

There is much interest big projects that consume much resource. Moreover, these affect the environment adversely by destroying trees and submerging valuable soil. Large numbers of people in the project site are displaced. Rehabilitation of such displaced persons is tardy and they are put to hardship. Moreover, there is a sense of deep loss when they are told to quit the place of residence of generations for some unknown destination. There is much debate on the feasibility of linking major rivers in the country, which is supposed to prove beneficial in the long run. However, this could have a severe impact on the ecosystem all along the links that could upset the fragile environment of these places spread over a vast area. Caution and detailed evaluation are needed before launching such projects, which could have adverse affect on the environment.

'Small is beautiful,' is still of many projects. Tanks of villages could be easily desilted to assure better storage. Bunds could be built to prevent rainwater runoff and recharge underground springs so that water could be pumped up when needed. There is much to be done in water conservation—drip irrigation, sprinkler and so on. Small community projects would involve the locals fully. They could see for themselves the progress of any project and suggest improvements. Thus, such small projects are not only cost-effective but also have full local support and cooperation.

DISASTER MANAGEMENT

As citizens, we are all consumers who would like to keep our lives and property safe when some disaster, either man-made or natural, strikes any place. The Centre and the States should by now have in place disaster management teams, which could be mobilized at a moment's notice. Permanent measures are needed to save consumers from disaster so that the citizens escape from the effects of any disaster without much damage. For example, people living in and around low-lying areas of rivers should be provided with alternate accommodation or high bunds built to prevent spill off of excess water from the river. Moreover, the river water could be regulated through a system of small dams and regulators. Presently, leaders and officials rush to a scene of disaster to supervise and make immediate arrangements to help the victims of a disaster. On the other hand, they do not have time to visit such places during normal times and suggest permanent measures so that the effect of any disaster is minimal. This is what every consumer wants in order to safeguard his/her life and property. We have to invest in long-term measures to prevent/minimize the effect of a disaster. For example, permanent cyclone shelters built near the coastal areas of Andhra Pradesh and Orissa help the villagers to take shelter when an alarm is sounded of an impending cyclone.

POLLUTION CONTROL

Despite so many laws ours is one of the most polluted countries. Some industries and civic bodies are dumping garbage indiscriminately and also releasing untreated or partially treated sewage underground or into water-bodies. This pollutes the water as well soil and making these unusable. Consumers should bring pressure by boycotting products made by polluting industries. The government appointed inspectors working for the State/Centre Pollution Control Board should do their job sincerely and without any corrupt practices. Polluting industries must be penalized heavily with fines and the CEO jailed. After sufficient warnings, such units should be closed for the public sake for a safe and clean environment.

There are still bitter memories of the Bhopal gas tragedy that killed thousands and injured thousands. If only the personnel of the company, who were working then, had issued timely warning, many lives could have been saved. Every industry should follow the pollution laws in letter and in spirit, as this is a statutory requirement. What needs to be appreciated is the fact that by controlling pollution, an industry needs to invest less in pollution control equipment and the process yield too would improve. The State as well as Central Pollution Control Boards should have more teeth and should act proactively to control pollution.

Pollution Control→Cleaner environment→ Better process yield

The distasteful practice of dumping unwanted, and often dangerous, products from the developed world to the developing world should stop. The third world people too have a right to live in a cleaner environment. Toxic waste is being imported that is dumped in some developing countries. Toxic ships are sent to India and other developing countries for breaking them down and recover scrap. This is a hazardous business that exposes workmen to toxic wastes.

Central Pollution Control Board (CPCB)

Technical publications on various subjects relating to prevention and control of water and air pollution are:

- Control of Urban Pollution Series (CUPS)
- Programme Objective Series (PROBES)
- Comprehensive Industry Document Series (COINDS)
- Assessment & Development Study of River Basin Series (ADSORBS)
- Coastal Pollution Control Series (COPOCS)
- Laboratory Analytical Techniques Series (LATS)
- Monitoring of Indian National Aquatic Resources Series (MINARS)
- National Ambient Air Quality Monitoring Series (NAAQMS)
- Ecological Impact Assessment Series (EIAS)
- Pollution Control Legislation Series (PCLS)
- Hazardous Waste Management Series (HAZWAMS)
- Resource Recycling Series (RERES)
- Groundwater Quality Series (GWQS)
- Information Manual on Pollution Abatements and Cleaner Technologies Series (IMPACTS)
- Environmental Mapping and Planning Series (EMAPS)
- Trace Organic Series (TOS)

For ordering publications contact:
Administrative Officer (Public Relations)
Central Pollution Control Board
Parivesh Bhawan, East Arjun Nagar
Delhi-110 032
Tel/Fax: 011-22301932
Website: *www.cpcb.nic.in*

Environment concern

The consumers of tomorrow would show more concern for ethical and environmentally friendly products and services. They want more parts to be recycled so that virgin materials could be conserved. For example, recycled paper would find many uses in our daily lives. They expect industries to work with government to protect the environment. Environment Impact Assessment would receive better attention so that any project is assessed for its impact on the environment.

Market forces

The future of consumerism is bright. However we should proceed to build our own Indian consumerism that need not be a carbon copy of the advanced countries' model. We should have choice for goods/services but not so many that our resources are put to the wrong use. Our priories should be right—to help the poor and the underprivileged to improve their quality of life. But this need not happen at the cost of the middle and upper class who should voluntarily desist from conspicuous consumption where there are still lakhs of people who go to bed hungry. Consumers should be united to drive out poor and dangerous quality products/services despite low prices and incentives. They should never patronize fakes and duplicates whatever might be the incentive. In fact, they should help the authorities in catching the fake/duplicate stuff makers as well as the adulterators who endanger lives by selling spurious drugs and poor quality food and oils.

LIVING WITH TECHNOLOGY

We have to be prepared accept technology that helps to improve the quality of life. There is no need to fear such technology to make life easier. For example, e-banking has come to stay with us since it has plus points. "Technology is like a steamroller. If you are not on the steamroller then you are destined to become part of the road," stated an expert who warned those who are apprehensive about the new inventions ushered in by technology. We should welcome technology where it helps us.

Technology→Serves consumers better→It is means to an end and not an end in itself

When consumers are used to better quality/grade/service, it's rare that they accept anything less by way of compromise. In the coming years quality will continue to receive the importance it deserves. Quality will become the number one factor, as always, in any purchase decision. Price once paid is forgotten but not the quality of a product/service that serves a consumer continuously till end of life cycle. Independent test houses would give out unbiased reports about any product that interests consumer for better decision-making. Involving the consumers who play a vital role in the feedback chain would strengthen the quality feedback loop:

R & D→Production→Quality Control→Distribution→Consumer feedback→Corrective measures→Back to R & D

We are far behind the 'service-oriented' service that needs to be upgraded. Service personnel should be really service minded and show concern for consumers without whom they don't exist. Every department/office/organization/company/dealer/service/retail outlet should think of the interests of consumers. 'Customer is King' should become a reality in India in the coming years. Prompt settlement of complaints- exchange, replacement and refund — should become routine like in the advanced countries. Separate customer service centres should operate, at least in big stores. Every government office should have a redress cell that's responsive and enables it to give what the consumers want without delay and hassles. Guarantee/warranty terms should be in simple language and pro-consumer rather than pro-company. Longer warranty terms should be the selling point for companies who want to establish the fact that they are reliable and long lasting.

Consumer education

This is an area that needs more attention. The government and the private sector along with consumer activists must strive to educate the consumers on their rights. Pamphlets and audio-visual shows to be organized in towns and villages to educate the consumers. They should know how to file a complaint with the consumer forum. The consumers should be able to unfathom the 'hidden agenda' of those out to confuse them. Consumer organizations should actively generate test reports and ratings of goods/services used commonly by ordinary consumers.

Consumer education→Key to understanding→Better decision-making→Feedback to supplier→Continuous quality improvement

Know your consumer rights:

- *Right to safety*
- *Right to be informed*
- *Right to choose*
- *Right to be heard*
- *Right to seek redress*
- *Right to consumer education*

Protection of your rights is our duty. Beware of misleading advertisements.

Issued by: Directorate of Information and Publicity
Government of NCT of Delhi.

Safety consciousness

Consumers should be aware of the need for safety. They should never buy electrical goods that are not certified. 'Safety first' should be the motto. No compromises should be made about the safety aspects of any equipment. There is no place for neglect or carelessness when a precious life is in danger. That's why a helmet should be worn by a rider of a two-wheeler, whether that is required as per government rule or not. Even the pillion rider should wear a helmet for self-protection. Riding more than two persons on a two-wheeler is risky and must be avoided. Where seat belts are provided, it is mandatory for the driver as well as the front seat passenger to use seat belts that provide protection in cause of a collision or accident. Riding over rooftops of buses and trains is a dangerous practice; so too is crowding of trains, buses, boats and ferries.

Consumerism of advanced countries→Take what is good for Indian consumers

SOCIAL CONCERNS

As enlightened consumers, they should discourage use of child labour at home and at the workplace. Any instance of employment of child labour, especially in hazardous industries, should be brought to the notice of competent authorities for remedial action. Animal care is another area that needs to be looked into. Treatment of animals should be the concern of citizens who should see to it that they are not harmed needlessly.

Instances of exploitation of employees should be brought to the notice of officials charged with inspection of the workplace. It's also necessary that the workmen be treated kindly and with consideration. They should not be made to work for long hours or in poor lighting or bad quality of air. The workers deserve regular breaks for various needs as well as lunch and tea. Social concerns should not be wished away by informed and concerned consumers, who in fact ultimately decide the fate of any company producing goods and services. The ultimate weapon of boycott could be used against a company that ignores social factors for the sake of making a profit.

Consumers are required to be careful about their choices. They should encourage reputed brands known for their after-sales service. Customer service could be the deciding factor in some instances, all other factors being equal. An informed consumer can take better decisions than the one who relies upon a dealer to tell him/her about the product's features.

Stakeholders (shareholders) of a company too are consumers. They can raise their voice against poor quality products/services, neglect of environmental concerns as well as exploitative labour practices at the Annual General Meeting (AGM), the forum where the management and the stakeholders meet every year. They should exert pressure on the management to control pollution and green the factory/company premises. Any labour related issues too should be highlighted at the AGM. Certain enlightened companies donate money and give free services to charitable organizations and NGOs working for the upliftment of children and elders. Some of them sponsor greeting card. Others promise to donate a part of the earning on a product to a socially relevant cause. NGOs sometimes collect left over food, which is still good to be consumed, from hotels and large canteens and serve it to the needy like street children, old and sick persons and orphanages. There are others who sponsor sports events, cultural events and picnics and outings for the underprivileged. Enlightened companies get involved in upgrading and maintaining public parks and gardens. Such corporate involvement in the community will increase in the future. Companies are known for their commitment to the community when a disaster strikes or a national emergency like war, cyclone, widespread disease, flood or drought strikes the land.

Social responsibility

"But the social responsibility of business is to tame the dragon — that is to turn a social problem into economic opportunity, into productive capacity, into human competence, into well paid jobs, and into wealth," stated the management *guru* Peter. F. Drucker. *Business World* magazine, sometime back, took into consideration 'community and environmental responsibility' of a company as one of the attributes for ranking a business. A few companies state that commitment to customers is a major component of their corporate policy. The giant IBM Corporation, U.S.A., states:

> *"Our primary measures of success are customer satisfaction and shareholder value. We are sensitive to the needs of all employees and to the communities in which we operate."*

Here is an Indian example from Zuari Cement:

> *"Zuari Cement's social consciousness further extends to maintenance of parks, sponsoring bus-shelters. Not just employee satisfaction. Much beyond."*

National Organic Chemical Industries Limited (NOCIL) states:

"A plant so rare to find you'll have to get by 4,75,000 trees." This shows the company's commitment to the greening of the environment where they have 'greened' land adjoining their plant with trees.

A nation-wide quality movement is not a reality yet. For this to happen we need one or two charismatic leaders and/or their outstanding organizations that work for the welfare of the consumers. Certain business leaders have taken the lead by making quality products and services so as to make 'Made in India' label visible all over the world. Some of them swear by fair trade practices and demonstrate their commitment to the environment and social/community causes. Others are taking a lead in transparency and openness about their company and are committed to ethical practices and ethical products. We need political leaders that promise good governance as well as commitment to the environment. They should focus on consumers as they are the ones who bring them to power so that they work towards the people's well being. Delivery mechanism of economic development should be faster and more efficient. E-governance and other novel methods to make governance more transparent with good practical systems and procedures should minimize corruption.

"The real danger is not machines will begin to think like men, but that men will begin to think like machines," stated Sydney. J. Harris showing his grave concern at the dehumanizing of human beings in this machine/cyber age. Any progress and development should take into consideration human beings. We want these to be with a 'human face'. There is still concern with liberalization and globalization as it has not been people-friendly but too capitalistic with the economy as the focus and not people's welfare. We need to stress on the paramount need to conserve resources for the

future. Alternate energy sources and more fuel-efficient machines and equipment should be developed that would have long-term beneficial effect. Pollution control should receive priority at the level of decision-makers.

A true measure of good consumerism is that people should be happy with the products/services that enhance their standard of living and makes life a lot easier. We need people who have vision of the future of human kind: *"Where there is no vision, people perish,"* proverb that warns people not to lose sight of vision and dreams for a better life. We should be all concerned with the well being of Earth that supports life.

It would be proper to remind ourselves what our Prime Minister Pt. Jawaharlal Nehru stated on the eve of our Independence:

Dedication:

"At the stroke of midnight hour, when the world sleeps, India will wake to life and freedom ... at this solemn moment we take the pledge of dedication to the service of India and her people and to the still larger cause of humanity..." Pundit Jawaharlal Nehru Addressing the Constituent Assembly, midnight, August 14, 1947.

We should remember always:

"There is nothing you cannot be,
There is nothing you cannot do,
And there is nothing you cannot have.
All you have to do is believe in you."

APPENDIX

CONSUMER ORGANIZATIONS

A list of consumer organizations is given below. This list is not complete or comprehensive. This is given for information and guidance only.

1. Citizen Consumer and Civic Action Group, No. 7, 4th Street, Venkateshwara Nagar, Adyar, Chennai-600 020.
2. Consumer Education and Research Centre (CERC), Thaltej, Ahmedabad-800 054.
3. Consumer Guidance Society of India, Hutment, J. Municipality Road, Opposite Cama Hospital, Mumbai-400 001.
4. Consumer Unity of Trust Society (CUTS), D-120, Bhaskar Marg, Bani Park, Jaipur-302 016.
5. Consumer Voice, D-203, Saket, New Delhi.
6. Mumbai Grahak Panchayat, Grahak Bhavan, Sant Dhyaneswar Road, Behind Cooper Hospital, Mumbai-400 056.

[**Note:** A few organizations like the CEI, CII, and FICCI have their own consumer cells devoted consumer matters].

BIBLIOGRAPHY

Here is a list of books/magazines that could prove useful for those interested in further reading. This is by no means complete or comprehensive. This is a suggested list only. The reader could use the search engine like Google and Yahoo to search the web-based sites, Internet, for information on any topic that is of interest to a consumer. This information will have to be updated regularly. Moreover, TV channels, newspapers and magazines do convey information about consumer related issues from time to time. The reader will find it useful to keep his/her knowledge up-to-date on consumer affairs.

BOOKS

ANTONY, M.J., *Consumer Rights,* Hind Pocket Books, 1995.

BALACHANDRAN, S., *Customer-Driven Services Management,* Response Books, 2004.

DAVID, H. BANGS, JR., *Creating Customers,* Vision Books, 1993.

DAVID FISCHER *et al., Products Liability: Cases and Materials,* Half.com

DEDHIA, NAVIN S., *Quality from Many Perspectives,* Part I, Part II, D.L. Shah Trust, 1998.

EDITORS *at* DARNELL, *Building Profitable Customer Relations,* SBP Management Press, 1998.

FAROOQ AHMED DR., *Consumer Protection in India —Problems and Prospects,* APH Publishing Corporation, 1999.

HIMACHALAM DR., *Consumer Protection and the Law,* APH Publishing Corporation, 1999.

ISABELLA SZMIGIN, *Understanding the Consumer,* Response Books, 2003.

JURAN, J.M., *Quality Control Handbook,* 4th Edition, 1988.

KEITH DENTON, D., *How to Give Quality Service to Your Customers,* Universal Bookstall, New Delhi, 1996.

MARIEKE DE MOOIJ, *Consumer Behaviour and Culture,* Response Books, 2003.

MUKESH M. PATEL, *Practical Tax and Investment Planning —Smart Strategies for Tax Savings for Assessment Year 2007-2008,* Published by Taxman (2006).

MURTHY, D.B.N., *Managing Quality: A Practical Guide to Customer Satisfaction,* Response Books, A Division of Sage Publications, New Delhi, 1999.

PUSHA GIRIMAJI, *Consumer Rights for Everyone,* Penguin Books, 1999.

RAKESH SETH, KIRTI SETH, *Creating Customer Delight: The How and Why of CRM,* Response Books, 2005.

SCHIFTMAN, L.G., *Consumer Behaviour,* Prentice-Hall India, 1999.

VERMA, M. M. DR. and AGARWAL, R.K., *Consumer Behaviour,* Kings Books (Regd.), 1999.

MAGAZINES

Consumer Voice, New Delhi, www.consumer-voice.org, e-mail: editorial@consumer-voice.org. 24×7 Helpline 0124-3989-8080

Insight, The Consumer Magazine, Consumer Education and Research Society, Ahmedabad, bi-monthly.

Quality Progress, American Society for Quality, Milwaukee, USA, monthly magazine.

The Consumer, Folio, The Hindu, October 1999.

INDEX